SETTING THE BAR

PREPARING OUR KIDS TO THRIVE IN AN ERA OF
DISTRACTION, DEPENDENCY, AND ENTITLEMENT

SHANE TROTTER

BV
PRESS

BV
PRESS

First Barbarian Virtues paperback edition November 2021

For information about special discounts for bulk purchases, please visit www.trottershane.com

ISBN 978-1-7375-9970-8 (paperback)
ISBN 978-1-7375-9971-5 (ebook)

Printed in the United States of America

To my kids, the Ace-man and my Brixie girl.
I just hope I make you proud.
And to Neely. I don't know where I would be without you.

Contents

SECTION I
THESE DAYS

"There are these two young fish swimming along, and they happen to meet an older fish swimming the other way, who nods at them and says, "Morning, boys, how's the water?" The two young fish swim on for a bit, and then eventually one of them looks over at the other and goes, "What the hell is water?""
—David Foster Wallace

"Our most private thoughts and emotions are not actually our own. For we think in terms of languages and images which we did not invent, but which were given to us by society."
—Alan Watts

CHAPTER 1

KIDS THESE DAYS

"Push back against the age as hard as it pushes against you."
—*Flannery O'Connor*

I'm riding my bike to work. The sun is rising and the air has that crisp September morning scent. I always enjoy these morning rides, but today my joy borders on bliss. A curious sense of connection washes over me. It's one of those rare, *Forrest Gump* moments when the grandeur of life hits you all at once and the mundane is suddenly transcendent—when, for reasons you can't explain, you find yourself smiling at the sky like a dog basking in the sun after a long winter.

I turn the corner and find myself approaching a group of high-school students waiting on their bus. You likely have memories of yourself doing the same—standing on the corner talking, joking, laughing—being a kid. Throw that image out. What I see is six kids sitting (yes, sitting) on the curb silently scanning their phones. Their heads are tilted to the side lazily, mouths open, faces empty, and thumbs swiping steadily in search of distraction. To say they are entranced is not sufficient. Each is a solitary island unconcerned for the life form just inches away. They exude a lobotomized disinterest in the world—completely removed.

I could run up in a pink tutu and start skipping in circles around them and they might never notice. In fact, they don't even register this bald, red-bearded bicyclist, until I am right next to them. Upon seeing one former student's surprised recognition, I succumb to the first grumpy old man comment that crosses my mind: *"You could talk to each other, you know."*

Not my finest moment. I'd prefer not to be the kind of guy who heckles unsuspecting youth. Yet, on this morning, I am the grouch spouting condescension on deaf ears. So much for bliss. I pedal away with an all too familiar question bouncing around my head:

"What are we doing to these kids?"

I've asked myself this question almost every day for a decade while working in high school, first as a teacher and now a high school campus Strength and Conditioning Coordinator. Every generation faces their share of *kids these days* pushback. In 1816, *The Times of London*, called for parents to stand guard against a disturbing new form of dance called "the waltz," which was sure to erode the fabric of society. Likewise, adults who lived through the Great Depression and Second World War no doubt looked on in disgust as their children listened to rock and roll and were spoiled rotten by the addition of a fourth television channel. I'm sure even our nomadic ancestors couldn't help but scoff at the behavior of their youngest generation.

"Crull, quit that foolish cave painting and help your sister collect walnuts. Kids these days!"

Yet, the reality remains that our youth development culture has been spinning out of control for some time. Through no fault of their own, more people than ever are coming of age fragile and unprepared for the rapidly changing world they will inherit. The rumblings of crotchety old men everywhere, while not telling the whole story, certainly bear a good degree of truth. Our children are entitled, soft, and lacking much sense of purpose other than to satisfy their most superficial desires. The modern youth development paradigm focuses on providing the highest level of comfort and entertainment possible. We obsess on providing outcomes, but too often ignore the quality of the people we are creating.

Compare our children to those throughout history. How would today's kids measure up against those of the civil war era or the 1930's,

40's, and 50's? Certainly, they are more likely to hold edified social views. We can't overlook the racism, misogyny, and homophobia that characterized most of history (and which persisted well after those often-glorified 1950's). However, progressive beliefs on race and gender equality are, largely, the consequence of cultural osmosis. For most, they are inherited perceptions that require little effort and, therefore, they are a poor judge of a generation's character. As psychologist Daniel Gilbert put it, " . . . condemning Thomas Jefferson for keeping slaves or Sigmund Freud for patronizing women is a bit like arresting someone today for having driven without a seatbelt in 1923."

For the sake of my thought experiment, let's presume past generations shared our current belief in the equality between the races, sexes, etc. How would today's youth compare in regard to defining and adhering to their own standards? How would a 14-year-old today compare with one in 1947 in regards to discipline, resilience, courage, gratitude, perseverance, toughness, patience, ingenuity, physical fitness, honesty, loyalty, or citizenship? Who would you rather have by your side in hard times? Who is more likely to replace the toilet paper roll when it runs out?

Still, this book isn't about creating a hypothetical generational round-robin tournament. I want to explore how we can live better today. What attitudes and skills matter? What pitfalls do we need to avoid? In short, who do we want to be and how can we better prepare future generations to create great lives?

And this is where we find the most damning evidence of a failing culture. Despite experiencing a higher standard of living than any generation in history, our children's mental and physical health are worse than ever. As a look at the numbers will show, new technology and failing youth development norms are combining to lead our children towards a staggering level of physical and mental degradation:

- Obesity:
  - Obesity has tripled since 1970 in American youth ages 6-19.
  - Today, nearly one in five kids are obese.

- A 2016 Harvard study predicted that of students age 2-19, 57% will be obese by the time they are 35.
- Mental Disorder
  - There was a 37% increase in teen depression between 2005 and 2014.
  - One in five youth now have a severe mental impairment.
- Suicides:
  - There has been a 33% increase in the suicide rate for kids 10-19 from 1999-2014 and girls in this range are now three times as likely to commit suicide.
  - Between 2010 and 2015, the number of suicides for adolescents aged 13-18 jumped 31%.
  - As of 2015, the second leading cause of death for both the 15-24 and 25-34 year old age brackets is suicide.
- Drug overdoses:
  - Prior to 2000, annual drug overdoses never reached 20,000. They've climbed steadily reaching over 67,000 in 2018.
- School shootings:
  - Between 1970 and 2000, annual school shootings never exceeded 50.
  - In 2018 there were 116 school shootings. In 2019 there were 111.

In January of 2020, before COVID-19 lockdowns, I gave a presentation to my staff on the depressing state of our nation's wellbeing and how we might create a culture that better met our students' needs. Afterward, teacher after teacher came up to me to share their own experiences and reaffirm the changes they'd noticed in students over the past few years. One administrator informed me that, at that moment, our high school had over 50 students institutionalized in a mental health facility.

The evidence speaks to an environment that provides youth with material needs but fails to give them the tools for building a fulfilling life. We have less inequality, less violence, more medications, more mandatory sensitivity training, more pleasure, and fewer pains. So, what the hell is wrong with us?

This question will remain front and center throughout sections one and two, but before we can answer that, we need to better understand our current environment and why its norms are something that we all have to contend with.

RAISING KIDS IN THE AGE OF NOISE

Raising kids has never been easy, but our environment couldn't make it any harder. A hundred years ago your great grandparents were probably raised on a farm, in a small town, or in a close-knit city neighborhood. They grew up attending school, farming, and, when possible, exploring the land around them. More than likely their peers shared the same core values and basic life expectations. Everyone said "please," "thank you," "yes sir," and "yes ma'am." Children wouldn't dream of talking back or storming to their room and slamming the door. There were no Kardashians to keep up with, no Netflix series to binge, and no video games beckoning kids to play into the early morning hours. Nope, that was cow milking time.

Still, kids played plenty, but it was a more old-school sort of play— self-organized, active, and in-person. From a young age they biked around town, started pick-up games, and simply played for the sake of playing. For those who got into organized sports, it was simple. There was football or soccer in the fall, basketball or wrestling in the winter, and Track and Field, Baseball, or Softball in the spring and summer. There were no skills coaches, select teams, weekend showcases five hours away, or any demand that they specialize at age seven, lest they be left behind to spend every Saturday playing badminton with Grandma on the front lawn.

Nearly every family ate dinner together each evening. There were no fast-food chains. Eating out was a treat and the only convenience food was the apple you picked off the tree in your backyard. Families were more likely to talk at dinner, and relax with books, music, or games in the evening.

Most of all, there were no smartphone feeds beckoning our children to scroll the day away while warping their expectations about how life should be.

But, Dad, everyone else has the brand new Lebrons.

I want to grow up and be a famous YouTuber like Ninja. Nowadays, all you have to do is get really good at video games and you can make millions.

None of my friends have chores. Why can't you just let me be like the other kids?

All the while Mom's social media feed is a revolving door of the loving moments that seem to define all her friends' relationships with their children.

Oh look, Jenny's son is signing his letter of intent to play on an eight-year-old select soccer team and he is only seven. Is Junior falling behind?

Look at the Johnsons having a great time at the State Fair. My family just walked around whining about the heat while staring at their phones.

All those manicured moments and staged poses masking the reality of their own hard experience parenting in this world. Of course, social media doesn't just subtly delude us with the belief that every other family is a harmonious bastion of love and support. It knocks us over the head with all the world's crazy in its daily deluge of comments and self-aggrandizing posts.

I cherish the time I get waiting in line to drop off and pick up my kids each day. That is how they know I love them.

Oh, that is a sweet picture of Sally, but she really shouldn't be forward facing in her car seat until she's 14.

The smartphone has changed parenting and daily life more than anything else, pulling all of us into its intoxicating vortex and preying on desires to be seen as a good parent. As much as this constant commentary influences our expectations, our phones have had even more impact on the way we spend our time. For children especially, the compulsion to scan glowing screens and curate a virtual image is replacing the desire to live and engage in the activities that develop capability, meaning, and a sense of reality.

We all understand that modern technology is addictive, but I never fully grasped the immense power of the screen until a couple years ago when I noticed my twenty-month-old was getting lost every time the TV was on. At this point, my son Ace had never really watched television. He'd seen Sesame Street and Barney, but this was not the norm. At under two, he was mesmerized by blowing the buds off a dandelion or filling a bucket and dumping it out. For someone so easily entertained and who didn't yet know what he was missing, we didn't see the need for television yet.

One evening, as I made dinner and my wife watched the news while feeding our baby girl, Brix, I noticed that Ace was at the base of the TV, spellbound by a furniture superstore commercial, like the puppy from *101 Dalmatians*. But he wasn't seeing talking dinosaurs or flying elephants. It was the boring geriatric-centered commercial set they play during the evening news. As the next commercial began, he remained unshakably transfixed, as if he'd been waiting his whole life for them to develop this Fibromyalgia medication.

I redirected him to his toy room around the corner. He began playing, but like Odysseus to the Siren's song, he kept walking out and becoming hypnotized by the screen. I'd say his name, but it wouldn't break through. So I'd tickle him while returning him to his toys around the corner. This cycle repeated. When it came time for him to pick up his toys before dinner, he'd be on a mission to grab the little broom and dustpan that he left by the dinner table and then, as if struck by Cupid's arrow, he'd abruptly shift; his eyes glazed over and dizzy-looking, then bob from side to side as his eyes and mind became engulfed in the screen.

Since then, we've noticed the same thing any time the television is on. Ace is now four and a talking, running, climbing wild man. But if a cartoon nursery rhyme looped for twenty-four hours straight, he'd sit there all day without speaking until he finally fell asleep. I'd always known that television and video games were compelling forms of entertainment, but I didn't fully grasp the biological draw humans have to bright, colorful screens.

The TV isn't all bad, however. Most of us grew up watching *The Sandlot* and *The Lion King,* and today we can't wait to talk to friends about what just happened on the latest streaming series. Shared stories have always been a part of the human experience, serving to convey culture and bond communities. The issue isn't our easily-quarantined televisions, but that these screens are in our pockets and are designed to learn from each of our unique choices. Now they can prompt us to the next juicy morsel—the one our past behavior demonstrated to be too alluring to pass up.

The power of modern devices is felt everywhere, particularly in schools. Take the experience of master teacher, Debbie Stevenson. In her almost 40 years as a teacher, she has taught everything from elementary to high school, riding the ebbs and flows of society from the Cold War, to the internet age, to the smartphone. When I asked her how kids had changed most over her career, she highlighted her experiences on standardized testing days:

> Standardized testing procedures have hardly changed since I was a little girl (a problem I will address in section 3). I remember I couldn't wait to finish my test so I could grab my book and get lost in a story. I was not typical, however. When testing time finally ended and my focus was broken, chaos erupted around me. This characterized my experience teaching. The second the last test was turned in, the class slipped into pandemonium. Kids couldn't sit still anymore. It was like trying to corral a zoo for however long you had them before lunch.
>
> But that changed in the years before my retirement. Now, the students finish their tests and they just sit there, anxiously staring at those still working—willing them to finish so the class will be allowed to get their phones. Since the

smartphone, it is as quiet after the last test has been turned in as during the test itself, and that is terrifying.

Insert smartphones into any gregarious class and you will find the same. Without boundaries, these magical tools use us, co-opting our time, distorting reality, and deterring real connection. While problems within youth culture have been brewing for some time, smartphones have taken these issues to another level. Today's youth experience is so defined by these devices, in fact, that Generation Z (the generation born between 1995 and 2012) is often referred to as iGen.

Dr. Jean Twenge, the psychologist who coined the term iGen, has been studying generational characteristics for over 25 years. According to her, changes between generations tend to be gradual indicating slight deviations in previously noticeable trends. As she says, "beliefs and behaviors that were already rising continue to do so. Millennials, for instance, are a highly individualistic generation, but individualism had been increasing since the Baby Boomers . . . ."

Smartphones changed that, however. "Around 2012, I noticed abrupt shifts in teen behaviors and emotional states," Twenge notes. "The gentle slopes of the line graphs became steep mountains and sheer cliffs, and many of the distinctive characteristics of the Millennial generation began to disappear."

Both in attitude and experience, today's teens are a stark mutation from the oft-criticized millennials that preceded them. Most disturbingly, iGen, born between 1995 and 2012, displays a radical decline in independence. "12th graders in 2015 were going out less often than eighth-graders did as recently as 2009." Today's high schoolers are less likely to date, drink, sneak out, drive, or begin working at age 16. And this was true well before COVID-19, when students became even more acclimated to living inside their bedrooms.

We're seeing a generation that is simply losing the desire to do anything, much less become self-sufficient adults. They are fine staying home and scrolling social media while parents meet all their needs. The result is that they are physically safer, while in far worse mental health. According to Twenge, "Rates of teen depression and suicide have skyrocketed since 2011. It's not an exaggeration to describe iGen as being on the brink of the worst mental-health crisis in decades."

It is easy to shake our heads at youth and their screen-dominated lives, but they didn't choose the culture they were handed and they aren't well-suited to resist it. Can you imagine being 14, today? You are a freshman in high school and all you really want is to be liked. Mom and Dad talk about grades, character, college and all that, but your whole world revolves around being significant to a bunch of other 14–16 year olds. You don't care if they worship material possessions or display an unhealthy degree of narcissism. You want them to like you and to do that, you need to be like them.

You have to have four social media accounts. You have to check them constantly so that you aren't missing out. You have to constantly engage with the newest apps. You have to be competing with friends throughout class on the latest, greatest phone game. Most importantly, you have to be constantly curating awesome profiles that show everyone how witty, pretty, funny, careless, defiant, woke, or (enter your significance-driven identity here) you are. Overwhelming.

But while smartphones amplify our issues, we can't hold them fully responsible. As we'll explore, parenting norms have been changing for some time. New terms like helicopter parenting (always hovering over kids) have entered the lexicon and are now being replaced with newer terms like bulldozer parenting, which describes the growing number of parents who are intent to mow down all obstacles from their child's path.

Occupational Therapist, Victoria Prooday has written extensively on the parenting trends that dominate youth development today. In her piece, *Reasons Today's Kids are Bored at School, Feel Entitled, Have Little Patience and Few Real Friends* Prooday highlights some of the destructive parenting norms that she often encounters. Kids are less autonomous, while more celebrated than ever. They get everything they want the moment they want it, dictate to their parents what foods they'll eat, expect to be constantly entertained, and despite ubiquitous social media, have very limited social interactions. It is a perfect cocktail for dysfunction.

My fear as I write this is that I will come across as the bitter old grouch who sits on his porch barking at kids to *"get off my lawn."* But I would love to see more kids playing on my lawn. Morning bike rides notwithstanding, I work very hard to understand students where they are and not hold them responsible for the youth development paradigm they have inherited. I've found that kids today are funny, caring, open-minded, and eager to become capable and self-reliant when this standard is clarified for them. Furthermore, I am always pleased to see resilient outliers whose examples fly in the face of my generalizations. These bright spots are worth understanding and building upon, but they do not negate our issues.

The typical modern youth experience—from the school environment, to the parenting norms, to the broader cultural value structure—is ingraining limiting beliefs and destructive habits that leave our kids ill-equipped for the challenges that lie ahead of them. The point isn't to blame students, teachers, or parents, but, rather, to understand the confluence of factors that brought us here so we can adapt better. Amid this environment of ever-expanding temptations, rapid technological change, and mass marketer manipulation, the costs of going with the flow will be higher than ever before. But "the flow" is harder to resist than you might imagine.

THE PULL OF NORMAL

"Wrong does not cease to be wrong because the majority share in it."
                                                    —*Leo Tolstoy, A Confession*

On March 2, 1962, Wilt Chamberlain set an NBA record that still stands, scoring 100-points in a single game along the way to a 169-147 victory over the New York Knicks. It has been over 50 years since then and this record has never been approached. Even with the addition of a three-point shot, the closest single game total falls 19-points shy—the late Kobe Bryant's 81-point explosion in January of 2006.

Chamberlain's incredible 100-point game was aided by a whopping 28-points from the free throw line, the most ever in an NBA game. This record is especially significant given Chamberlain's reputation as a horrible free-throw shooter. Over the course of his career, he only made 51.1% of his free throws. To put this in context, the NBA league average has been over 70% every year in its history. But on that rainy Pennsylvania night, Chamberlain shot 87.5% from the foul line. You might assume that the fates just aligned perfectly that evening—he got a hot hand and everything went in. But Wilt owed his success to a new technique he'd been trying—the mechanically advantageous underhand, or "granny" free-throw.

This often-mocked shooting motion allows for a more consistent shot arc. Yet, it remains stigmatized by modern NBA players and coaches. When legendary free throw shooter (and granny shot advocate) Rick Barry talked to Shaquille O'Neal about using the "granny" shot to cure his free throw woes, Shaq said he'd rather never make one. Chamberlain himself soon switched back to an overhand free-throw and returned to his unreliable ways. As he explained, "I felt silly, like a sissy, shooting under-handed. I know I was wrong. I know some of the best foul shooters in history shot that way . . . I just couldn't do it."

It makes no sense. Chamberlain knew he was making a bad choice that would make him a liability, particularly at the end of games, when trailing teams often foul opponents in order to stop the play clock. Even despite his remarkable first-hand success with the granny shot, Chamberlain chose a less successful route, because it was more socially acceptable—because it was cooler.

Malcolm Gladwell explains this unwillingness to be different using sociologist Mark Granovetter's *Theory of Thresholds*. Most people have a high threshold for change. You can show them all the evidence in the world, but they won't be the first to change, or even the second. This is human nature. We value social norms over self-interest almost every time.

When the norm is fast food at lunch and dessert for breakfast, most fall in line with what everyone else is doing. When the norm is to let kids stare at screens all day, not give them chores, or run yourself ragged with year-round select sports, then this is what most families do because there is social justification.

Our environment pulls most people away from the behavior they'd like to adopt and impedes their ability to notice other possibilities. We confuse the way things are with the way they should be. There have never been more possibilities for learning, innovating, and living differently. But despite increased opportunities for adaptation, most believe that the normal path must be fine because everyone else is doing it.

Humans usually default to whatever the environment promotes. For example, you'd expect that the percentage of organ donors would vary little from country to country. Yet, behavioral economists Eric Johnson and Daniel Goldstein found that countries tend to fall in one of two categories: very low organ donor participation (30% or less) or very high (85% or more). These differences weren't a consequence of national values, education level, or any other societal differences. Many culturally similar neighbor-nations like Austria and Germany varied dramatically with 99.8% and 12% donor participation, respectively. The difference was that in low participation countries people had to opt-in to be a donor. By contrast, high participation countries set participation as the default choice and required those who did not want to participate to opt-out. These vast differences were almost entirely the result of a default setting. It takes a lot of energy and intention to behave differently.

We must begin this book with an understanding of the overwhelming power of culture. Sure, there are individual measures we can take to promote better development in our children, but each of those changes is far less likely to take root against the tide of a community that continuously throws roadblocks in the way. Any behavior that goes against the tide of culture will be hard to start and harder to maintain.

You may be thinking that cultural norms aren't so important—that you'd be the type of person to adopt the granny shot. And you may be. But in high school you wouldn't have been. Social pressure is especially significant to adolescents, who will go to great lengths to model normal behavior, whether in regards to classroom discussion, communication style, or the way they use their smartphone. They see the world in terms of what is "normal" in their peer group. The disheartening reality is that even the very best parents often have to scale their parenting relative to the norms of the day or risk eliciting a far worse rebellion (some degree of rebellion seems inevitable and appropriate). Thus, as "normal" becomes more extreme, good parents feel compelled to gradually slide in that direction. For better or worse, we gravitate towards the patterns of the world in which we live.

It is time for a paradigm shift in the norms that drive our youth development culture and, thus, our culture at large. While this book is meant to be helpful to individual parents, teachers, and citizens, it is a book about culture. Culture has always been born and reborn around youth development. The central fixation of every society has been the raising and developing of the next generation. This is where the community comes together to establish values, to reaffirm what it stands for, and to convey what they think is most essential. When that shared purpose dissipates, you have a failing culture.

To clarify, I'm pushing two seemingly contradictory arguments, which I'll address throughout this book:

1. We have to respect the power of culture and take note of the broader cultural trends because those shape our habits, beliefs, and behaviors whether we like it or not. That means we have to fight to craft a culture that will pull more people towards creating a fulfilling life. I'll highlight the pitfalls and examine the areas where our efforts will make the most impact.

2. You can't rely on mainstream culture to bring you anywhere worth going. Environment may be influential, but our environment also doesn't have to seal our fate. In fact, great people are almost always those who are willing to question norms and chart their own course. Change always begins with individuals. Therefore, regardless of what happens in society, my goal is to inspire you to craft a better path. Whether you are a teacher, parent, coach, uncle, grandparent, or concerned citizen, this book will offer a new lens on human development. Your role in helping to clarify a more fruitful path has never been more important (or difficult).

Because of the power of culture, the volatility of our moment, and my love for big-picture thinking, most of my emphasis will go towards clarifying and correcting at the cultural level. This serves individuals best by giving them the context to fully understand modern challenges. But it also recognizes the unfortunate reality that most people aren't comfortable grappling with. Our culture's current path is not tenable.

AN UNCERTAIN FUTURE

"The real problem of humanity is the following: we have paleolithic emotions; medieval institutions; and god-like technology."
—E.O. Wilson

A book about kids is necessarily a book about the future. We are living through the fourth industrial revolution. Sounds ominous and for good reason. More than any time in human history, our future will be defined by constant technological disruption.

In the last thirty years we've watched as email made messaging instant, newspapers, C.D. 's, and taxis became obsolete, and phones began prodding us to check them over 100 times a day. Entertainment is now streamed to our TV without the need for cable contracts and shopping increasingly happens online, with packages brought to our doorstep and groceries brought to the curbside for pick-up.

How might life change in the next thirty years as Hyperloops turn a three-hour drive into a fifteen-minute pod ride, 3-D bioprinters allow us to print human organs, and deep fake technology allows any novice to fabricate videos of people doing and saying things they have not done or said? Will our civilization and its already archaic systems be capable of handling these challenges? And how will we adapt as technology learns to do more of the jobs that we never thought it could?

The reality is we have no idea what the future has in store—only that the pace of change and the volatility of the job market will continue to accelerate. With such uncertainty, it is difficult to determine the specific skill sets our kids need to master. They might spend five years learning Mandarin only to find that a new earpiece translates other languages into your native tongue in real time.

My children, Ace (now almost five) and Brix (age three) will be 32 (my age) in the years 2049 and 2050, respectively. There is no road-map our schools can create for solving our issues, much less those of the world of 2050. There is no path parents can point to that is sure to bring kids success. As millions of debt-ridden recent college graduates will tell you, even the once-vaunted college route is no longer a sure thing. Future success will be dependent on our kids' ability to adapt, overcome adversity, and see new opportunities. More than ever, the value of wanting to learn and learning well will define our children's lives. As author Mark Manson explains:

> Processing information and understanding something is not only more valuable than ever before, but the value compounds over time. The lessons you learn today will improve your ability to learn important and useful lessons tomorrow. Similarly, the cost of *not* being able to learn well is compounding as well. Failure to learn from today's experiences

will be even more costly tomorrow because you will be left that much further behind.

One way to think of the stratification in society at the moment is that there is an increasing gap between those who learn well and quickly and those who do not. That gap comes in all sorts of guises: not just income gaps, but also gaps in health, well-being, divorce rates, addictions, and so on.

Each new innovation changes the job landscape, but even more, it changes the way we live our lives and interact with one another. No one could have foreseen the social costs of a do-everything smartphone device and an information economy built to increase time on screen. Email increases efficiency but also changes people's expectations, blurring the lines between work and life. Few expected that having more choices (often billed as a perk of modern living) would tyrannize us in so many ways. The paradox of choice is that with more choices we make worse decisions, we're less satisfied with each, and our willpower is drained by the fatigue of constant decision-making.

Practiced learners and critical consumers will tend to adapt well to the unforeseen ailments that characterize modernity. For them, challenges are surmountable. Trials are evidence of a need for adaptation. They can enjoy the benefit of innovation without incurring every cost.

As the pace of change increases, so will the gap between these adapters and those who are swept away by the current normal. There has never been more opportunity for learning, yet also never more distraction and confusion. Right now, our youth development paradigm is confused and distracted. We are setting a generation up for failure. Rather than rationalizing this intuition away, let's use it as an inflection point. Let's define the values that lead to fantastic lives and fight to give our kids the tools to thrive in an uncertain future.

CHAPTER 2

A FAILED YOUTH DEVELOPMENT PARADIGM

"No man was ever wise by chance."　　　　　　　*—Seneca*

At just after 11 p.m. on Saturday, June 15th, 2013, Ethan Couch jumped behind the wheel of his father's red Ford F-350. His own Harley Davidson package F-150 was in the shop. With seven friends aboard, two who sat exposed in the truck bed, the sixteen-year-old sped down a rural two-lane road at over 70 miles-per-hour.

Further down Burleson Retta Road, Breanna Mitchell's Mercury Mountaineer sat stalled on the shoulder. Mitchell, a 24-year-old chef at a private club, had been working late and was on her way home when her tire blew and she swerved into a mailbox. The homeowners, Hollie and Eric Boyles, came out to help along with their 21-year-old daughter, Shelby. A fourth helper, Brian Jennings was driving home from his son's graduation party when he noticed Mitchell's car and stopped to assist. Eric Boyles grabbed the mailbox and took it to his garage, which is where he was when he heard what sounded like an explosion.

Couch had been showing off by driving on the wrong side of the road. He overcorrected while transitioning back to his lane, slamming his F-350 into Mitchell's SUV. Gas, burning rubber, torn metal and human bodies littered the road. One Tarrant County Sheriff's deputy recollected the scene looking "more like a plane crash than a car wreck." Mitchell, Jennings, and Boyles' wife and daughter were dead before emergency personnel arrived. All seven of Couch's passengers survived, but Sergio Molina, one of those in the truck bed, was paralyzed and now communicates by blinking.

The investigation revealed that Couch had stolen two cases of beer from a local Wal-Mart about an hour before. His blood-alcohol level was 0.24% (three times the legal limit) and he tested positive for both Valium and marijuana. Couch pled guilty to four counts of intoxication manslaughter and two counts of intoxication assault, but his defense team wasn't lying down. In a move that earned animosity from every corner of the globe, Couch's lawyers claimed that he couldn't be held responsible for his behavior because he'd never been held responsible. His parents had fought all of his battles and used their considerable wealth to buffer out any blemishes he acquired along the way.

When Ethan drove himself to school at age 13, the school's founder, LeVonna Anderson went to discuss her concerns with his father, Fred Couch. Fred threatened to buy the school and, soon after, unenrolled Ethan. At 15, the police found Ethan parked at the Dollar General with a Miller Lite, a bottle of Grey Goose, and a naked 14-year-old girl. When the officer asked Ethan what he was doing, he responded, "What's it look like I'm doing?" Despite breaking at least six laws, his parents helped finagle the charges down to a minor-in-possession and minor-in-consumption.

As the psychologist who treated Ethan's family after the accident, Dr. Dick Miller remarked, rather than the golden rule, Ethan was taught: "We have the gold. We make the rules." Ethan's lawyers claimed he was a victim of his upbringing. How could Ethan know there were limits when he'd never been given any? Dr. Miller even came up with a name for Ethan's condition: "affluenza."

A media hailstorm ensued. Ethan Couch became the poster child for all that was wrong with the American justice system. A separate set of rules for the wealthy. A get out of jail free card for the privileged. Here was a spoiled young man who'd been running wild without any concept of a line. His utter disregard for the law and human decency wrought destruction in countless lives. Now the court was being asked to continue the trend. They were being asked to reduce his consequences because he had been so sheltered from consequences that he couldn't have known any better. And they did. Ethan Couch was sentenced to ten years of probation and sent to a beautiful California rehab facility where his parents flew first class to visit him each week.

If you are human, this verdict disgusts you. Your heart aches for the victims and your blood boils when you think about the Couches and their ridiculous legal defense. Yet, the thing is, we all know that, despite its gimmicky name, affluenza is a real phenomenon. Spoiled kids with no limits tend to become entitled narcissists. Parents who fight all their children's battles and remove consequences tend to create dependent, immature young adults who have no sense of reality. In this sense, you don't have to be rich to fall victim to "affluenza." You just have to be coddled.

This is the problem with our modern youth development paradigm. It promotes treating every child like they are the center of the universe, somehow deserving of our constant adulation and certainly needing us to solve every problem for them. The new norm is to over-provide, overprotect, and to always find the excuse for a child's behavior. Everyone is responsible, except for the youth.

If he were raised in a different setting, Ethan Couch might have been a great kid. If he was fortunate enough to receive boundaries and consequences he might have grown into a hardworking, productive member of society. Ethan's environment contributed to his behavior just as any drug-dealer or thief's environment promotes theirs. Like you, I empathize more with an impoverished thief, yet both simply manifest the way their environment interacts with their biochemistry. When it comes to behavior, nature and nurture are the only two factors at play, and as we can't very well influence nature, our focus should be on nurture. Ethan Couch was nurtured to be an incredible asshole.

Still, this doesn't excuse his behavior. In fact, the best thing we could have done for Ethan Couch is to hold him fully accountable. Maturation is fundamental to happiness and the most essential lessons often have to be learned the hard way.

Our goal must be to pull behavior up—to influence the majority towards living better. This is why we have to set standards and focus on behavior regardless of a person's circumstances. In fact, this is the greatest form of respect: to treat each person as if they are capable of taking responsibility for themselves. When the boundary of ultimate responsibility is blurred, dysfunction follows. It is important to understand people's backgrounds, meet them where they are, and support them. Yet, prior circumstances can't be a justification to cut someone off from consequences.

We don't examine Ethan Couch's background to excuse his behavior. Rather, it is a useful archetype for helping us recognize the five ingredients of our dysfunctional youth development paradigm. These are:

1. **Low Expectations**: Treating youth as perpetual children rather than adults-in-training. As such they are always innocent and never responsible.
2. **Blunted Feedback**: Under the guise of kindness, we remove honesty and accountability that would prompt appropriate adaptations.
3. **Victimization**: We program youth to interpret every adversity as the consequence of their own unique deficit, thus, justifying their demand that others solve problems for them. They learn to see others as responsible for each problem, rather than themselves.
4. **Deferred Responsibility**: Having determined external circumstances are responsible for their challenges, youth learn to expect other people, institutions, and technologies to solve their problems and they quit when circumstances present even a modest challenge.
5. **Empty Values**: Youth are fed a materialist culture that prioritizes possessions, pleasure, and outcomes over deeper human

needs. Within this cultural value system, giving kids what they want is always seen as the greatest good (unless that conflicts with a parent's protective instincts).

We aren't Tonya and Fred Couch, but modern norms are closer to them than we'd like to think. And these ingredients of dysfunction are not reserved for rich exceptions like Ethan Couch. In fact, wealthy parents can be some of the best at identifying and avoiding these pitfalls. In our affluent modern societies, the ingredients of dysfunction are part of the mainstream culture perpetuated through our media influencers, television shows, and institutions. They have infected our schools where even the least privileged youths fall victim to them.

BULLDOZER PARENTING

"My dear child, I do not worry about the bleakness of life. I worry about the bleakness of having no challenges in life."
—Ayaan Hirsi Ali, Letter to my Unborn Daughter

I recently sat down with a high school principal. It was April, near the end of a school year and I could tell she was tired. As our conversation went on, she told me about three separate incidents that she was currently addressing. All three featured a kid caught under the influence of drugs or in possession of drugs. In each instance, the student confessed. One, she explained, brazenly detailed how he had illegally obtained Adderall, crushed it up, and mixed it with cough medicine and a Monster energy drink. Despite these students' confessions, all three punishments were being appealed by their parents.

More than any educator I've ever met, this principal connects with students, loves them, and sees the best in them. She did not threaten the students and wear them down with coercive interrogation tactics. The students freely admitted their offenses after being caught. Yet, in all three scenarios, the parents felt entitled to demand more of this principal's time and energy, pulling her away from the other 2,400 students and 150 teachers, and even calling her character into question in order to prevent their kid from facing consequences.

Working in high schools over the past decade, I've experienced hundreds of anecdotes like this. It has become common for parents to spend their days tracking their child's every move. They monitor their high schooler's grades online, tell them when to study, when to make up a test, when to go in for extra help, or even when to sign up for the SAT. In their eyes, they have to, or Junior just won't do it. Once, after I explained to a mother why I'd prefer that her sixteen-year-old son email me to ask for an extension rather than her, I got the response: *"I'm just glad he cared enough to ask me."*

With this ever-present safety net, it is no wonder high school students are more dependent than ever. They expect their parents to wake them up, manage their schedules, prepare every meal, buy them everything they want, and solve every problem. When a 17-year-old isn't getting as much playing time as he wants on the varsity team, more often than not, Daddy and Mommy set up a meeting with the coach. If a teacher catches a student cheating, she can expect parents to point the finger at other students, to normalize academic dishonesty, and to demand that she makes a new test so their baby can try again. Likewise, an inordinate number of parents hold teachers responsible when their kids don't get a certain grade. When a student scores poorly on tests and doesn't turn in half their work, parents often set out to change the teacher's behavior, rather than their child's.

But the problem isn't any one parent's demand to bump up a grade, excuse cheating, give more playing time, or award varsity status. The problem isn't any one email that starts out with, "I'm not one of those crazy parents, *but . . . .*" Crazy has always been here. The bigger issue is the frequency of this madness and the way schools have cowered down to these demands. In a time marked by outrage and immediate gratification, education has failed to draw the line and define a better vision.

Before critiquing modern education, I want to acknowledge that it houses some of our most selfless, caring, and supportive citizens. I know teachers who spend hundreds of dollars decorating classrooms and creating projects for their students. They give up their lunch each day to offer math tutorials and bend over backwards to try to make a difference despite the obstacles. Furthermore, there are countless examples of amazing school programs doing amazing work for their communities. Nothing I say is meant to diminish or disregard that sterling work.

However, the exceptional minority is too often characterized as the majority in response to anyone who would question the quality of our schools. These outliers have been made the poster child of education, meant to preclude any dialogue about what is going wrong. But these amazing teachers would be much more effective in a better system. One great teacher is just a drop in the ocean—meaningful, perhaps life-changing in individual cases, and yet, not enough. Their impact can't compare to the broader educational culture that students exist within.

What we have is a system (which we will look at in detail in chapters 11 and 12) driven to create the illusion of education without all the inconvenience of learning. Everyone scrambles to guarantee outcomes with little concern for the skills that made those outcomes desirable in the first place. And the kids suffer for it.

I'll be the first to argue that our school systems are out of touch with our modern needs (see section 3). Fixing education is far more complicated than just holding kids accountable. Still, no youth development program is worth anything without honest feedback and the expectation that youth take responsibility for themselves.

BLUNTED FEEDBACK

In the late 1950's, University of Oregon Track Coach, Bill Bowerman, conceived of a new way of running that he believed would help his athletes win races. He coached his athletes to extend their stride and land on their heels, rather than initiating ground contact at the mid and forefoot as they naturally would. But this would hurt. People don't naturally heel-strike because it is too painful, so Bowerman built shoes with a thick, padded sole. He then went on to co-found Nike and change the way we all run, walk, and move.

Before Bowerman's padded heel, humans all ran pretty much the same. As Christopher McDougall says in his book, *Born to Run,* "Jesse Owens, Roger Bannister, Frank Shorter and even Emile Zatopek all ran with backs straight, knees bent, feet scratching back under their hips." They had no choice: "the only shock absorption came from the compression of their legs and their thick pad of mid-foot fat." If you watch children run, it is the same. According to Dr. Kelly Starrett, they all run identically until around the first grade.

Adolescent running styles vary greatly and not just because the shoe world embraced thick soles. Flip-flops, "slides," and slip-on shoes with no back also conspire to change our natural movement. Every step you take in slip-ons requires your big toe to press down in order to keep the footwear from falling off. Over time, the plantar fascia at the bottom of the foot shortens, thus working its way up the chain to create tight ankles, calves, and overstressed knees. Living in the south, I'll see children who spend the better part of their year trouncing around in these movement destroyers. They have, miraculously, mastered running around without losing their flip-flops. Of course, this only expedites the loss of safe, beautiful movement and ensures pains that will discourage an active future.

Humans run. It is quite natural. Yet today, if you decide to embrace this hobby, you'll assume that you need thick padding, arch support, and all sorts of magic tape. Running is now considered hard on the body. In order to run, as humans have done the entire history of humanity, you'll need to employ the latest in expensive, foot-cushioning technology.

After years of changing natural movement by excessive chair-sitting and flip-flopping, we compound the damage by running with a heel strike that would be far too painful without two-inch padded soles. Immersed in our protective mechanisms, we run completely blunted from any feedback. We eliminate the slight aches and discomforts that would typically prompt minor, real-time corrections. We are completely ignorant to our missteps until the compounded effect manifests in a painful blowout. It could have all been pre-vented, if we'd only been able to deal with the consequences earlier in this chain of events.

Likewise, it is becoming more common to eliminate every minor pain and struggle from the experience of today's children. By blunt-ing their natural feedback mechanisms, we allow dysfunctional pat-terns to calcify. We may be pacifying our children now, but we are allowing them to reinforce patterns that will prove far more painful than the hard lessons we've worked so hard to shield them from. And these patterns will require a great deal of time and effort to undo. Without feedback, there is no correction. But when we are connected to natural consequences, we make millions of micro-adjustments, growing as a natural effect of living.

THE SHIFTING PARENTING PENDULUM

While our current trajectory is worrisome, we should be careful to avoid the fiction that parents of the past had it right and that us wretched moderns have simply fallen away from virtue. In many re-spects modern parenting norms are far superior to those character-izing the majority of history where children were to be seen and not heard and brutal physical abuse was a sign of good parenting. In his book, *The End is Always Near,* Hardcore History's Dan Carlin re-minds us that, all the way into the 20th century, students were rou-tinely beaten with implements like the "'disciplines' (whips made of small chains), and 'flappers' (school instruments with a pear-shaped end and a round hole, designed to raise blisters)." Through most of history, flogging your child showed that you cared enough to redirect them. *Spare the rod, spoil the child.*

During many eras, children were simply a commodity to be farmed out to other families in need of workers. Carlin quotes one nineteenth century Victorian lady who wrote: "Yes, certainly the baby shall be sent as soon as it is weaned and if anyone else would like one, would you kindly recollect that we have others."

These weaning duties were often contracted out, as well. Wet nurses have been nursing and caring for other people's children for thousands of years. In 1780, the chief of police of Paris estimated that out of 21,000 children who were born in Paris each year, only 700 were nursed by their mothers. Most often children were stripped from these wet nurses (the only mother they had ever known) and returned to their birth-parents as soon as they were old enough to work.

Thank goodness the pendulum has swung away from abuse and neglect. But we've landed at the opposite extreme and that isn't ideal either. The past few generations experienced a developmental paradigm that prioritized all-encompassing protection and providing the maximum for each child. The privileges of adulthood became automatically transferred with the passage of time, while many of the responsibilities, capabilities, and values that once defined adulthood, were neglected.

We all want to be good models and raise good people. Even Fred and Tonya Couch thought they were doing right by Ethan. The issues stem from bad metrics. The priority of parenting has moved to the extreme of providing and protecting at the expense of important considerations like creating capable, purpose-driven people who are inclined to contribute to something greater than themselves.

Providing and protecting are essential responsibilities up to a certain threshold. If a young child has no food and wanders crime-ridden streets, then remedying these challenges is the priority. However, creating capable, values-driven people is also the parent's duty. Once primary needs are met, this should become the overwhelming parental priority. The parenting pendulum has swung too far towards coddling and is in desperate need of re-balancing.

Some may argue that parents are actually more concerned with creating capable people than ever before. We've all seen those parents obsessed with pushing their children to be better athletes—the five-year-old who goes to a pitching coach or the eight-year-old who spends every free moment with tutors and music teachers. There is

TIMELESS GUIDING DIRECTIVES OF PARENTING:	CURRENT GUIDING DIRECTIVES OF PARENTING:
Create & Contribute	*Provide & Protect*
Create competent, useful people with the skills necessary to be autonomous	*Provide in abundance; your job is to make sure you satisfy as many of your child's wants as possible*
Create resilient, responsible people who will expect to solve problems and earn what they get	*Protect from any pain*
Create honest citizens inclined to find a purpose bigger than themselves	*Ensure that your kid gets the outcomes that society has deemed worthy*
The child's effort and conduct is the greatest measure of parental success	*The child's immediate comfort is the greatest measure of parental success*

even a growing trend where students transfer schools their junior year to improve their class ranking.

However, these patterns are usually an extension of the parental desire to provide outcomes. Rather than letting adolescents take responsibility for themselves and creating the expectation that they become capable of directing their own experience, parents manage their children's lives like sports agents or campaign managers. Everything becomes about guaranteeing some predetermined worthwhile outcome.

Students may have a better class rank at their new school, but it is at the expense of rigor, competition, and quality of instruction. Johnny may have a perfect SAT and an impeccable GPA, but does he have any sense of what work brings him to life and any sense of what pursuits will matter most? Cindy may throw a great rise ball, but did she develop an ability to put the team first or an inclination to maintain physical activity throughout her life?

In the effort to guarantee outcomes, we often sacrifice authenticity and maturity. Grades are inflated, All-Conference teams hold twice as many players as positions on the field, and celebrations have multiplied, but we've lost sight of the *purpose* behind all those things youth spend their lives doing. We've slipped into an environment that demands outcomes while forgetting the value of each experience. Author and teacher, David McCullough Jr. says it best in his 2012 commencement address, *You Are Not Special*:

> We have come to love accolades more than genuine achievement. We've come to see them as the point and we're happy to compromise standards or ignore reality if we suspect that is the quickest way or only way to have something to put on the mantelpiece—something to pose with, to crow about—something with which to leverage ourselves into a better spot on the social totem pole. No longer is it how you play the game, no longer is it even whether you win or lose or learn or grow or enjoy yourself doing it. Now it's, "so what does this get me." As a consequence, we cheapen worthy endeavors. Building a Guatemalan medical clinic becomes more about the application to Bodin than the well-being of Guatemalans. It's an epidemic.

The modern paradigm prioritizes outcomes with little consideration for the underlying beliefs and values that tend to generate high-quality living. We define the status-markers and comforts that we think mark success without clarifying a vision of the kind of person who can thrive even when conditions aren't perfect. These patterns have only gotten worse as social media embeds itself deeper into mainstream culture and both parents and children feel the pressure to perform for a virtual world.

Still, these critiques could be taken too far. Under-protection and neglect are not the point either. In her book, *Grit,* psychologist Angela Duckworth makes a case for why grit—a combination of

	UNDEMANDING	DEMANDING
SUPPORTIVE	*Supportive and Undemanding* = **Permissive**	*Supportive and Demanding* = **Wise**
UNSUPPORTIVE	*Unsupportive and Undemanding* = **Neglectful**	*Unsupportive and Demanding* = **Authoritarian**

passion and perseverance—is the most important factor in a person's success or failure. She identifies four common parenting styles, only one of which reliably builds grit. She categorizes parents as either supportive or unsupportive and either demanding or undemanding. The combination of these elements creates four categories:

Duckworth reports that " . . .study after carefully-designed study has found that the children of psychologically wise parents fare better than children raised in any other kind of household." By contrast, the overprovide and overprotect paradigm tends to fall under quadrant 1, the permissive category with the exception of a slightly authoritarian tendency in regards to safety. Overprotective parents tend to be so eager to solve their children's problems and protect them that they ingrain an inflated sense of helplessness. By never allowing children the freedom to take appropriate risks, they discourage the curiosity and willingness to fail that lie at the root of all lifelong learners. Children come to see themselves as more limited and fragile than they really are.

Ironically, learned helplessness can also result from the opposite extreme. When children are neglected and constantly presented with challenges that they do not have the means to overcome, they may grow to feel helpless to their circumstances.

As usual, the best path is to seek a balance—a yin-yang—a healthy interplay between seemingly contradictory ideas. There is an ever-evolving tension between the need to embrace a youth's current developmental limitations and the need to scaffold them to the next level. Supportive parenting and demanding parenting can and should go hand in hand. Parents must be the authority, but that authority has to come from wisdom rather than power. Children need both limits and freedom—expectations and love.

THE KIDS WON'T RAISE THEMSELVES

"It's not what you do for your children, but what you have taught them to do for themselves, that will make them successful human beings."
                                                            —Ann Landers

The first year or so of a child's life, they are completely helpless. They cry and you come running. *"She's hungry!" "Poopy diaper!" "Ace is poking her in the eye!"* Crying is her only survival skill and we don't fault her for that. She is, after all, an infant.

Slowly, however, things change. She begins walking, pulling things down, and understanding crucial words like *hot* and *no*. She, also, aggravatingly, learns to say *no*. With extreme parental persistence, she'll even clean up her toys and say, *"Go Bears!"* At this point, parenting can never be the same.

That baby girl is still the apple of your eye, requiring consistent meals, changings, wiped noses, and profuse love, but her whimpers no longer warrant backflips. The pendulum is swinging towards the need to establish expectations and create capabilities. This must mark a shift in the whimper-response cycle. Henceforth, the parental credo becomes: *I will not reward whining.* This does not mean *I will not be conscious of my child's emotional state.* There are plenty of justifiable tears that prompt you to comfort her and there are often times where she is crabby just because she is hungry or tired. Yet, there is a difference between signaling needs and manipulating you to get what she wants.

She'll demand more sweet potato and despite the abundant supply, you'll point to her untouched broccoli and chicken. She'll give a pouty face when you say to clean up, and you'll only become more persistent. She'll cry to get her way and you'll calmly explain, "*No, ma'am. We don't whine.*"

Giving her what she wants is always easier. You don't make her pick up her toys because you don't want to do the work. You don't deny her because you are callous. In fact, it hurts your heart. You refuse to give her what she wants because you love her and you know best. You are the parent.

Clearly, a three-year-old shouldn't be held to the same standard as a fifth-grader or even a kindergartner. If you want to better understand the unique quirks of early developmental stages, I recommend Dan Siegel and Tina Payne Bryson's *The Whole Brain Child.* My example is only meant to illustrate the duty of parents, teachers, and other adults to, often, not give children what they want. It may sound obvious, but kids should not rule the world. Despite the Rousseau-inspired narrative that kids are all born with clear eyes, pure hearts, and a depth of perspective that has been beaten out of us wretched adults, the truth is that youth are mostly just shortsighted and impulsive. They have a very limited understanding of the world's complexities and, quite naturally, feel an inflated sense of their own wisdom. Humility, nuance, and maturation tend to only follow lots of experience—lots of failure. It takes many years to figure out that you don't know shit.

While it appeases children to get their way in the short term, this creates deep problems in the long run. According to Occupational Therapist, Victoria Prooday, today's children are missing:

- Emotionally available parents
- Clearly defined limits and guidance
- Responsibilities
- Balanced nutrition and adequate sleep
- Movement and outdoors
- Creative play, social interaction, unstructured time, and boredom

Prooday contends that these fundamentals of a healthy childhood have been replaced with:

- Digitally distracted parents
- Indulgent parents who let kids "Rule the world"
- Sense of entitlement rather than responsibility
- Inadequate sleep and unbalanced nutrition
- Sedentary indoor lifestyle
- Endless stimulation, technological babysitters, instant gratification, and the absence of dull moments

These trends are hard to fight because they are "normal," ubiquitous, and they get everyone what they want in the moment. Parents get freedom and quiet, clean, safe children. Children get their desires placated. But the costs are waiting down the road.

We may be giving kids what they want, but we are ingraining habits and beliefs that will plague them their entire lives. We have to be willing to refuse a youth's immediate desires for their benefit. Gifts and treats are wonderful, of course, but within limits and within a grander vision of what best develops the person.

Kids aren't oblivious, either. If you establish clear expectations and explain why you believe your approach will help them become a more dynamic, awesome adult, they'll come to appreciate that. But you cannot expect them to find the best developmental practices on their own. Youth will always choose flickering screens and Happy Meals over mowing the grass and eating vegetables. There is nothing kind about giving in.

KINDNESS 2.0

"I judge you unfortunate because you have never lived through misfortune. You have passed through life without an opponent— no one can ever know what you are capable of, not even you."
—*Seneca*

Kyle Maynard's legs end at his knees and his arms end at his elbows. He was born with a rare condition called congenital amputation.

When Kyle was two his father decided that the family would stop helping him eat. If Kyle was going to someday live on his own and have a
full life, then he'd have to start finding ways to overcome his disability.
He began using a prosthetic spoon and later a knife and fork.

This approach came to characterize Maynard's upbringing, even
when his grandmother watched him. As Maynard explains:

> My Grandma Betty had this dark green jar she used to ask
> me to get sugar out of, except the catch was, as an amputee,
> I used both arms to grip things, and I could only fit one arm
> inside the jar. I'd sit there for hours, repeatedly failing to
> balance the scoop on my one arm. I'd get it right to the edge
> then lose it. After 50 more tries, I'd get it back near the top
> before I'd lose it again. Eventually, and sometimes to my sur-
> prise, I'd succeed. It not only helped with my dexterity and
> focus, but it also helped build my will.

Maynard would go on to climb Mount Kilimanjaro and Mount
Aconcagua, win two Espys for his efforts as a mixed-martial-arts
fighter, and become a best-selling author and entrepreneur who com-
mands thousands of dollars per speaking engagement. What separates him from others is not that he was innately gifted, but that he

was especially lacking in physical gifts. He had more cause to pity himself than most could dream. Yet he had the fortune of growing up in a family that chose to teach lessons rather than reinforce obvious excuses. By having to face more adversity, he had more opportunity to grow willpower—perhaps the most trainable and important quality for success in the modern world.

With an understanding of the power of mindset, it becomes clear that those most insulated from adversity (the Ethan Couches of the world) are some of the most disadvantaged. They pass through life without an opponent. No one can know what they are capable of, not even them.

More than anything, our failed youth development paradigm results from a perversion of kindness. It often appears kind to give people what they want, whether that is a grade they didn't earn, "kids food" for dinner, unlimited video games, or the absence of expectations. On occasion, this might not be such a big deal. But as a pattern, following the overprovide and overprotect youth development paradigm is one of the least kind things we can do.

When we understand what constitutes a fulfilled life, our definition of kindness must change. Kids need a lot of experience not getting what they want. They need experience withstanding setbacks and persevering when the road is tougher than expected. These tend to be the most transformative experiences.

Of course, there is a lot more to this conversation than chores, high expectations, and broccoli. The challenging thing about life is there are no hard and fast rules. Each situation differs. I've drawn attention to the general trends of a failed youth development paradigm and tried to fit them into a schema that makes it easier to recognize maladaptive patterns. Yet, we should be cautious not make the story too simple. There is a time to provide, to protect, and even to just calm the hell down and enjoy the ride.

So, rather than give definitive directives, throughout this book I will present deeper principles of human development that apply across many contexts. First among these, is antifragility.

CHAPTER 3

ANTIFRAGILITY

"The things that hurt, instruct."   —*Benjamin Franklin*

The water was getting cold. I'd been in the shower for 30 minutes and if I didn't get out soon, I'd be late for work. My boss would be calling my phone, anxious to get supplies for the day's landscaping job. I didn't take this lightly. After all, it was my perfectionist streak that brought me to this point. But I couldn't leave. Not until I remembered the name of the second baseman that the St. Louis Cardinals had just traded for.

It was the summer of 2009. I could have googled the answer and there was a sports page on the dining room table, but I had to remember his name for myself. I had to remember it before getting out of the shower, or I might go to hell.

It would appear I'd lost my mind. Believing you'll go to hell because you can't recall a baseball player's name isn't a far cry from "My dog told me to kill my wife." Yet, I was as rational as ever. I knew how insane this was. Yet, I couldn't, or, rather, wouldn't get out. The fear was too real.

Mark DeRosa! That was it. I dressed in record time and flew out the door.

For years, I dealt with a form of obsessive-compulsive disorder (OCD) known as Pure Obsession, or Pure O. It began when I was 19. At first, there was just a general sense of anxiety that I couldn't shake.

I spent enormous time and energy trying to come up with mental defenses that could make it go away. Rather than the ticks and cleaning rituals that most associate with OCD, I mostly just obsessed and occasionally wrote notecard reminders with lists like: Ignore, Trust, Balance, Confidence.

At times the anxiety was manageable and I'd even forget about it, however briefly. But over time it manifested in increasingly irrational and constant obsessive fears that were magnified with each step I took to push them away.

We all have random uncomfortable thoughts, but typically see them for the arbitrary mental conjurings that they are and move on. For example, you have almost certainly been driving down the interstate at 70 miles per hour, when it occurred to you: *At this speed, if I pull the wheel hard in either direction, I'll be sent flipping to my death.* It is a sobering realization that serves as a momentary reminder about the focus that driving demands. You think the thought and then turn your attention back to the countless other more interesting and useful thoughts. You'd have no idea how many of these musings you had unless you began believing that they were going to happen just because they popped into your head. Such unwelcome impulses, to jump from high balconies or shout obscenities in polite company, are so common that they've earned a term—the *Imp of the Perverse*—named after the Edgar Allan Poe short story of a man who couldn't help confessing to a murder.

For me, the realization that high speeds require sensitive steering adjustments brought a terror that, at any moment, I might be possessed by a perverse impulse that sent me flipping. I was in no way suicidal, but knowing my history with Pure O led me to not trust myself. I did not so much fear anything as I feared my response to the fear. I knew that I would never flip my car on purpose, but feared that because of my experiences with anxiety, just having the thought made it a threat. I assumed that since I couldn't get rid of the thought, I had to stand guard against it. I'd fight like mad to convince myself that, with 100% certainty, there was no way I'd ever be so reckless. But the harder I fought, the more my anxiety levels increased.

On one 10-hour road trip from Ft. Worth to my parents' house in St. Louis, the anxiety got so bad that I had to pull over at a rest stop. After a ten-minute break, I got back on the road and coached myself home like Maverick helping Cougar get back to the aircraft carrier at the beginning of Top Gun.

There were more insane internal battles than I care to remember. The specifics are irrelevant because they were only symptoms of a thought pattern. I'd obsess on a bizarre fear convinced that the presence of my unique disorder turned the impossible, or highly unlikely, into a possibility—one that required mental combat to keep me from unravelling. Like the mythological hydra, every time I fought back at the irrational thoughts, they'd grow more, increasingly bizarre heads.

You may be picturing a feeble, panicked college student who spent his free time rocking in the fetal position. But, to the contrary, I appeared to be flourishing. I had a large, strong social circle, I volunteered as a Lacrosse Coach at my old high school, and I loved my studies, sporting a 4.0 G.P.A. throughout college. My issues were mostly self-contained, leaving few clues other than the growing pains typical of a young adult struggling to figure out who he would become. The experience is hard to understand unless you've been through it. I had confidence and conviction. I knew what I believed. I knew what was rational. And yet, I spent the majority of every day consumed by irrational fears.

If this sounds like an awful affliction, I'm here to tell you, it was the most important period of my life. I would have never willingly chosen to spend three years in constant anxiety, trying to convince myself that I could hold it together. But, having worked past it, I'm now more terrified to think of who I might be if life had followed my own narrow plans. Or if I'd jumped to numb the painful feedback with pharmaceuticals rather than learn to correct the patterns that were wreaking havoc.

This challenge prompted me to funnel my obsessive mind towards human psychology, philosophy, and a broader view of health.

It led me to explore meditation, gratitude, and many other self-development practices and it spurred a passion for exploring the principles of human thriving, which continues to stoke my curiosity and sense of purpose. Without those years of anxiousness, I'd be less as a father, husband, friend, leader, writer, and human. And you would likely not be reading this book.

GROOMED FOR SUCCESS

"Life instantly improves when you don't blame other people and focus on what you can control."
                                                    —*James Clear*

The son of a successful businessman and philanthropist, Theodore Roosevelt grew up among the New York City elite. Add to this his exceptional natural intellect and the 26th president's later success seems a foregone conclusion. But for young Theodore, success was never likely.

Roosevelt was an exceptionally feeble boy—near-sighted and asthmatic to such a degree that he found himself on the verge of death more than once. He was timid and shy, and developed a tendency to try to use his frailty to elicit pampering. But his father, Theodore Roosevelt Sr., believed this would be crippling for Theodore. One day, he pulled his son aside and told young Theodore that he may have the mind, but he didn't have the body and "without the help of the body, the mind cannot go as far as it should." That day, an inspired young Theodore decided to "make his body." He embraced a lifestyle full of resistance training, boxing, hiking, rowing, and every manner of physical exertion, which he famously termed the "strenuous life."

Roosevelt would eventually become a governor, a rancher, a hero of the Spanish-American War, and a courageous president known for attacking corruption and charting middle courses that upset both Democrats and Republicans. Regardless of your opinions about his politics, he accomplished more in a year than most people could in a lifetime.

His transformation did not take place overnight and it didn't create an easy path. He continued to deal with asthma well into his twenties and he fell into a deep depression after his first wife and mother died on the same day. Roosevelt's political career was no less tumultuous. Critics on both sides sought to quiet the bold maverick. But Roosevelt learned to relish resistance and used it to spark inspiration. Before a 1912 campaign speech he was shot in the chest, but still insisted on addressing the crowd for the next 90-minutes. Foolish as this may have been, it was this commitment to "tire out" rather than "rust out"—to overcome apparent limitations—that made it possible for him to become more than a sickly boy with a bad heart.

Roosevelt's advantages certainly opened doors, but it was his disadvantages, and a wise father, that allowed him to become the dynamic figure we remember today. His life was changed by his father's insistence that he honestly engage his current limitations and take responsibility for becoming capable of more. Like Kyle Maynard and so many other successful people, Roosevelt's disadvantages were the gift that revealed his route to transformation.

Similarly, a 2003 survey of Great Britain's 69,000 self-made millionaires found that half came from unprivileged backgrounds and about 40% were dyslexic, four times the national average. A naive reading might prompt parents to hope for dyslexia in much the same way that baseball-crazed fathers hope for left-handedness. But clearly dyslexia doesn't provide any direct advantages. The struggles of dyslexia are just prompts to ingenuity and tenacity. Because human attitude and persistence matter most, we find that in people *with the right mindset*, disadvantages almost always create greater strength.

Decorated former Navy SEAL, Jocko Willink, articulates the success mindset beautifully in his book, *Discipline Equals Freedom: Field Manual*:

> The people who are successful decide that they are going to
> be successful. They make that choice and they make other

choices. They decide to study hard. They decide to work hard . . . They decide they are going to take on the hard jobs. Take on challenges. They decide they are going to lead when no one else will. They choose who they are going to hang around and they choose who they will emulate. They choose to become who they want to become—they aren't inhibited by nature or nurture. They overcome both.

Whether Jocko's statement is true or not, our children and society will be far better off when they hear and believe it. Some people do have great disadvantages that are harder to overcome and others have advantages that make their route to success much more likely. I don't mean to discredit that reality in any way. In fact, just the opposite. I want you to see how big of an advantage a person's upbringing can give her, especially in regards to mindset. The greatest advantages and disadvantages come from mindset.

The question we should be asking, then, is what makes a person inclined to decide that they are going to be successful and to believe they can make it so? Cultivating that mindset, more than anything else, will determine our childrens' success.

THE ADAPTATION PRINCIPLE

"It is likely that most of what you currently learn at school will be irrelevant by the time you are 40 . . . my best advice is to focus on personal resilience and emotional intelligence."
—*Yuval Noah Harari*

Traditionally, we think of resiliency along a spectrum that ranges from very fragile, like glass china, to very durable, like a bullet proof vest. But author and statistician, Nassim Taleb, coined the term *antifragile* to describe a third category that is not only resistant to stress, but is actually improved by it.

Bullet proof vests may be able to withstand bullets but they are still better off not being shot. Gore-tex resists water, but it is not improved by rain. Humans, on the other hand, are antifragile. After years of attracting what seems like every possible sickness, adolescents begin to fight off infections with increasing success. Our immune systems require stress to prompt the adaptations that strengthen and protect us. Likewise, our bodies become stronger when we engage in physical stress and our minds grow more capable and confident when we face a steady dose of appropriate mental challenges.

There is, of course, a sweet spot. Jumping in front of moving cars or beating children will do more harm than good. Too much stress can be devastating. But too little and we wither into a feeble, limited version of ourselves.

The more fragile someone is, the more their available experiences must shrink in order to keep them from shattering. A baby has access to only a very limited experience set. If they try to cook, drive, or bathe themselves, they'll die. Similarly, fragile adults won't allow themselves to date, speak in public, start their own business, learn Brazilian Jiu-Jitsu, or do much of anything. It then follows that by cultivating antifragility, you are cultivating the freedom to live more fully. With more antifragility we have more opportunity to grow by trying new experiences and more courage to go where those experiences lead.

We are fragilizing the modern world. The rise of safety culture, the self-esteem movement, and the subsequent demands for "safe spaces" and "trigger warnings" have deluded many into believing that any painful experience leaves us irreversibly traumatized—that major hardships (however loosely defined) imbue us with an intractable pathology, which infects every future thought and action. This sentiment took purchase long ago. As psychologist, Daniel Gilbert, explains in *Stumbling on Happiness*:

> For at least a century, psychologists have assumed that terrible events—such as having a loved one die or becoming the

victim of a violent crime—must have a powerful, devastating, and enduring impact on those who experience them . . . . But recent research suggests that the conventional wisdom is wrong, that the absence of grief is quite normal, and that rather than being the fragile flowers that a century of psychologists have made us out to be, most people are surprisingly resilient in the face of trauma.

We're adaptive beasts, whose biology anticipates inevitable hardships. And we aren't just capable of overcoming stress, we need it. People who don't allow themselves to face hardships don't feel better, but are, in fact, more sensitive and more afflicted by each minor inconvenience. The absence of stress pits our antifragile systems against us.

Immigrants who grow up in the developing world experience a far lower rate of auto-immune disorders than the general population. Their children, by contrast, born into hygiene-crazed Western lifestyles, develop these disorders at the same high rates as other citizens. Without any exposure to hostile bacteria, the immune system begins attacking healthy cells. Similarly, we've discovered that the best way to ensure children don't develop peanut allergies is through frequent early exposure to peanuts.

The same rules apply for our emotional development. In an over-sanitized, comfort-obsessed environment, the body, mind, and emotions whose natural instincts are to find problems and solve them, will create problems that don't exist. When adversity is reduced and pleasure is increased, minor pains are magnified to make up the difference. We maintain a baseline level of discomfort regardless of how comfortable life gets.

The problem isn't hardship, it is convincing people that hardships are traumatizing—that our disadvantages define us and that we should be shielded from whatever makes us uncomfortable. There is a self-fulfilling nature to believing that we are more fragile than we are. We begin to fear what we have no reason to fear and to avoid what we have no reason to avoid.

My Pure O didn't get better until I started to consciously train better patterns of thought by committing to meditation and a form of Cognitive Behavior Therapy (CBT) known as exposure therapy. What I eventually found was that I had to change how I responded to anxiety. I had to learn not to fight or flee when I felt the symptoms of anxiety. These were only thoughts, after all. They had no power to do actual harm. If they were so eager to keep dropping by, why not just invite them in to stay a while. It turns out the best way to treat anxiety is to stop fleeing or fighting fears and, instead, to seek them out.

CBT is the most effective, enduring treatment there is for a vast array of mental disorders: depression, anxiety, PTSD, eating disorders, and more. It works by identifying and deconstructing unhealthy beliefs in order to reprogram what it calls mental distortions—patterns of perception that wreak havoc on those who hold them. In their book, *The Coddling of the American Mind,* Jonathan Haidt and Greg Lukianoff argue that the exact same mental distortions that CBT works to untrain are being indoctrinated in our universities and flowing out into mainstream culture. They identify Three Great Untruths that are being reinforced in our younger generations:

1. The Untruth of Fragility: *What doesn't kill you makes you weaker.*
2. The Untruth of Emotional Reasoning: *Always trust your feelings.*
3. The Untruth of Us vs. Them: *Life is a battle between good and evil people.*

These untruths contradict psychological research on well-being, they contradict ancient wisdom, and they harm the individuals and communities who embrace them. At their core, these untruths are the product of an immature, delusional view of reality. People are not simple. Feelings often betray us. And living a good life should not and could not be painless.

Supreme Court justice John Roberts explains this well in a commencement speech to his son's graduating class:

> From time to time in the years to come, I hope you will be treated unfairly, so that you will come to know the value of justice. I hope that you will suffer betrayal because that will teach you the importance of loyalty. Sorry to say, but I hope you will be lonely from time to time so that you don't take friends for granted. I wish you bad luck, again, from time to time, so that you will be conscious of the role of chance in life and understand that your success is not completely deserved and that the failure of others is not completely deserved either. And when you lose, as you will from time to time, I hope every now and then your opponent will gloat over your failure. It is a way for you to understand the importance of sportsmanship. I hope you'll be ignored so you know the importance of listening to others, and I hope you will have just enough pain to learn compassion. Whether I wish these things or not, they're going to happen. *And whether you benefit from them or not will depend upon your ability to see the message in your misfortunes.*

If we don't give our children the gifts of struggle, they'll be disproportionately bereaved by the smallest hardships. Life won't be better because they somehow avoided normal human trials, they'll just be more sensitive to every slight. Most devastating, they'll be far less likely to persist in the pursuits that would build confidence and expose them to transformative ideas and people. Thus, they'll be less likely to seize future opportunities for growth. They'll not only be shells of their potential, but they'll lack the initiative to change.

Still, there is always a balance. Focusing on antifragility is only effective when there is genuine care and stress only makes us stronger when it oscillates with periods of rest and recovery. Again, we can

look at Theodore Roosevelt Sr.'s example, as described by Theodore
Roosevelt in a letter from 1900:

> I was fortunate enough in having a father whom I have al-
> ways been able to regard as an ideal man. It sounds a little
> like cant to say what I am going to say, but he did combine
> the strength and courage and will and energy of the stron-
> gest man with the tenderness, cleanness, and purity of a
> woman. I was a sickly and timid boy. He not only took great
> and untiring care of me—some of my earliest remembrances
> are of nights when he would walk up and down with me for
> an hour at a time in his arms when I was a wretched mite
> suffering acutely with asthma—but he also most wisely re-
> fused to coddle me, and made me feel that I must force my-
> self to hold my own with other boys and prepare to do the
> rough work of the world. I cannot say that he ever put it into
> words, but he certainly gave me the feeling that I was always
> to be both decent and manly, and that if I were manly no-
> body would laugh at my being decent . . . I would have hated
> and dreaded beyond measure to have him know that I had
> been guilty of a lie, or of cruelty, or of bullying, or of un-
> cleanness or cowardice. Gradually I grew to have the feeling
> on my account, and not merely on his.

As Roosevelt's reflections about his father indicate, cultivating antifragility doesn't call for callousness or faux bravado. It is not an
absence of compassion, but in fact wisdom—an understanding of the
tools required to make a good life.

We must remember that the goal of youth development is to create strong adults—people of purpose, capable of standing for what
is right and solving hard problems—not perpetual dependents who
think more comfort is the way to a better world. The primary objective of youth development is to create great people.

CHAPTER 4

THE DANGER OF OVERPROTECTION

In 1996, as a second-grader living in University City, a St. Louis neighborhood, I walked nearly a mile to and from school each day. After school, my friends and I would head to the park where, having no cell phone to check-in with, we would play until whatever time we were supposed to be home. We spent nights and weekends walking to each other's houses, rollerblading around the schoolyard, playing games at the park, and even walking into the Delmar loop (a busy entertainment district) to buy Pokémon cards at the comic shop. By fifth grade, I was babysitting a pair of five-year-old twins who lived down the road. In sixth grade, we moved to a suburb on the Illinois side of the Mississippi River where there was always a cadre of neighborhood kids playing in the driveways or the street. We'd walk back from the bus stop every day, often congregating on the fields of the nearby elementary school for pickup football and most weekends we met for a variety of night games.

My upbringing wasn't some wellness utopia. There were also hours of after school television and nights spent at friends' houses bingeing junk food and movies. But I did have a great deal more freedom and opportunity for exploration than most have today. I didn't know it at the time, but even as I enjoyed these hallmarks of childhood, they were becoming rare experiences for many. As you've undoubtedly noticed, those pangs of nostalgia you get when you see kids running through the neighborhood are increasingly rare.

To many, the reason for these changes is obvious. *The world was different back then. We know more now, and Shane . . . how do I put this? . . . Your parents should have been charged with neglect.*

Today, they might be. Demands for constant supervision have grown so normal that in 2018 the state of Utah felt compelled to pass a law protecting parents from being charged with neglect for letting their children walk the neighborhood or play at the park alone.

But our growing concerns with safety aren't the result of rising danger. By almost every metric from robbery and assault to kidnappings and homicides, crime has been steadily declining since 1990. Mass media saturation would have you believe every 3rd person is a violent sex-offender who steals packages off your doorstep, but in reality, life has never posed fewer physical threats. Every house is now childproofed, every parent at the park is neurotically scanning for threats, and every person on the street has a smartphone. The issue isn't that times have changed, it is that we have changed.

In *The Coddling of the American Mind,* psychologists Jonathan Haidt and Greg Lukianoff reference an "Is Your Child Ready for First Grade" checklist from a popular 1979 human development text. Unlike its modern equivalents, the list paid little attention to math and reading skills instead focusing on physical and emotional development milestones. Among the 12 questions listed was:

> Can he travel alone in the neighborhood (four to eight blocks) to store, school, playground, or to a friend's home?

As recently as 1980, this capacity was seen as a prerequisite to entering the first grade. The understanding of past eras wasn't just that children should be allowed more freedom, but that they *needed* to develop self-reliance—that the most important skills came from experience and that children who weren't empowered to take care of themselves would not develop the confidence and emotional stability to be capable of succeeding in life.

Today the pursuit of evermore safety has become an incontestable trump card. In matters related to our children, all you have to do is utter the word safety and every other consideration is mute. Mainstream society is under the spell of what Haidt and Lukianoff call "safetyism."

SAFETYISM

Beginning around the 1980's, the birth of cable news networks brought a steady flow of alarming news stories to every home. Parents immersed themselves in coverage of high-profile kidnapping cases and learned about the dangers of house fires, bullies, and swimming within 30-minutes of a meal. The safety-craze grew extreme as parents were constantly reminded of everything that could go wrong.

And when we return, the common household items that could kill your kids.

And when we return, the silent killer that has one mom demanding answers.

And when we return, the story of one mom whose child never woke up.

Amid the guilt and paranoia, parents became convinced that their children required incessant supervision. A sort of virtue signaling took hold of parenting culture where parents competed to be more aware of potential risks and gossiped about parents who failed to demonstrate an abundance of caution. *Did you see that Sally's kids didn't have gloves on? It was like 50 degrees and windy.*

Still, many sensible improvements came from safetyism. We fenced in pools, required seatbelts and car seats in cars, removed lead from paint and began slathering little ginger babies like me in sunscreen. The results were hard to argue against. By 1990, 48% fewer kids between five and fourteen died in accidents than had in 1960.

The problem was that there was no distinction between reasonable caution and paranoia, or any sense of the significant costs of overprotection. Soon neighbors were calling the police when they saw children walking home alone or even playing in the backyard unsupervised.

In 2014, South Carolina mother Debra Harrell was arrested for allowing her nine-year-old daughter to play at the park while she worked the day shift at McDonalds. After spending most of the summer scrolling a laptop in corner booths, the nine-year-old asked if she could start going to the park where there were splash pads, playgrounds, plenty of shade, and a steady supply of kids to play with. Her mother agreed and gave her a cell phone in case she needed anything. On the daughter's third day playing at the park an adult asked her where her mother was. *"At work,"* she replied. The outraged adult called the police who then deemed this nine-year-old "abandoned." Her mother was arrested for unlawful conduct towards a child.

That same year Kim Brooks left her four-year-old son in the car while she ran into a store to get him headphones before their flight. She was well aware of the dangers of leaving children in hot cars. On a 75-degree day a closed car becomes unbearably hot. Every year 30 to 40 children die from being left in hot cars. Brooks was also aware, however, that, while tragic, these deaths were almost always the result of a changed schedule. Dad usually goes right to work, but today he's supposed to drop his son off at daycare. When sleep-deprived Dad gets in the car, he goes on autopilot. He heads into work and leaves his child in the car for hours. Gut-wrenching, but completely different than running in for headphones. As Brooks explained, she did a logical risk calculation:

> I noted that it was a mild, overcast, 50-degree day. I noted
> how close the parking spot was to the front door, and that
> there were a few other cars nearby. I visualized how quickly,
> unencumbered by a tantrumming 4-year-old, I would be,
> running into the store, grabbing a pair of child headphones.

And then I did something I'd never done before. I left him. I told him I'd be right back. I cracked the windows and child-locked the doors and double-clicked my keys so that the car alarm was set. And then I left him in the car for about five minutes.

She returned to find her boy safe as ever, playing his iPad game. They made their flight and thought nothing of the event until they landed and her husband told her to check her voicemail. A bystander had seen her running into the store without her son, videoed her absence, and then contacted the police. Brooks was charged with contributing to the delinquency of a minor and warned that if she fought the charge, she may risk losing her children.

In her desperation, Brooks called Lenore Skenazy, the founder of Free-Range Kids who was famously dubbed "America's Worst Mom" after she let her nine-year-old ride the subway home alone. Despite her reputation, Skenazy is a proponent of reasonable caution. She and her son had been rehearsing his solo ride for years. It was a rite of passage that he badgered her about. On the big day, she picked out a good location to leave him, Bloomingdales, and gave him $20, a subway map, and a long reminder of what to do if something went wrong. Skenazy wanted him to enjoy the same independence she had at his age and determined that the mild risks were offset by the confidence and self-reliance he would build.

Skenazy believes in being smart, she just doesn't buy the new parental dogma that children require constant supervision. When Brooks called her, Skenazy had already heard a different version of this story many times.

Brooks recounts a few wonderful Skenazy insights from their conversation:

> "Listen," she said at one point. "Let's put aside for the moment that by far, the most dangerous thing you did to your child that day was put him in a car and drive someplace with

him. About 300 children are injured in traffic accidents every day—and about two die. That's a real risk. So if you truly wanted to protect your kid, you'd never drive anywhere with him. But let's put that aside. So you take him, and you get to the store where you need to run in for a minute and you're faced with a decision. Now, people will say you committed a crime because you put your kid 'at risk.' But the truth is, there's some risk to either decision you make."

She stopped at this point to emphasize, as she does in much of her analysis, how shockingly rare the abduction or injury of children in non-moving, non-overheated vehicles really is. For example, she insists that statistically speaking, it would likely take 750,000 years for a child left alone in a public space to be snatched by a stranger.

"So, there is some risk to leaving your kid in a car," she argues. It might not be statistically meaningful but it's not nonexistent. The problem is," she goes on, "there's some risk to every choice you make. So, say you take the kid inside with you. There's some risk you'll both be hit by a crazy driver in the parking lot. There's some risk someone in the store will go on a shooting spree and shoot your kid. There's some risk he'll slip on the ice on the sidewalk outside the store and fracture his skull. There's some risk no matter what you do. So why is one choice illegal and one is OK? . . .

There's been this huge cultural shift. We now live in a society where most people believe a child cannot be out of your sight for one second, where people think children need constant, total adult supervision. This shift is not rooted in fact. It's not rooted in any true change. It's imaginary. It's rooted in irrational fear."

To be fair, parenting a young child is terrifying. For the first six months they can't even hold their neck up and then they spend the next three years putting everything in their mouth and finding creative ways to climb as high as possible. I once left the garage open when I went to work, knowing that my wife, Neely, was about to leave with the kids. Five-minutes later I got an angry call. Neely had gone to the bathroom and when she came out, she couldn't find our daughter Brix, who was one at the time. Then she saw the door leading to the garage had been opened. She sprinted through it and grabbed baby Brix as she wandered toward the street.

Every parent has experiences like this that seem to reinforce the neurotic norms society tells us to adopt. It doesn't have to be rational for us to feel better when we can see that our children are safe. The thought of my beautiful baby girl being harmed makes me want to scoop her up and hold her tight forever—safe from any danger. But I know that I must resist that impulse, for her sake. She and Ace need the freedom to explore and expand their limits in order to build appropriate antifragility. The current epidemic of fear isn't just harmless caution. It impedes development, discourages essential experiences, and instills mental distortions in our children that are far more of a threat than the worst-case scenarios constantly playing in every parent's mind.

LIABILITY AND SAFETYISM

In the early 1900's a playground movement swept through America. Communities reeling from the ails of rapid urbanization sought to honor children's need for physical play by increasing the number of public parks and recreational facilities. Responsibility for these new facilities typically fell to local school boards and parks and recreation departments. But among them there was much less paranoia about risk than we see today. One movement leader professed the wisdom of the time:

> It is reasonably evident that if a boy climbs on a swing frame and falls off, the school board is no more responsible for his action than if he climbed into a tree or upon the

school building and falls. There can be no more reason for taking out play equipment on account of such an accident than there would be for the removal of the trees or the school building.

As of 2001, New York City public schools cut tree branches to keep students from climbing trees and a California school banned running on the playground. One federal handbook even concluded that playing in nature is too risky, stating: "Earth surfaces, such as soils and hard-packed dirt, are not recommended because they have poor shock-absorbing properties." The handbook goes on to caution that "Seesaw use is quite complex . . . ."

As author and lawyer, Philip K. Howard, explains in *The Lost Art of Drawing the Line*, America's lawsuit culture was born of a well-intentioned attempt to perfect the legal system by giving every victim a means of legal recourse. Rather than entrusting judges to enforce a standard of law that gave people confidence in where the lines were, we adopted a new expectation that every case would be brought to jury. But this meant that every interaction, no matter how well-intentioned, became subject to a lawsuit. Suddenly a volunteer baseball coach could be sued when a child was hit by a line drive; friendly neighbors could be sued when someone got hurt playing in their backyard; and the city could be sued if someone fell off a slide. Rather than inevitable quirks of living, accidents became opportunities to assign blame and seek profits.

The problem is that lawsuits are usually based on an opinion like: *It should have been safer; they should have noticed*; or *my child deserves more individual attention*. Sometimes these opinions have merit, but by definition value judgments are impossible to prove right or wrong. While it is most likely that a jury will be sensible, sometimes they aren't. Often defendants are held against an impossible utopian standard.

The coach should have known that Suzie wasn't skilled enough to play in the infield.

Her parents should have been watching them the whole time.

Each time this happens, more healthy activities are blanketed in anxiety. Public confidence decreases and shared notions of common sense become murkier. Before long, we've pulled all of the humanity out of life. Not because climbing trees or see-sawing is too dangerous, but because there is too much liability. Something could happen and that risk is just not acceptable.

Over and over, leaders in America saw that not taking enough precautions was the cardinal sin. Allowing someone to get hurt was the ultimate sign of poor leadership. Thus, anxious authorities began sacrificing every expectation of personal responsibility in deference to new expectations of fanatical safetyism.

This insanity has pervaded every sector of society. As a campus Strength and Conditioning Coordinator, I sat through a mandated four-hour yo-yo training. American health is worse than ever, yet our cultural incentive structure pushes P.E. curriculums to eliminate wrestling and dodgeball, while adding yo-yoing. The cost, as usual, is to the people we over-protect. By eliminating the possibility for minor short-term pains we've invited a litany of far larger long-term consequences.

THE COST OF EXTREME SAFETY

For truly it is to be noted that children's plays are not sports and should be deemed as their most serious actions."
—Michel de Montaigne

Anthropologists have noted that in hunter-gatherer societies children "play and explore freely, essentially from dawn to dusk, every day—even in their teen years." In play we interact with different personality-types, bond through common experiences, exercise, and foster curiosity, authenticity, and a sense of flow with our environment. While it is important for adults, play is the most essential thing our children do other than eating and sleeping. Which explains why it is the first thing they do after their primary needs are met.

As Jonathan Haidt details in his book, *The Happiness Hypothesis*, the psychologist John Bowlby formulated Attachment Theory after observing differences in play and relational styles between well-adjusted and maladjusted children. Attachment Theory holds that the primary biological directives driving childhood behavior are safety and exploration. Staying safe ensures survival. Exploration and play ensure that children develop the necessary skills for adulthood. According to Bowlby, when children feel adequately safe, they are freed to explore. But when their perceived level of safety drops too low, a switch flips, and like a thermostat detecting temperatures that have dropped below the prescribed setpoint, they cease play and seek out their parents or another trusted adult. Once the need for safety is reestablished through adult affection and reassurance, the child feels safe to explore again. The goal of this dance is to gradually scaffold the child to ever-greater personal confidence and competency so they can become independent and capable of biting off far greater challenges. Attachment theory is a great model for the necessary balance between providing and protecting children and helping them become capable, resilient, and admirable people.

According to play psychologist, Dr. Peter Gray, play is the primary means by which children:

1. Develop intrinsic interests and competencies
2. Learn how to make decisions, solve problems, exert self-control, and follow rules
3. Learn to regulate their emotions
4. Make friends and learn to get along with others as equals
5. Experience joy

When children play, they are conducting experiments that help them better understand the world. They learn nuanced lessons that exceed their linguistic capabilities, build confidence, and create a foundation for cultivating future passions. Children who are habitually harnessed in a sedentary, controlled, screen-saturated environment are kept from millions of these essential experiments.

Particularly for pre-adolescent children, the majority of play naturally errs toward free play—that is "play that is freely chosen . . . directed by the participants and undertaken for its own sake"—as opposed to structured play where rules are imposed by external authorities and driven by a goal other than the activity itself. As Dr. Peter Gray, observes:

> (Kids) seem to be dosing themselves with moderate degrees of fear, as if deliberately learning how to deal with both the physical and emotional challenges of the moderately dangerous conditions they generate . . . . All such activities are fun to the degree that they are moderately frightening. If too little fear is induced, the activity is boring; if too much is induced, it becomes no longer play but terror. Nobody but the child himself or herself knows the right dose.

This intuitive process is essential to their building antifragility and it is only possible when authorities stay out of the way.

Today, safety-obsessed parents tend to push structured activities where adults set expectations and manipulate their children's behavior to elicit some predetermined "good" outcome. Most of our children's time is spent indoors either in an adult-directed activity or safely pacified by the magnetic pull of a screen. What little time they do get outdoors is increasingly adult-led and spent in highly structured sports development environments. From their play, to their standardized school curriculums, to the answers they google before contemplating, there is always some program to tell kids what to do and rarely a time for discovery.

Despite the emphasis on bringing academic benchmarks to kindergarten, it is developmental experience and exploration that matters most in early childhood. In one experiment, Jean Piaget, the most renowned developmental psychologist, showed children two identical glasses, each with water filled to the exact same height. All of the kids identified that these glasses had the same amount of water. But when one of the glasses was poured into a tall-skinny glass right before their eyes, nearly every kid under six or seven claimed that the tall glass had more water. No amount of explanation could convince them otherwise.

As Piaget showed, it is futile to try to teach young children concepts like the conservation of volume. Their minds won't understand until a certain stage of development and at that point they will figure it out naturally just by playing with cups of water. I can't help but think of this every time I see a three-year-old being subjected to T-ball hitting lessons or flashcards. Parents grow frustrated prodding the little guy to "focus!" They'll push a task for months, accomplishing no more than they could have in three-minutes had they just waited a year. Other children will naturally bridge the modest gap when they are developmentally ready.

This is not to demonize parent-child activities or to suggest kids should be neglected all day. My four-year-old and three-year-old both love matching games, flash cards, books, puzzles, and even hitting a ball off of a tee. But, for young children, especially, we are best leaving the pressure and the goals out and encouraging free discovery.

In *Antifragile,* Nassim Taleb references biologist E. O. Wilson's suggestion that the archetypal soccer mom presents the biggest obstacle to her child's development because she interferes with their natural passion for living things. As Taleb expands:

> . . .soccer moms try to eliminate the trial and error, the antifragility, from children's lives, move them away from the ecological and transform them into nerds working on pre-existing (soccer-mom-compatible) maps of reality. Good students, but nerds—that is, they are like computers except slower. Further, they are now totally untrained to handle ambiguity.

Our modern norms eliminate obscure risks while creating fertile ground for physical and mental imbalance. Kids who don't climb trees, play in the rain, chase balls, scrape knees, walk the neighborhood, and spend unsupervised time with their peers are deprived of an essential developmental nutrient. Youth who sit and stare at screens all day are far more likely to be overweight, anxious, and depressed. We may keep kids safe and entertained, but we are programming them for limited lives. The absence of exploration breeds neuroses far more debilitating than the bumps, calluses, and hurt feelings that are so integral to proper development. When looking with a broader scope, the greatest danger to your children is that of taking no risks.

We obviously should not be reckless, either. There is no reason to have kids hang around street-corners known for drug-dealers or to let your five-year-old play with electric saws. But kids need to run, jump, and face modest risk; otherwise, they will be both fragile and passionless.

In most respects it is actually safer to encourage children towards a gradual progression of freedom and risk than to follow safetyist norms. Such kids will be healthier, more socially adjusted, and more capable of adapting in unpredictable situations. That's a pretty good formula for longevity.

So much of safetyism is just an illusion. We pretend that we can eliminate risk but our world is far more chaotic than we like to imagine. Academics, bureaucrats, and news outlets make sense of events after the fact. They like to create neat little stories and neat little plans that give them a sense of control. However, these post hoc creations almost always oversimplify reality and make us more fragile to the inescapable volatility of life. We create endless regulations and get training in specific protocols only to find that they don't apply to the ground-level needs. Plans can never be nimble enough to overcome the need for human competence. We are deluded into a false sense of security and become more likely to follow Google Maps right off a cliff.

This phenomenon is well documented. The Federal Aviation Administration (FAA) found that forcing pilots to turn over more responsibilities to automation led to more flight accidents and deaths. Under-challenged pilots grew less capable of adapting when their automated systems failed. Likewise, every year more people die at regulated crossings than while jaywalking. Many European towns have even found that traffic accidents decreased when they eliminated the white lines that marked lanes and that roads were safer when they removed traffic signs. This "naked streets" movement is based on the counterintuitive realization that we are actually safer when assessing risks ourselves. We are the only mechanism sophisticated enough to adapt to all that life will throw at us. For optimal safety we need to hone our skills through years of play and exploration.

Still, the opposite approach reigns. We are so afraid that someone might trip and fall that we create a flat, boring world with nothing to trip on. But this doesn't make us safer. Having no reason for alertness and no experience problem-solving, we stumble over the twig that has fallen onto our serene path. Pitfalls that would have been effortlessly parried had we allowed ourselves an organic life experience now pose significant threats.

A study of Swedish children showed that kids are over 50% more likely to have a distal forearm fracture than in 1950. They aren't experiencing more injuries because they jump, climb, and run more. On the contrary, these children are presented with fewer opportunities for a forearm fracture than ever before and that is the problem. Because of their limited experience doing normal human things, mundane activities are now threatening for them. By fragilizing our kids, we make them both more likely to be hurt and less likely to live fully.

And this phenomenon isn't reserved to the realm of the physical. When we eliminate mental discomfort, our kids don't feel better, they are just more likely to be harmed by normal experiences. They learn to avoid the very experiences that would be most meaningful and instructive.

PROTECT THY FEELINGS

"Pain is the source of all values. To numb ourselves to our pain is to numb ourselves to anything that matters in the world. Pain opens up the moral gaps that eventually become our most deeply held values and beliefs. When we deny ourselves the ability to feel pain for a purpose, we deny ourselves the ability to feel any purpose at all."
—*Mark Manson*

Safetyism didn't stop at boo-boos and child predators. It spurred the self-esteem movement, which convinced parents and educators that self-esteem—a measure of the extent to which you *feel* good about yourself—was the bedrock of success and happiness. This oversimplification is best summed up by the balloon lecture that I and most other Millennials were subjected to in elementary school. Teachers across the nation would tell a story about a young boy going through his day. When he got in trouble or forgot his homework his balloon deflated symbolizing decreased self-esteem. But when he was praised, had fun, or was given something, his balloon grew. The implication was that we should just blow everyone up with as many good feelings as possible while making sure no one's balloon ever got deflated. Hello overprovide-overprotect parenting paradigm.

It was now the adults' duty to make sure that no one could ever make Johnny feel bad about himself. He needed a trophy after every rec-league season so he felt like a winner. His grades needed to be inflated so he felt smart. His teachers needed to understand why he misbehaved so *they* could change their approach and *they* needed to use positive reinforcement so Johnny didn't feel bad about misbehaving. If he was frustrated, an adult needed to step in before he got down on himself. And if he was ever uncomfortable advocating for himself, then an adult needed to so he didn't miss out on any opportunities.

Generations have now been raised under such thinking, yet depression, anxiety, and suicide have only increased. As psychologist

Roy Baumeister and his team concluded after decades of research on the self-esteem movement:

> . . . over time unconditional positive regard has taken the form of suggesting that parents and teachers should never criticize children and indeed should praise children even for mediocre or trivial accomplishments, or just for being themselves. Always praising and never criticizing may feel good to everyone concerned, but the data we have reviewed do not show that such an approach will produce desirable outcomes.

This is obvious to anyone who understands antifragility. It would be like claiming the best way to make physically healthy people was to *always massage them and never have them exercise.* This would keep them most comfortable at every specific moment, yet they would never develop the strength to walk around a grocery store, much less bring in the groceries. Their aversion to discomfort would make them far less comfortable in the long run.

Ironically, the self-esteem movement deters the development of true confidence. You can only believe empty praise for so long. Eventually life's feedback breaks through. Confidence grows from action and exposure to failure—from learning that struggles are not fatal and that other people's opinions don't always matter. Obsessively monitoring self-esteem levels only distracts from building the capability and self-awareness that really matters.

But we should be careful not to disregard the power of positive feedback or to overstate the importance of emotional stress. As usual, the best path is more nuanced. A Japanese study found that there were different types of self-esteem producing vastly different effects. Healthy self-esteem is internally derived and characterized by a sense of authenticity. People with healthy self-esteem tend to be engaged in "committed activities" and they focus on "efforts for self-development." They feel good about themselves because they know who they are and are confident in their ability to improve.

By contrast, unhealthy self-esteem is characterized by a sense of superiority and entitlement. These people tend to base their self-esteem on "approval from others and appearance." Unfortunately, social media and modern self-esteem tactics are programming our youth for unhealthy self-esteem. We train kids to focus on external validation at the expense of honing their own internal compass.

The difference between healthy and unhealthy self-esteem mirrors Stanford Psychologist Carol Dweck's research on Growth Mindset vs. Fixed Mindset. As we'll see in chapter 15, healthy self-esteem is fostered in growth-oriented climates where people are frequently exposed to challenges and receive praise for virtues like effort, rather than for the outcome they achieve.

When we inflate people's sense of self-importance and insulate them from feedback, they are less likely to seek and learn from constructive criticism, work well with others, and enter challenges that pose a risk of failure. Their self-concept is fragile because it is completely dependent on other people's opinions. Thus, they are more easily swayed by fickle peer pressure and less capable of sacrificing for a greater purpose.

We can't allow the pursuit of superficial feelings to distract us from the ultimate goal: creating high quality people. This is the best approach for cultivating healthy long-term self-esteem. Building a true sense of confidence might require a few instructive low moments. As Baumeister et. al explain in their self-esteem analysis, there are plenty of instances where the only appropriate response is to feel bad:

> After all, Hitler had very high self-esteem and plenty of initiative, too, but those were hardly guarantees of ethical behavior. He attracted followers by offering them self-esteem that was not tied to achievement or ethical behavior—rather,

he told them that they were superior beings simply by virtue of being themselves, members of the so-called Master Race, an idea that undoubtedly had a broad, seductive appeal. We have found no data to indicate that indiscriminately promoting self-esteem in today's children or adults, just for being themselves, has any benefits beyond that seductive pleasure.

The empty self-importance we've worked so hard to instill in our children only serves to numb them from essential feedback that would pull them to become greater versions of themselves. It degrades our standards and lowers our collective capacity to embody worthwhile virtues.

If the highest value we can conceive of is physical and emotional safety, then we may successfully avoid many pains. But that comes at a price. We will be less curious, less connected, less capable, less courageous, and less admirable. We will be less and that brings far greater pains.

CHAPTER 5

HAVING MORE VS.
BEING MORE

*"Unless we keep the barbarian virtues, gaining the civilized ones
will be of little avail."*   *—Theodore Roosevelt*

What important truth do very few people agree with you on?

According to Peter Thiel, the billionaire tech entrepreneur and philanthropist, this is the best interview question you can ask. What do you believe that most people don't? As Thiel explains in his book, *Zero to One*, "It is intellectually difficult because the knowledge that everyone is taught in school is by definition agreed upon. And it's psychologically difficult because anyone trying to answer must say something she knows to be unpopular."

I'm sure many respond to Thiel with impressive sounding economic theories or, perhaps, a regurgitation of Thiel's own famous outside the box beliefs, like his assertion that many high-achieving young adults would be better off skipping college. If you randomly polled people on the street with this question, you'd probably get a lot of responses like, "Everything happens for a reason," "Nice guys actually finish first," "school doesn't prepare you for life," and the occasional, "9/11 was a government conspiracy." Next!

Being naturally skeptical of conventional wisdom—a quirk of being raised by a Clint Eastwood loving, doctoral philosophy professor who once graced the cover of Black Belt Magazine—I'd have no problem coming up with a list of my own unorthodox beliefs. I think normal citizens have no business selecting the most qualified person to be president (read Federalist 68 and you'll see that the U.S. founders warned against the modern perversion of our electoral college, where electors "prostitute their vote"), that all cultures are not equal, and that we are all better off in a society with some kidnappings, broken bones, and bullies. The cost of removing the possibility of every social ill is a world we do not want to live in.

But, before I risk offending more readers, I'll move to the truth I'd respond with:

Most people believe that the traditional markers of progress—more comfort, convenience, luxury, entertainment, and overall ease of life—are an undeniable good. They believe that with fewer inconveniences and more pleasures life will improve. However, I believe that as modern life becomes more convenient and comfortable—as it becomes easier and less chaotic—and as we are more entertained and face fewer hardships, humanity en masse grows more depressed and plagued by a sense of emptiness. Certainly, there are some universally positive innovations, like the smallpox vaccine and robot vacuums. And it isn't that Uber Eats and Google search aren't awesome in their own right, but the collective effect of mass diversions has been to breed less capable, less connected, less fully-activated humans.

As Yuval Noah Harari puts it in his latest book, *21 Lessons for the 21st Century*:

> We have bred docile cows that produce enormous amounts of milk, but are otherwise far inferior to their wild ancestors. They are less agile, less curious, and less resourceful. We are now creating tame humans that produce enormous amounts of data and function as very efficient chips in a huge data processing mechanism, but these data cows hardly maximize the human potential.

Our failed youth development paradigm is fueled by the misconception that, if it were possible, a life without responsibility would be optimal. The best life would just be for our children to win the lottery at age 22 so they never have to work for anything. In reality, nothing could be less fulfilling. Happiness is a lot more complex than just increasing pleasure and decreasing pain.

Sure, peanut butter cookies and pizza are awesome. Yet, we all intuitively grasp that a never-ending supply of cookies, reality TV, or whatever indulgence you crave won't add up to enduring happiness. These *lower pleasures*, as philosopher John Stuart Mill called them, are not bad, per se, but they grow destructive when we make them the point of life. Lasting fulfillment is much more dependent on self-actualization, which psychologist Abraham Maslow described as, "the desire to become more and more what one is, to become everything that one is capable of becoming." Maslow saw the process of moving toward self-actualization as the chief need of a human life.

The Greeks had another word: eudaimonia, which roughly translates to human flourishing or "life well lived." To them, happiness wasn't an immediate subjective state that came and went like the fleeting pleasures of pecan pie a la mode. Eudaimonia was the pursuit of a well-balanced ideal—one that became richer and more nuanced as we mature. To the Greeks, the life well lived was not an abstract passing notion. It was their north star—the chief aim of existence. They wrote books, developed hero-cults, and birthed philosophy as we know it, all in an effort to better understand this pursuit.

Today, we think a lot about happiness, but the culture at large is uncomfortable with topics such as *the life well lived*. Our failure to clarify a concept of happiness that goes beyond immediate gratification lies at the root of our mental health crisis. We've failed to clarify a more inspiring vision than feeling good all the time and, consequently, many grow up to find that life feels bland and meaningless.

HUMAN NEEDS

For years, the general narrative surrounding addiction and overdose were that these were strictly a chemical phenomenon. If there was a heroin overdose, the obvious cause (proximate and absolute) was heroin. Studies repeatedly demonstrated that when rats were offered both normal water and water with morphine, cocaine, or some other drug, they returned to the drugged water over and over, often resulting in an overdose. The assumption became that these drugs were irresistibly addictive.

Yet, Dr. Bruce Alexander and his colleagues saw a flaw in these studies. Rats are a social species, like us humans. But the rats who were used in all these studies lived isolated in tiny metal cages called Skinner boxes. They had no room for exercise, no sunlight, and no interaction with other rats. Dr. Alexander's team created a different environment that they called Rat Park. This large, open rat haven featured cans to hide in, chips to move about, wheels for exercise, and many other rats of both sexes. As you'd expect, Rat Park soon brimmed with rat babies. These social rats were then exposed to the same experiments as the caged rats held in the typical solitary confinement setting. However, unlike the caged rats, social rats tried the morphine solution, but rarely returned to it. These studies were replicated many times with the same results. Rats weren't interested in drugging themselves into oblivion when their deeper needs were met. A fulfilling environment seemed to counteract what was once considered an irresistible biochemical addiction.

I'm not suggesting that heroin isn't dangerous or addictive, just as I don't think we should ignore the dangers of limitless smartphones, junk food, and pharmaceuticals. What seems apparent is that these supernormal stimuli help form a larger Skinner box that is deeply out of touch with our human needs.

In his book, *Tribe*, war reporter Sebastian Junger notes an amazing pattern throughout history—humans love times that demand physical hardship, sacrifice, and heroism. Despite the pains, losses, and personal sacrifices required, mental health often improves in times of disaster. Whether the Bosnian civil war, the Battle of Britain, or Hurricane Katrina, we've watched as humanity rallies together, finds meaning, and experiences improvements in emotional health and wellbeing. When interviewed later, survivors almost universally reported missing the purpose and connection that the crisis brought to their lives.

Similarly, during the colonization of the Americas, there is no record of anyone from the native tribal populations ever trying to join the rich American colonies. Yet, on countless occasions, colonists threw off the trappings of their comfortable lives to join indigenous tribes. Something about the modern world seems to be leaving many starved of something essential. As Junger posits, "Humans don't mind hardship, in fact they thrive on it; what they mind is not feeling necessary. Modern society has perfected the art of making people not feel necessary."

For the vast majority of our time on earth, humans have lived in small bands of 50 to 150 people who relied on one another for survival. These bands hunted animals, fished, gathered plants, and moved in accordance with the patterns of nature.

Many of our modern issues stem from the significant discord between our environment and the experiences our biology evolved to expect. When you are born, every ounce of your DNA expects a hunter-gatherer lifestyle. We are not hardwired with any adaptations for a world dominated by bureaucracy, Coke, and smartphones—where you spend your daylight hours seated in rows waiting on an hourly bell to dismiss you to your next chair. This is actually a bizarre reality that our adaptable systems try hard to normalize. We are humans born into a world that expects us to behave like fish and all the while we wonder, "Why do my lungs burn?" You can only expect so much surrounded by an environment that ignores your bio-evolutionary needs.

According to Sebastian Junger, "Human beings need three basic things in order to be content: they need to feel competent at what they do; they need to feel authentic in their lives; and they need to feel connected to others. These values are considered 'intrinsic' to human happiness and far outweigh 'extrinsic' values such as beauty, money and status."

For our hunter-gatherer ancestors, competency, authenticity, and connection were the natural extension of daily life. The tribe hunted together, raised children together, starved together, feasted together, mourned together, and laughed together. Rites of passage forged common values and clarified the capabilities that earned adulthood. Tribesmen had little opportunity for posturing and superficiality. There were no illusions of utopia or that you should expect to feel good all the time. The hardship and loss characteristic of every human life was expected, openly embraced, and a source of shared humanity.

Today, we experience a higher standard of living than any people in human history. Our homes are cool in the summer and warm in the winter. Amazing technology allows us to play in virtual worlds, hear and see loved ones at the push of a button, and fly around the world while eating meals we had no hand in preparing. We're more likely to eat ourselves to death than starve to death. And unlike kings and queens a couple centuries ago, today's parents do not expect half their children to die in childhood. Yet, despite our material abundance, depression, anxiety, and general hopelessness have been steadily rising across the developed world.

I'm not suggesting you should give up your possessions and run away to the Amazon. I want you to fully appreciate this magical modern world with its low infant mortality rates, central air, and *Game of Thrones* memes. But to help our children thrive in the modern environment, we have to work to honor the needs programmed by our long nomadic past.

WHAT DO WE WANT AND WHY?

My father observed that humans have four instinctive behavioral responses: fighting, fleeing, feeding, and sex. The Four F's. These primal urges pull and prod us to fulfill our biology's chief mission—keeping our DNA alive. But we also have a realm of experience that transcends our basic instincts for self-preservation.

We expend valuable energy dancing and playing, we take immense pride in manipulating our food so that others can't help but eat more of it, and, sometimes, we even run into machine gun fire despite an overwhelming urge to flee. As the psychologist and father of sociology, Emile Durkheim explained, humans are governed by two often competing operating systems. We are what he called *Homo Duplex*—an animal compelled by carnal self-serving impulses, but also by the need to transcend ourselves through our relationship with society.

It is this desire, to be a part of something bigger, that has inspired almost every civilization to create art, music, sports, myth, and a sense of morality. But different societies take these pursuits in very different directions. Each culture is influenced by an infinite number of interrelated factors that conspire to produce very different attitudes, beliefs, and behaviors.

If you were born in ancient Sparta, for example, you would value courage and toughness over fashion and fine dining. You'd be more likely to pursue a glorious suicide mission than the riches of foreign conquest. If you grew up on a ranch in Montana, you'd probably value time in nature over big city amusement. You'd be more likely to spend an evening by the campfire than a night on the town. And if you grew up in China, you'd probably value order and tradition over individuality. You'd be more likely to grow up wanting to run a business than dreaming of becoming an actress, athlete, or rock star.

Each of these preferences indicates a differing value structure. While we often think of values in abstract, idealistic terms, our values are not necessarily the lofty virtues we advertise. Joe may claim to value education, but if he spends his evenings watching reality TV, scrolls Instagram photos all day, and won't be troubled to open a book, practice a skill, or even download an informative podcast, then other values rank higher for him. It isn't that Joe wouldn't like to be smarter or wiser. He would just *prefer* not learning over changing his behaviors.

According to author, Mark Manson, our values are the preference hierarchies that direct our choices, like a computer code that outputs our decisions. They tell us what to pursue, how to interpret events, and what matters. There are many different reasons for our values, but the largest influence is culture. The Spartan would *prefer* to die honorably than to stay home and miss a battle. An 18-year-old American living today would view that choice through a very different lens. That is the power of culture.

Culture tells us where to look for meaning and identity. It tells us what pursuits matter and what to care about. This raises the question: what dominant forces are creating our beliefs, expectations, and inclinations? Who are we becoming and why?

> *"If we understand the mechanism and motives of the group mind, it is now possible to control and regiment the masses according to our will without them knowing it."*
> —Edward Bernays

It takes a village to raise a child, or so the saying goes. But our villages have undergone a rapid deterioration over the past decades. They show all the markers of growth—the new schools, restaurant chains, and *Super Targets*—but with a marked loss of connection and identity. Communities are no longer the vehicles where culture spreads and evolves so much as they are the playing field where consumerist forces manifest.

Now more than ever before, our cultural values are being formed by people we've never met. Parents and community organizations have watched their influence steadily decline as an explosion of mass marketing and mass entertainment came to define our world. Today, these intertwined industries are the primary source of our values. They've transformed every sector of society and re-shaped the goals that drive our lives.

Americans consume more food, material items, and entertainment media than any people in history. This is not by accident. Our staggering abundance began with the birth of free market capitalism and the industrial revolution that it spurred. In a market economy, businesses compete to create the highest quality products at the cheapest price. This has stoked incredible efficiency and life changing innovations like refrigerators, vaccines, and automobiles. But as our quality of living went up, a greater portion of the economy became dedicated to increasing consumption for its own sake.

We saw the rise of processed sugary foods, porn, and eventually an attention economy where media outlets were rewarded for keeping us scrolling longer. If a desire could be tapped it would be, and then it was refined to become as irresistible as possible. Hypernormal stimuli came to dominate the environment exploiting our impulses at every turn. But we weren't just surrounded by more temptation than ever. An elaborate marketing industry developed based upon an explicit intent to influence people to crave, consume, and then crave more.

Perhaps no one was more responsible for the birth of marketing than Edward Bernays and his uncle, the groundbreaking psychologist, Sigmund Freud. Most of us think of Freud whenever there is an unfortunate slip of the tongue—*Yes ma'am. Thank you. This is the breast steak . . . I mean best steak I've ever had.* But Freud's influence goes far beyond explaining an embarrassing slip of the tongue—the so-called "Freudian slip." Freud believed that most human behaviors are controlled by unconscious drives and that despite the illusion of conscious choice, we tend to be pulled by our feelings. We behave as our subconscious feelings tell us to and, like a lawyer, our logical mind goes about rationalizing this course post hoc.

Bernays saw the opportunity in his uncle's revelation. If he could use modern technology to prey on those unconscious drives, he could manipulate mass behavior. He put these theories to work creating propaganda to increase support for World War I. But Bernays's real impact came after the war when he realized that the principles of propaganda could be used to influence mass movement during peacetime.

Before Bernays, advertisers focused on making people aware of products that they might want. Potential customers were seen as rational individuals who would hear about a product and decide whether they wanted it or not. Bernays demonstrated that by understanding the unconscious mind, advertisers could implant desires. Companies began adding marketing departments to conduct research on human persuasion. They made a science of pulling on our pain points and planting messages in every sector of society. Soon sports arenas, newspapers, and magazines were littered with ads and catchy jingles bounced around our brains. But modern marketing didn't really take off until after World War II, when an explosion of television consumption exponentially expanded the ability for advertisers to shape our thoughts and desires.

Today, the reach of these forces has multiplied. Marketing experts estimate that Americans see anywhere from 4,000 to 10,000 advertisements per day. With the advent of smartphones, Google, and algorithms capable of making sense of mass data collection, companies now exploit our individual vulnerabilities, sending personalized marketing packages right to our pockets—each with the same message: *Here is something you need to be happy. You have a problem and our product is the solution.*

Don't get me wrong, I enjoy this stuff too. I was over the moon that Brixie's stroller could do advanced Jiu-Jitsu to convert itself into a car seat. And while it initially felt like a luxury, her noise machine was re-purposed as my noise machine. *She never appreciated it anyway.* My hypocrisy doesn't stop there. I look forward to pleasures like a good cigar and a glass of bourbon. I dream of someday getting a pool, a ping-pong table, and an RV. And that smartphone I've been demonizing is among my most essential possessions.

There are a lot of great products out there that really can enhance our lives. My critique is of the association many have developed between self-worth and material possessions and between happiness and pleasure. Prioritizing these ends stands in the way of deeper fulfillment. We all know money doesn't buy happiness, yet our actions speak to a very different belief system complete with rituals, sacred texts, saints, and even a holy season.

If the religious analogy seems extreme, consider the verbiage used by marketing consultant, Victor Lebow, at the beginning of this consumerist revolution, in the Spring 1955 issue of the *Journal of Retailing*:

> Our enormously productive economy demands that we make consumption our way of life, that we convert the buying and use of goods into rituals, that we seek our spiritual satisfactions, our ego satisfactions, in consumption. The measure of social status, social acceptance, of prestige, is now to be found in our consumptive patterns. The very meaning and significance of our lives today expressed in consumptive terms. The greater the pressures upon the individual to conform to safe and accepted social standards, the more does he tend to express his aspirations and his individuality in terms of what he wears, drives, eats, his home, his car, his pattern of food serving, his hobbies . . . . We need to have people eat, drink, dress, ride, live, with ever more complicated and, therefore, constantly more expensive consumption . . . . We need things consumed, burned up, replaced, and discarded at an ever-accelerating rate.

Lebow's vision has come to fruition. Between birthdays, anniversaries, holidays, and the ever-expanding list of gift-worthy occasions, shopping has become everyone's part time job. All of our societal rituals revolve around purchases. If you are graduating soon, you need a class ring (which you will wear for less than a year). If you're getting married, you need another ring, a wedding shower, a $20,000 venue, a $3,000 photo package, and a brand new thousand-dollar dress that you will wear once. If you're having a baby, you need a baby shower, a bigger car, a wipe-warmer, fourteen sleeping contraptions, four million one-time photo-shoot outfits, the Jiu-Jitsu stroller, and two noise machines (get one for yourself and thank me later).

We've shortened the holiday that is about gratitude so we can get back to the store to shop for the holiday with loads of presents. We regret the Apple watch that was brand new three months ago, because there is now a newer version that alerts us of an impending fart.

Our culture is constantly telling us we need more comfort, more convenience, and more entertainment. And while I'd agree that Netflix, Amazon Prime, and pizza delivery are undeniably awesome, the problem is that, for most people, they are more than nice additions that enhance life on the way to a larger mission. They are the priorities that drive our daily lives. They have become our culture's collective *why*.

Why should I care about school?

So, you can get a better paying job and buy all the stuff you want.

Why do you work so much?

To get more of the things I need to be happy.

What do you do to be happy?

Eat sweets, scroll social media, shop, and binge television shows.

The pursuit of happiness is the defining objective of modern culture. But no matter how easy and full of pleasure our lives become, we aren't satisfied. The more society "progresses" the more our expectations grow. In other words, the more we pursue happiness the more it eludes our grasp.

This phenomenon has been called the hedonic treadmill. Each improvement in lifestyle becomes our new set point and our expectations rise making that old way of life, incomprehensibly meager. How did we ever live without a Roomba?

The hedonic treadmill explains why an oceanside drive is breathtaking to a vacationer, yet overlooked by the local resident and it's why the car you were so excited to purchase eventually becomes no more than a means to get from A to B. The hedonic treadmill is based on the same adaptive process as antifragility. We build a tolerance to whatever is normal in our lives. Whether stress or pleasure, we only notice the change *while* things are either getting better or worse.

No matter how magical our lives become it will not be enough. But there are more fruitful pursuits that make our lives meaningful and foster the competency, connection, and authenticity we need. Lasting happiness is better thought of as eudaimonia or self-actualization. Rather than accompanying the satisfaction of an external end-goal, eudaemonic happiness emerges within us as a consequence of pursuing better values.

The values guru, Mark Manson, developed criteria to distinguish between the "good" values that lead to consistent fulfillment and the "bad" values that wreak havoc in our lives.

According to Manson, good values tend to be:

1. Reality based: They engage with the world as it is rather than how we wish it would be.
2. Socially constructive: They have a positive or at least neutral effect on society.
3. Immediate and controllable: They are derived internally and, therefore, whether they are met or not is under our own control.

Examples: integrity, courage, learning, honesty, humility, empathy, toughness, adaptability, persistence, patience, health

By contrast, Manson concludes that bad values have one or more of the following characteristics:

1. Superstitious/founded upon rigid dogma (As we saw from the Lebow quote, materialist culture has intentionally sought to implant beliefs and take on the role of a sort of modern religion).
2. Socially destructive
3. Not immediate or controllable

Examples: being liked, pleasure, beauty, having money, having sex, being right, winning, comfort, convenience, being happy

None of these bad values are inherently bad outcomes. It is great to enjoy the exhilaration of winning and who doesn't like being liked? These are simply bad guiding values. We have no control over these outcomes. They are secondary concerns that are individually and socially destructive when prioritized over "good" values.

Unfortunately, both our most innate impulses and our marketing-saturated environment pull us toward unfulfilling values.

But let's not blame this all on big business. Businesses are often bastions of ingenuity and community. Marketing may have fueled this new religion, but for most of the players, our shift to consumer-ist values wasn't the result of some nefarious plot. Every business sets out to sell a good or service and if they can't influence us to consume their product then they will be replaced. The problem isn't that any one company worked to make sales. It is that business interests superseded every other concern. All our systems, from healthcare to politics to education, bowed to the whims of commerce. There was no institution working above the fray—no one standing up for human flourishing—no value above the market incentive.

As far back as 1947, English writer Dorothy Sayers, called upon education to check the influence of materialist culture and prepare society to live in a world of mass marketing, stating:

> For we let our young men and women go out unarmed in a day when armor was never so necessary. By teaching them all to read we have left them at the mercy of the printed word. By the invention of the film and the radio we have made certain that no aversion to reading shall secure them from the incessant battery of words, words, words. They do not know what the words mean; they do not know how to ward them off or blunt their edge or fling them back; they are prey to words in their emotions instead of being masters of them in their intellects.

Like Sayers, I believe education is the answer. Schools are the cultural nucleus best positioned to pull our values in a better direction. They should be the authority in human development dedicated to giving people the tools to take control of their lives, make sense of the world, and determine what pursuits will be most rewarding. But such goals are largely absent from the thought process of most educators. Our kids are woefully unprepared for the world we have created.

CHAPTER 6

FLYING TO OUR OWN DEMISE

"We have never been more in the thrall of human nature and its destructive potential than now, and by ignoring this fact we are playing with fire. The permeability of our emotions has only been heightened by social media where viral effects are continuously sweeping through us and where the most manipulative leaders are able to exploit and control us . . . . The potential for mayhem, stemming from the primitive side of our nature has only increased."
—Robert Greene

I stared off the dock at the bait fish frantically circling an underwater light. As if choreographed, hundreds of them repeated the same counter-clockwise pattern over and over with no end in sight. Their whole lives, it seemed, would be nothing more than this circle. Brayden, my destruction-bent nine-year-old nephew threw a pebble at them. In perfect uniformity the entire collective darted right, before rapidly returning back into formation to resume their obsessive task.

"Why are they doing that?" Brayden wondered aloud.

"Because of the light." my wife, Neely, responded.

"That's stupid." Brayden added.

Feeling the need, as usual, to shatter this simple moment with heavy life lessons, I interjected:

"It is just like humans and smartphones. These fish are driven by a biology that never could have expected a world of fluorescent, artificial underwater light. Like moths to the flame and humans to the infinite Instagram scroll, any other purpose has been overridden by a powerful, biological draw."

"Oh. Well, I'm going inside," says Brayden. Neely looks at me and shakes her head.

As ill-conceived as my message was for a third grader, it is a fundamental understanding for anyone concerned with living well in our bizarre modern world. Our biology did not expect this world of incessant, hyper-normal stimuli, where the natural rewards that once helped us survive and thrive are now available in extreme, unnatural doses, often completely removed from the evolutionary benefits they once ensured. We need some sort of framework for mediating the complexities of modernity and our staggering technological advancements or we may spend our days as aimlessly as those bait fish.

Imagine that moths were somehow granted the same brain power that humans have and given access to the same scientific heritage and social structures. A super-intelligent moth civilization now populates the earth. But these moths are not prepared for the billions of artificial lights in industrialized societies. Wouldn't it seem careless for these super-intelligent moths to ignore their inconvenient tendency to make kamikaze flights at fluorescent light bulbs? You'd expect their education system to devote a significant degree of attention to the dangers of flying towards light and how best to avoid this shocking demise.

Likewise, you'd expect our school systems to identify the primary threats to human flourishing and to work to offset them. The advance of technology has allowed for chemical combinations and constant sensory overload that our biology was not designed to handle. Our survival instincts tell us to gorge when we find high calorie food. We're not built for a world of all-you-can-eat buffets and homes filled with cookies and dessert cereals—where you can sit inside in nearly every waking moment—where messenger notifications constantly beckon and algorithms always deliver the perfect video "up next."

Among the vast number of hypernormal stimuli today, there are three particularly insidious forces that parents, schools, and developmental institutions must begin to counteract: the convenience food industry (Food Giants), the technology design industry (Big Tech), and the pharmaceutical industry (Big Pharma). In the absence of a unifying commitment to human flourishing, these forces have swept in to degrade us for their profit. In this chapter, I'll look at each of these industries and later, in an aside on practical parenting practices at the end of Chapter 9, I'll offer specific steps to combat their influence.

A PORTRAIT OF AMERICAN HEALTH

"We may be approaching a time when sugar is responsible for more early deaths in America than cigarette smoking."
—Dr. Lewis Cantley

According to the 2015-2020 Dietary Guidelines for Americans Report, "About half of all American adults have one or more preventable, diet-related chronic diseases, including cardiovascular disease, type 2 diabetes, and overweight and obesity." 38% of United States adults are now obese, which makes obesity (a step above the overweight classification) the most prominent BMI category. This number is expected to reach 44% by 2030. Most shockingly, a 2016 Harvard study predicted that of youth between the ages of two and nineteen, 57% will be obese by the time they are 35.

Much of the problem is that we underestimate the addictive nature of common industrial foods. Studies on lab rats show that rats will eat Oreos far past the point of satiation (to be fair these rats are almost certainly depressed). In another study, rats that were already addicted to cocaine and morphine chose saccharin, a calorie-free sweetener, 94% of the time. Even after upping the dose of cocaine, rats still preferred the sensation of intense sweetness. The combination of corporate strategy, cultural indoctrination, and chemical engineering has ingrained habits in most of society which are as hard to break as many more stigmatized addictions.

Michael Moss's Pulitzer Prize-winning book, *Salt Sugar Fat*, reveals the story of an industry that is well aware of its effect on global health. In 1999, heads of all the largest food companies—General Mills, Kraft, Coca-Cola, Kellogg, Frito-Lay, Nestle, Nabisco, Pillsbury, Cargill, and others—gathered at Pillsbury headquarters for a rare meeting among rivals to discuss the negative publicity circulating about their role in creating a health crisis. Many companies believed they were in for a reckoning and that they would have to change their products. But then the CEO of General Mills, Stephen Sanger, took the floor and communicated a clear directive. Stay the course. Fickle consumers could be easily duped. It was not a time for reinvention, but rather, a re-commitment to the manipulative arts that had allowed them to take over society in the first place.

Food manufacturers began to employ new tricks like promoting new, lower calorie options with loads of sugar added to make up for reduced fat. Moss outlines a vast array of tactics that these companies used to sink the hook even deeper into American society. Of all of these, baiting children remains the most important part of their marketing strategy.

The Food Giants prey on young customers who will badger exhausted parents until they slowly succumb to an almost entirely convenience food diet. We see this in the Play Places and Happy Meal toys at McDonald's, in Coke's ploy to be synonymous with every landmark event (they seemingly own the movie theaters), and most obviously in cereal commercials. Each cereal comes equipped with a Tony the Tiger, a Count Chocula, or even a silly rabbit who struggles to understand that Trix are only for kids.

Frosted Mini-Wheats even had the audacity to advertise that "a clinical study showed kids who had a filling breakfast of Frosted Mini-Wheats cereal improved their attentiveness by nearly 20%." Of course, this claim was debunked and Kellogg's was forced to stop advertising it. But the lie had already gained traction. Kellogg's market research indicated a full 51% of adults surveyed believed the claim was true, and true only for Frosted Mini-Wheats. Oy vey.

THE BATTLE OF THE BETTYS
FOR HOME ECONOMICS

There was a time when schools and parents would have never accepted modern eating norms. Before Betty Crocker, there was Betty Dickson. Unlike Mrs. Crocker, Dickson was a real person with real conviction. Having grown up on a farm in South Carolina, she believed in homegrown and home-cooked meals. After graduating college in the early 1950s, she began teaching home economics, and soon became the national model for this once essential course.

Betty Dickson taught students to make grocery lists, budget, and shop for the highest quality ingredients at the lowest prices. Most importantly, she taught them to prepare nourishing meals and to understand how vital this was to strong families and a strong nation. Cooking was considered a core competency. In her day, the Home Economics Association was instrumental in consumer activism. They fought the push of convenience food, and lobbied in Washington for "nutritious, inexpensive cooked food in the home and in school."

By the mid-1950s, however, the Food Giants were making inroads. They knew that if they could infiltrate the schools, they would be able to change the diet and food attitudes of a new generation. Through education they could redirect the habits of a nation. But how were they to overcome the strength of concerned parents and their allies in the Home Economics Association?

General Foods took the lead. First, they hired an arsenal of their own home economics "teachers." These always attractive young women were not employed in schools, but they set up everywhere else to show how convenience foods could emancipate women from the tyranny of food preparation. They held cooking competitions and conducted cooking classes to compete with those in public schools.

General Mills then created Betty Crocker to be the spiritual lead of a new cooking paradigm. Betty, who existed in name only, advertised incessantly, responded to fan mail, and constantly preached the values of the convenience kitchen: "Just Heat and Serve!"

Still, this influence would remain on the fringe as long as schools opposed it. The food industry had to somehow insert itself into the schools. In order to win the hearts of a new generation of home economics teachers, General Foods became the largest source of home economics scholarship money. In 1957 alone, General Foods gave over $288,250 to a college grant and fellowship program for future home economics teachers. To put this ample sum in the context of its time, in 1958 annual tuition at Kansas State University was $104 and $53 at California State University.

With the teachers indebted to them, General Foods could finally colonize the schools with its advertising machine. Over the next few years, the new teacher advocates radically shifted the home economics curriculum from teaching resourcefulness and the skills necessary for a healthy home to an indoctrination into materialism and convenience culture.

These were the opening salvoes of the marketing campaign that helped create our current health epidemic. The institutions charged with leading America's development were effectively on the convenience food industry's payroll from then on. Over time the other Food Giants made their way into schools with their own clever ploys, like General Mills' *Box Tops for Education* program. Families are encouraged to score points for their school by eating Pizza Rolls, Count Chocula cereal, and hundreds of other nutritionally devoid products.

Today, the food industry's infiltration of education is complete. Our schools rely more than ever on revenue streams from junk food. Vending machines line the halls. PTA parents sell cookies whose scent could rival the Siren's song. Districts negotiate contracts to sell specific soda products, clubs sell crates of candy to raise money, teachers promise pizza parties whenever they want compliance, and FCA meetings attract students with the promise of donuts. The anti-drug program D.A.R.E. even rewards students with a D.A.R.E. card that earns them a free soda at participating establishments. *Hey kid, stay away from cigarettes and have a free daily soda, on me.* We seemingly cannot conceive of any way other than junk food to incentivize behavior.

What you'll find in the cafeteria is no better (despite the ceremonial bowl of apples and bananas). Breakfast is chocolate milk, French toast sticks with loads of syrup, or a single-serving sugar bomb cereal. Lunch is nachos, white bread chicken sandwiches, sloppy joes, or square pizza. Without a trace of irony, schools call their cafeterias "nutrition departments," and boast of serving X number of nutritious meals a year.

Every conceivable moment of the educational experience has become an endless conveyor belt of convenience food and sweets. The solution to our eating crisis lies where it began. Education must honestly assess this environment and commit to their responsibility to become the authority in human development. They will face many disgruntled parents, students, and sponsors. But we must have the integrity to raise funds in different ways and to place a nation's health over fancy atriums, new uniforms, and expensive trips.

I'm not advocating nutritional puritanism. I enjoy ice cream, pizza, and a nice glass of bourbon as much as anyone else. These are fun deviations from my daily habits. But there is nothing nice or normal about the nutritional norms schools help facilitate. When people have no exposure to healthy habits—when eating real foods is considered a bizarre monastic experience that is only for "health freaks," then they suffer greatly. Our schools set the daily schedule and habits of an entire nation's children. We should make normal things normal, like a diet that predominately consists of foods that existed before the industrial revolution.

KIDS' FOODS

I sometimes speak at sports parent meetings to talk about the best ways for athletes to stay healthy and perform well. After one football parent meeting, an outraged mother sought me out. She took offense at my suggestion that parents could help their kids by limiting the amount of junk food available at home. As she said, *"I'm not going to not have chips and soda for my kids! Cheetos and Doritos are part of being a kid!"*

Eating is an emotional topic. Parents have memories of their own experience and, since the health consequences of eating habits are delayed, it seems harmless to let kids eat like they did. We tend to think of nutrition only in terms of physique and fat loss. From that lens, youngsters should take advantage of their fast metabolism while they have it. But you wouldn't give kids cigarettes in kindergarten and say, "They're kids! They won't have to worry about lung cancer until they're much older. Let them smoke. They like it!" The analogy isn't perfect, but it makes the point. It is considered normal to saturate kids in an environment that virtually ensures they'll deal with the chronic mental, physical, and emotional effects exacerbated by the Western diet.

Today, even health-conscious parents often cook separate dinners for their children. They'll work hard to change their habits and create a healthy lifestyle for themselves, only to cook their children something different every night. Mommy and Daddy are having salmon, asparagus, and sweet potatoes, and little Jasmine is having mac and cheese, fish sticks, and her nightly dessert afterward. These are considered "kids' foods." Other popular kids' foods include chicken nuggets, pizza rolls, frozen pizzas, and white bread and Velveeta grilled cheese sandwiches.

Parents often claim that their kids only like "kids' foods." They forget that until very recently, such foods did not even exist. The problem is not Bobby's unique palate but that Bobby's parents won't wait him out. He won't starve himself. Sure, there are things Bobby will just not like, but allowing him to not eat any vegetables because he says he doesn't like them, should not be an option. If parents don't insist on growing their child's tolerance for nutritious foods, he is almost certain to struggle with health.

We are creating our kids' conception of normal. We are creating their palate and distorting it to appreciate only the extremely sweet and processed. Take your kids out for ice cream on occasion, but avoid the daily deluge. Few gifts will be more valuable to our children than helping them become healthy eaters.

BIG TECH AND THE ATTENTION ECONOMY

"It is easier to fool people than to convince them they have been fooled."   *—Unknown*

Just as hyper-normal food stimuli can addict us to eating patterns that are self-destructive, hyper-normal social tools are tugging at our emotions and weakening the broader social fabric in the process. And like the industrial food takeover, money and power often incentivize these socially destructive technological developments.

Clickbait is big business. Internet ad revenue totaled $124.6 billion in 2019 up from $107.5 billion in 2018. Advertisers invest their money where people spend the most time. The more a site can get you to scroll, click, or stare at a page, the more dollars they will earn. In contrast to the classic journalistic approach, where higher quality work is expected to bring attention, technology designers have invested heavily in manipulating our biological vulnerabilities. Time spent on screen is not seen as the side effect of valuable work, but the explicit intent of the tech business model. We are not a customer to be satisfied. *We are the product* that is being sold to advertising agencies. Whatever gets our eyes to the screen is bait.

Former Google web designer Tristan Harris, founder of The Center for Humane Technology and the primary driver of the *Social Dilemma* film, has been vocal in exposing the goals that drive the technology industry. As he says:

"There's a hidden goal driving the direction of all the technology we make, and that goal is the race for our attention . . . The best way to get people's attention is to know how someone's mind works . . . Technology is not neutral." Harris claims that tech companies are competing in a race to the bottom of the brain stem. They invest heavily in neuroscience in order to exploit every vulnerability.

Harris was taught the tricks of this trade at Stanford's Persuasive Technology Lab. Some of these include:

- **Intermittent, variable rewards**: Checking your phone sometimes result in nothing, but often gives you information that elicits an emotion. The uncertainty of whether awards will be waiting or not keeps us coming back. This is the phenomenon behind slot machines, which make more money each year than professional baseball, movies, and theme parks combined. We now have a slot machine in our pockets at all times, which helps explain why most people check their phone over 150 times a day.
- **Social approval and reciprocation**: Like buttons and retweets get right at our evolutionary need for social acceptance, but steer us away from nuance and towards herd superficiality. Follows give us a subconscious tug to reciprocate.
- **Bottomless bowls and auto-play**: Perhaps the most effective tactic that technology companies use to keep you scrolling and watching longer is to keep the flow of juicy morsels uninterrupted, with precious little input from you, the user. Netflix plays the next video before you can stop the binge. Instagram allows you to swipe down forever. And for some reason every time you go to YouTube to get a video for a presentation, you spend two hours watching cathartic political rants or acoustic covers of your favorite songs. Every media company is busy collecting information on each of us to make the next item too irresistible to pass up.
- **Instant interruption versus respectful delivery**: As we saw with blood donors in chapter one, humans tend to default. There is no reason Facebook messages, emails, or texts have to be seen the second they come through, but we've come to expect this because the default setting is built so that all notifications beep and prod us as constantly as possible.

At the root of most of these methods is the manipulation of dopamine: a powerful neurotransmitter that causes you to seek out more of what gave you your last hit. It is the itch you must scratch. Our biology is magnetically pulled to texts, videos, likes, games, and the never-ending instant gratification that is offered by the slot machine in the palm of your hand. It is no wonder that recent generations have been transformed and defined by their screens.

THE GENERATION OF DIGITAL NATIVES

A 2015 Common Sense Media report found that teenagers averaged almost 9 hours a day of entertainment media, *excluding time spent at school.* Do the math. When are they not on their phone? These aren't just subtle cultural changes. Incessant screen entertainment strips kids of the qualities most vital for fulfillment, healthy relationships, and future employability. As Victoria Prooday, explains:

> Using technology as a 'free babysitting service' is, in fact, not free at all. The payment is waiting for you just around the corner. We pay with our kids' nervous systems, with their attention, and with their ability for delayed gratification. Compared to virtual reality, everyday life is boring.

In 2012, smartphone ownership crossed the 50% threshold. By 2015, 73% of teens had smartphones. In direct correlation, between 2010 and 2015, the number of teens who claimed to "feel useless and joyless" rose 33% in national surveys. Likewise, teen suicide attempts jumped 23% and actual suicides jumped 31%.

According to psychologist Jean Twenge, there is strong evidence that "smartphone use and depression increase in tandem . . . . " Her studies reveal that "teens who spent five or more hours a day online were 71% more likely than those who spent less than an hour a day to have at least one suicide risk factor." More time online is more time our kids are sedentary, isolated, and obsessing upon curating their image for an artificial world.

Critics of Twenge often point to a few studies which seem to indicate that increased screen time (broadly defined) does not cause mental disorders. However, when Jean Twenge and Jonathan Haidt re-analyzed this data and looked at smartphone screen time only (rather than all screens) and looked at girls specifically, they saw a clear relationship between heavy social media use and depression and anxiety. It appears that all screens are not equally harmful. Typical male use has less of a negative impact than typical female use, at least in regard to immediate mental well-being.

Girls tend to use social media more obsessively than boys who spend a lot more time on video games. While these games are also addictive, they're more likely to foster feelings of productivity and connection. Gamers share missions and problem-solve together. I am still concerned about addictive video games nudging out real world activity and ambition, but they do not seem to bring the immediate mental health harm that social media does.

Still, there are voices I respect who have tried to take the *too-clever* stance that since correlation does not mean causation, there is no decisive evidence that social media is harming our society. They'll point to the need for more evidence and try to equate the hysteria around smartphone culture to past fears of violent video games. But there is an obvious blind spot in anyone who tries to argue that new smartphone norms aren't contributing to decreased happiness and a divisive, alienating social climate. Such reductionist arguments are analogous to past claims that fats, calories, and lack of exercise are the cause of growing obesity and, thus, Coke is no more a part of the problem than almonds or any food or beverage of a similar calorie count. As we've seen, smartphones aren't the only cause of increased mental disorder, but they exacerbate every causal factor. Any study of happiness, success, or the conditions that contribute to human flourishing points to the development of emotional abilities and social conditions that smartphone culture diminishes.

But we should be asking a far better question than whether or not social media reduces happiness. Does it hurt our kids' ability to become competent, admirable, resilient people who have the tools and inclinations to deal with the tremendous challenges ahead of them? Is it making us more or less?

Distraction and manipulation are virtually impossible to mitigate without a framework that teaches us how to access technology's benefits without, ourselves, being used by that technology. Rather than playing to society's perception that all technology is progress, our schools should be the experts, helping to clarify and instill responsible tech habits. They should be on the cutting edge of the manipulator's methods, teaching both parents and students how to create structures that prevent manipulation.

THE CURES THAT ARE KILLING US

"Alarmed by something in the present we grab for a solution without thinking about the context, the roots of the problem, and the possible unintended consequences."   —Robert Greene

Billy Smith is a talented high school baseball player. As such, his parents send him to a pitching coach, a hitting coach, and recruiting showcases on any weekend that he does not have games. Between his year-round select club and the high school team, this is not often. Billy's parents have always put baseball first, but now that he is a junior in high school their obsession has grown too all-encompassing.

When he isn't playing ball, Billy's young brain ping-pongs between video games, social media, and other online activity. In addition to his smartphone consumption, he has two Monster energy drinks every morning and makes a couple of fast-food stops before the day is over. This doesn't include the donuts, Pop-Tarts, and candy that characterize his daily snacking. After a few bad grades, Billy claims that he can't focus. His mother takes him to a doctor who determines that Billy has ADHD. His daily cocktail now includes Adderall.

More recently Billy has become angry, rude, and prone to disrespectful tirades. He doesn't sleep well and he's losing interest in baseball. So, his parents take him to another doctor. Enter more pharmaceutical drugs.

The United States accounts for 45% of global pharmaceutical sales. We are one of only two countries in the world that allow direct-to-consumer drug advertising with product claims. Advertising tells us to go to the doctor and tell them we have some affliction and we want the drug that fixes it. *Ask your doctor about X.*

We are programmed to expect a quick fix anytime something feels off. Rather than explore whether the patterns of our insane environment might have anything to do with our problems, we assume there is something inherently wrong with us. When we can't sleep, we don't set a sleep schedule, avoid screens while in bed, learn to meditate, or explore the science behind sleep. We take melatonin or Ambien. High blood pressure isn't a call to reexamine our diet, stress levels, and lifestyle. We blame it on genetics and expect pharmaceuticals to solve the problem. Genetics often play a role, but the answer is rarely just medication. We have to be part of the solution, as well. Our pain is a feedback mechanism. If we listen, it can teach us about ourselves and point us in the direction we need to grow. The obvious, yet rarely professed truth is that, if it is possible to fix a disorder without drugs, that is preferable. Drugs tend to have side effects, whether we are aware of them or not. This is not something to invite nonchalantly.

For all its ills, the pharmaceutical industry has made many medical breakthroughs like lengthening lifespans for those with H.I.V. and leukemia, or, more recently, developing multiple COVID-19 vaccines in less than one year. But such miracles don't excuse the unethical tactics that have become commonplace throughout the pharmaceutical industry.

In his recent book, *Bad Pharma*, epidemiologist, Dr. Ben Goldacre addresses the methods Big Pharma uses to trick doctors and create a veneer of safety and acceptance around drugs that are destroying lives. As Goldacre explains:

> Drugs are tested by the people who manufacture them, in poorly designed trials, on hopelessly small numbers of weird, unrepresentative patients, and analyzed using techniques that are flawed by design, in such a way that they exaggerate the benefits of treatments . . . . When trials throw up results the companies don't like, they are perfectly entitled to hide them from doctors and patients, so we only ever see a distorted picture of any drug's true effects.

In 2012, Shire pharmaceuticals, the producer of market leader Adderall (which in a cartoonishly evil stroke, they named to explicitly state their goal of ADD medication for ALL), created an extremely successful campaign to convince adults they had ADHD. Adam Levine and other celebrities pointed adults to a quick quiz, which would inevitably reveal that ADHD had been holding them back. The idea was to make ADHD sexy and create the appearance that millions of adults had been silently sabotaged by this hidden curse, afraid of the stigma attached to their disorder. Against the prevailing scientific wisdom that ADHD often went away in adulthood, they now claimed a phenomenon called "Adult-Onset ADHD" was sweeping the nation. And who could argue against such a claim without appearing insensitive? We've been trained to feel uncomfortable voicing opinions about overdiagnosis or unhealthy cultural norms. Such commentary should be reserved for doctors, we are told. But, for a number of reasons, the medical establishment does not reliably give good advice.

We expect to be able to turn to doctors for health advice, but pharmaceutical companies go to great lengths to confuse doctors and prey on our faith in them. As Goldacre asserts:

. . . after leaving medical school, doctors hear about what works ad hoc, from sales reps, colleagues, and journals. But those colleagues can be in the pay of drug companies—often undisclosed—and the journals are, too. And so are the patient groups. And finally, academic papers, which everyone thinks of as objective, are often covertly planned and written by people who work directly for the companies, without disclosure.

It is not just that Big Pharma sells addictive drugs with side-effects that should make us wary. They will seemingly stop at nothing to convince people that they have issues that don't exist, requiring drugs that aren't as safe as advertised and don't do what they claim. They normalize introducing drugs with little benefit and great long-term cost, while distracting the public from healthier responses. They grease the hands of politicians and muddy every study to the point where no one has a clue whether disorders are real or imagined, whether drug treatment is necessary or preferable or what the real long-term consequences are.

In the instance of adult-onset ADHD, Shire's pharmaceutical reps worked to discourage doctors from weaning patients off of medication, as had been the popular wisdom, and to begin advising their adult patients about the benefits of lifelong Adderall. Why have a customer for ten years when you could have them for 60?

In the 1960s, after analyzing years of data sets, Dr. Keith Connors came to believe that 2-3% of youth suffered from what he called Attention Deficit Hyperactivity Disorder, ADHD. The American Psychiatric Association (APA) maintains that this remains the appropriate rate. Since the 1990s, however, Connors noted a disturbing over-diagnosis. By 2003, the CDC found that 7.8% of American children had been diagnosed with ADHD. Currently, over 15% of high school students are diagnosed as having ADHD (20% of boys), and over 3.5 million are medicated. As Connors asserted, "The numbers make it look like an epidemic. Well it's not. It's preposterous."

Perhaps we should question what we consider normal before concluding that one out of five boys have a hyperactive disorder. Maybe seven-year-olds should not be forced to sit all day. Perhaps moving, exploring, running, jumping, pushing, and playing are normal behaviors. At the very least, maybe some kids don't need drugs for their peculiar restlessness—just a different approach. As the late educational innovator, Sir Ken Robinson, put it, "If you sit kids down, hour after hour, doing low-grade clerical work, don't be surprised if they start to fidget. Children are not, for the most part, suffering from a psychological problem. They are suffering from childhood."

There are certainly instances when medication is warranted. But such legitimate cases do not negate the problems of flippant medicating or the deeper issue of a culture that thinks it is normal for most of its population to need drugs.

> *"Hyper-normal stimuli happen to be good for markets because on the supply side, if I want to maximize the lifetime value of a customer, addiction is good . . . but it is very bad for society as a whole."* —*Daniel Schmachtenberger*

Like most physicians, Dr. Sam Everington was trained to believe that depression was caused by a chemical imbalance. It was a linear equation. Low levels of some neurotransmitter were causing a patient's depression. He could then add these drugs to fix that. Yet, when he talked to patients, this simple, symptom-focused picture proved insufficient. Patients always had a deeper angst—a cause or, more commonly, an absence. The problem wasn't their brains, it was their lives.

Around the corner from Dr. Everington's East London clinic was an ugly space the locals called "Dog Shit Alley." For years this dark walking tunnel had been a breeding ground for graffiti, litter, and dog shit. Dr. Everington and colleagues organized a program to funnel groups of depressed people towards volunteering projects, like beautifying Dog Shit Alley. A site coordinator facilitated groups of around 20 depressed, anxious, or otherwise distressed people. Yet,

unlike traditional mental health initiatives, their goal was to interfere as little as possible. There would be no counseling, questions, or
specific agenda other than the project at hand.

After years of crippling depression, Lisa Cunningham was put
on the Dog Shit Alley project. She and her peers were tasked with
turning this wasteland into a beautiful garden of flowers and vegetables. Neither the alley nor the group's emotional well-being improved
overnight. Many plants failed. They had to learn about nature, about
the seasons, and about what plants would thrive in their environment. As Ms. Cunningham observed:

> You can't change how nature is . . . . Creating a garden takes
> time and an investment of energy and commitment . . . You
> might not feel you've made much impact in one gardening
> session, but if you do that every week, over a period of time
> you'll see change.

Slowly group members began to trust each other and open up
about their challenges. They'd go to the local café after gardening
sessions. The garden slowly bloomed and people would walk by and
thank them for their efforts. They began to feel useful and appreciated. They reconnected with people and community. And they reconnected with nature.

Ms. Cunningham credits nature itself for giving her back a "sense
of place." As she put it, "those two things that I had completely lost
contact with (community and nature) had come back into my life
again." After a few years in the gardening program, Lisa Cunningham
got off Prozac, lost 62 pounds, married a gardener, and is now opening her own garden center in Wales.

In his book, *Lost Connections*, Johann Hari details this story and
many others about people who have overcome crippling disorders.
Hari, who battled depression through most of his life, recounts how
over and over he'd get a prescription, feel better for a while, but then
eventually he'd slip back into a dark hole. The doctor would prescribe

more powerful drugs and the cycle would repeat. According to Hari, research suggests that there are nine causes of depression, only two of which are chemical. The rest deal with the way our environment interacts with our biology. As he contends, "The most effective strategies for dealing with depression and anxiety are the ones that deal with the reasons people are depressed and anxious in the first place."

The most important lessons for our schools and youth development institutions to teach are about how to thrive in our modern environment. We should be obsessed with understanding the human experience—who we are, how we think, what we need, where our blind spots are, and how to master ourselves so that we are best able to determine a fulfilling path and then walk it. But to make changes at a broader level, we have to first understand the flawed thinking that created our flawed youth development paradigm. Attempts to reform education will do more harm than good if we don't first correct the immature notions of progress driving mainstream initiatives. As we'll see, much of our problem is a proliferation of bad ideas and good intentions gone astray. For our children and our society to thrive, we have to dig deeper into the complex interplay between humans and society. Only then will we be able to define a better vision. The next section will lay the groundwork for that vision.

SECTION II

THE COST OF UTOPIAN DELUSIONS

"To break sharply with the past is to court the madness that may follow the shock of sudden blows or mutilations. As the sanity of the individual lies in the continuity of his memories, so the sanity of a group lies in the continuity of its traditions; in either case a break in the chain invites a neurotic reaction, as in the Paris massacres of September, 1792.

Since wealth is an order and procedure of production and exchange rather than an accumulation of (mostly perishable) goods, and is a trust (the credit system) in men and institutions rather than in the intrinsic value of paper money or checks, violent revolutions do not so much re-distribute wealth as destroy it. There may be a redivision of the land, but the natural inequality of men soon re-creates an inequality of possessions and privileges, and raises to power a new minority with essentially the same instincts as in the old.

The only real revolution is in the enlightenment of the mind and the improvement of character, the only real emancipation is individual, and the only real revolutionists are philosophers and saints."

—Will & Ariel Durant, The Lessons of History

CHAPTER 7

THE COST OF UTOPIAN DELUSIONS

"This is the tragedy of modernity: as with neurotically over-protective parents, those trying to help are often hurting us the most."
—Nassim Taleb

There has not been a kidnapping in 5 years.

Online trolling has been eliminated.

Politicians operate in full transparency.

And murder, assault, theft, vandalization, and crime at every level virtually ceases.

This utopia is the world of David Eggers' book, *The Circle*, named after the Google-esque tech company at the center of its plot. After inventing *TruYou*, a system that eliminates any need for passwords and makes it impossible to steal identities, The Circle grows to dominate the entire technology industry from social media and messaging to security and voting. Early on, things don't seem much different from our own screen-dominated world. However, when The Circle develops barely visible cameras that can be stuck anywhere and then linked to a searchable database, they begin focusing on expanding the possibilities of what can be known.

Before long live footage of the entire world is accessible with a few keyboard strokes. You can see anything, search anyone, and catch every crime, lie, insensitive comment, or nuanced opinion. Transparency becomes its own dogma as The Circle's progressive leader adopts the position that privacy is a theft of knowledge. *All that happens must be known.* Because people only hide the bad parts, right?

Public pressure begins to demand that politicians wear cameras all day, but of course this only further dumbs down their work as they seek to behave so inoffensively as to appease everyone. Each person obsessively curates an agreeable virtual image, "participating" neurotically in an effort to prove their commitment to the norms of the herd. Life becomes a performance.

Eggers' terrific book (which was regrettably turned into an awful movie) conveys an essential lesson: In the age of infinite technology, naive good intentions are likely to be far more dangerous than bad intentions. But this has always been the case.

At the height of its colonial dominance, it was said that the sun never set on the British Empire. Of all its colonies, none were as prized as India. After conquering Delhi in 1803, British settlers poured in. But many complained about the venomous cobras that slithered throughout the city. The British government decided to solve this problem by offering to pay Indian villagers for every dead cobra. The logic was simple. *Cobra bad. Kill cobra.* But native Indians began breeding more cobras in order to earn more rewards. The British caught on and canceled the payment program, but this only spurred angry natives to release their cobras into the wild. Within a short time, Delhi's cobra population tripled.

Far from the exception, these *cobra effects* are almost always the rule of sweeping attempts to make life safer or, even more illusively, *fair.* We've already seen cobra effects in over-automated airline protocols, over-regulated streets, over-cushioned shoes, over-sanitized environments, and, of course, overprotected kids. While this phenomenon is nothing new, it is more of a threat now than ever. Modern technology makes the consequences of naive goals exponentially larger and mainstream society (most notably, schools) show a disturbing tendency to prioritize naive objectives. Today, utopian delusions are at the center of almost every mainstream goal.

We want everyone to have high self-esteem, respect, maximal safety, and free access to the most valuable commodities. We want to create a legal system so sophisticated as to quantify the exact price of each person's pain. We want an education system that ensures every student receives the same lessons at the same quality with the same workload but which also modifies work to accommodate every individual difference. We want to be so enlightened, so *woke*, that we detect every conceivable disadvantage and offset each with an individualized, proportional response. Despite all the "good" driving these wants, the refusal to confront reality invites unintended consequences that often dwarf the benefits of our efforts.

I'm not saying that we shouldn't dream. After all, airplanes and immunizations once seemed impossible. It is important to strive towards collective progress. But we have to engage with the world and with human nature as they are, rather than how we wish them to be.

> *"No one defends gulags today, but the world remains full of suckers for the false utopian promises that bring gulags into existence."*
> —Rod Dreher

For most of history, societies have recognized a basic order to the world. They saw themselves as a part of this world, subject to its cycles, and dependent upon its functioning well. Consequently, they built their cultures on philosophies and religions which tried to make sense of the natural order and bring the person into harmony with it.

But the scientific revolution challenged this. Suddenly thinkers began to see the world like a mathematical equation, with fixed variables that could be understood and manipulated to create specific outcomes. We no longer saw ourselves as part of a reality that transcends us but as the philosopher and mathematician Rene Descartes said, as the "masters and possessors of nature." Whatever was inconvenient or uncomfortable could and should be reshaped to fit our desires.

In this view, history was no longer an instructive lens into the nature of human societies and the human experience, but an account of the flaws that should be fixed. History showed us all the imperfections that could be ironed out with better engineering. We see this hubris taken to its extreme in Karl Marx's claim that "Communism is the riddle of history solved, and it knows itself to be this solution."

But, like all utopian delusions, Marx's solution to history has yet to play out because it tries to reduce reality to something predictable and quantifiable. It seeks to eliminate the human component—to reduce individuals to mechanisms who would behave perfectly if it weren't for their imperfect societies. Most notably, it is deluded by the belief that maximal happiness can be delivered through social engineering.

This isn't to say social leaps aren't possible. After all, the scientific revolution produced the enlightenment ideals that made our republic possible. When we balance new ideas with respect for the wisdom of tradition and the limitations of human understanding, we create room for social, political, and economic progress. This brings the possibility for innovation but with an appropriate humility.

But whenever people have put too much trust in their ability to recreate social orders, they inevitably find that they've shattered something integral to the social fabric and the human spirit. As Will and Ariel Durant express in their classic book, *The Lessons of History:*

> No one man, however brilliant or well-informed, can come in one lifetime to such fullness of understanding as to safely judge and dismiss the customs or institutions of his society, for these are the wisdom of generations after centuries of experiment in the laboratory of history . . . .
>
> It is good that new ideas should be heard, for the sake of the few that can be used; but it is also good that new ideas

should be compelled to go through the mill of objection, opposition, and contumely; this is the trial heat which innovations must survive before being allowed to enter the human race. It is good that the old should resist the young, and that the young should prod the old; out of this tension, as out of the strife of the sexes and the classes, comes a creative tensile strength, a stimulated development, a secret and basic unity and movement of the whole.

Real progress isn't just about what sounds nicest, it is about what functions best—what is most compatible with human communities, human nature, and the human needs. This obvious truth is lost when we try to force modern notions of "progress." Social progress is almost always a function of individual maturity. Our utopian-driven culture incentivizes just the opposite.

DEFINING THE DELUSIONAL

Utopian goals suffer from some combination of the following:

1. They are good for us, but only if accomplished through human maturity.
2. They are not actually good for us because they deprive us of an essential stressor.
3. They are not possible because they ignore human nature (and therefore attempts to accomplish them deprive us of an essential stressor).
4. They might be possible, but accomplishing them requires us to cross the threshold where costs exceed benefits (for example, what would society have to do to bring the annual number of kidnappings to zero?).
5. They exaggerate a problem and, thus, provoke a disproportionate response (where costs exceed benefits).

Let's take the example of anti-bullyism, perhaps the most popular and least criticized movement in 21st century education.

Following the Columbine high school massacre, schools across the country dedicated massive energy into anti-bullying programs. Everyone agreed (and still agrees) with the anti-bullying movement's ethical foundation: *bullying is wrong and we should try to create kids who are less likely to bully.* This is what's tricky about utopian ideas. Arguing against them requires honesty, nuance, and an understanding of the complex interplay between human nature and society.

School psychologist Izzy Kalman has been one of the lone voices explaining why anti-bullying policies exacerbate the bullying problem. As he explains:

> I did a great deal of classroom observation. I noticed that the teachers who expended the most energy, experienced the most frustration, and accomplished the least amount of academic teaching were those who took on the responsibility of managing the social complaints of their students. Their students quickly discovered that they could get them to spend half of their class time conducting investigations, pronouncing verdicts, and sending guilty parties to the principal's office. These teachers didn't realize that they were unwittingly intensifying the hostilities between the students, causing them to fight endlessly, and actually preventing them from figuring out how to solve their social problems on their own.

Forcing teachers to solve every conflict invites what psychologists call triangulation. As Kalman explains, the student who is deemed the "bully" feels mischaracterized and becomes angry at both the adult and the "victim." He learns to dislike school and distrust teachers. The "victim" becomes convinced of their moral righteousness and is more likely to continue antagonizing the "oppressor" while expecting the protection he has grown dependent upon. Most disastrously, the "bully" is now more likely to seek retribution against the "victim." Research finds that kids who seek intervention from authorities the most are subsequently bullied the most.

Many children grow up with parents who manage every conflict for them. Then, those parents and their children are told to expect a school environment where kids are protected from any bullying, however defined. But authorities can't possibly police every issue. Most bullying takes place online or in those inevitable, necessary moments where adults aren't lurking. When squabbles happen, students are far less capable of coping. They are more fragile to their tormentors' abuse (which, in the 21st century, is far more likely to be verbal than physical) and they feel resentful of the authorities who failed to protect them.

Anti-bullying initiatives expanded the scope of what was considered bullying, encouraged students to seek adult intervention as a first recourse, and created the expectation that an adult would and should always step in to solve student conflicts. This movement deprives youth of opportunities to learn de-escalation tactics, mediate minor disputes, develop emotional resilience to slights, and take any responsibility for the conflicts they find themselves in. This encourages students to perceive themselves as helpless victims and to drastically expand what they consider traumatic or unkind.

FINDING THE WITCHES

"Nothing in all the world is more dangerous than sincere ignorance and conscientious stupidity."
—*Dr. Martin Luther King Jr.*

In 2018, scientists from Harvard, Dartmouth, and New York University published a study where thousands of participants were shown a succession of dots ranging from extremely blue to extremely purple. Their task was simple. Participants were to look at each dot and determine whether it was blue, or not blue. Each person looked at one thousand dots on their own individual computer monitor. Through the first 200, true blues were frequent, yet over time they gradually became scarce. The last 100 dots were almost all purple. But scientists found that as they reduced the number of blue dots, participants found them with the same frequency. They saw just as many blues in the last 100 as in the first 100 dots. The mind, expecting to see a constant range of blue dots, began to shift its definition of blue to fit the expected outcome.

The study went on to apply the same model to other circumstances. Participants were asked to look for threatening faces and they detected just as many when the number of threatening faces was reduced. They were asked to read business proposals and identify the unethical ones. As the number of unethical proposals was reduced, participants continued to find just as many. Their sense of ethics seemingly shifted. In each scenario they thought they were consciously discerning, but in fact their mind was compelled to fulfill an unconscious default pattern.

As the researchers explained:

> Levari et al. show experimentally that when the "signal" a person is searching for becomes rare, the person naturally responds by broadening his or her definition of the signal— and therefore continues to find it even when it is not there. From low-level perception of color to higher-level judgments of ethics, there is a robust tendency for perceptual and judgmental standards to "creep" when they ought not to.

Scientists named this unique flaw in human perception: *prevalence induced concept change*. It is particularly important to our understanding of how good intentions grow destructive both to society at large and the individuals they try to protect.

Every utopian delusion creates a witch hunt, whether for bullies, liability, or some form of inequality. They pursue purification—the

elimination of an evil—and in the process they expand the definition of that evil so that it encompasses a range far beyond what is
reasonable.

With anti-bullyism, definitions of bullying have expanded dramatically. Students are trained to be more sensitive to slights, feel more
victimized, and believe the effects are more devastating than they
are. The obvious, while politically incorrect, truth is that bullying lies
along a spectrum. At the extreme end are rare events that should provoke a response from adults or capable, good-natured peers. But at
the mildest end are many natural interactions that would have hardly
registered a couple decades ago—the social maneuvering, shit-giving,
and friend-to-friend honesty that is so essential for both the social-
ization of individuals and the community's standards. When schools
demonize these natural social behaviors, authenticity, competency,
and connection (the human needs) are discouraged.

Even bullies in the middle of this bullying spectrum are a necessary part of the childhood ecosystem. They provide opportunities
for non-bullying protector types to develop moral courage and their
milder harassments often help their "victims" correct antisocial behaviors that would otherwise plague them far worse. Too many kids
have been so insulated from natural feedback that they become in-
sufferable tyrants. Whether snobbery, whininess, or a narcissistic
god-delusion, kids benefit from peer correction far more than adult
suggestion. The oft-uttered expectation used to be that, *someday
someone meaner than me will come along and teach you the lesson
you need.* And the bullies too are subject to this correction. Their peer
interactions often prompt them to change, giving other kids examples of redemption and human complexity.

So, what do I suggest we do about bullying? It depends on each
situation. There is no blanket response. Life is complex. People are
complex. We don't want leaders who follow a mechanized script. We
want nuanced-thinking, growth-oriented leaders who grow wiser
with each experience. And we don't want harmless, scared young
adults who think more safety is always best. We want capable, strong

people who develop the empathy to help those who need it, the power to fight for what they believe, and the wisdom to utilize that power with proportionality and pragmatism.

THE REAL VICTIMS OF UTOPIA

> *"Once the mind has accepted a plausible explanation for something, it becomes a framework for all the information that is perceived after it. We're drawn, subconsciously, to fit and contort all the subsequent knowledge we receive into our framework, whether it fits or not. Psychologists call this "cognitive rigidity". The facts that built an original premise are gone, but the conclusion remains—the general feeling of our opinion floats over the collapsed foundation that established it."*
> —*Ryan Holiday*

As we saw in the Blue-Dot experiment, when oriented to find something, the human mind tends to find it. Today we see manifestations of this phenomenon in both political extremes. Xenophobes and other bigots see confirmation of their prejudiced beliefs everywhere they look. Once they've convinced themselves that *these people* are lazy, *those people* are untrustworthy, or *they* are all idiots, their mind will filter events to confirm that prejudice.

Likewise, the social justice warrior movement encourages adherents to detect every conceivable slight or bigotry. They find racism, sexism, and fascism even where they do not exist. With a mind programmed to scan for injustice, they create new conceptions of wrong-doing, like unchecked privilege, cultural appropriation, toxic masculinity, and failing to give trigger warnings prior to discussing potentially sensitive subjects.

Currently, woke social justice culture is harvesting hostility by training all of us to be upset by problems that they have invented. It may appear nice to be so sensitive that you perceive that someone somewhere could possibly prefer your white three-year-old daughter did not dress up like Moana for Halloween, but how many people would be offended if they weren't told to be by such a large, zealous movement? And if you are among the infinitesimally small group of people who would have naturally taken offense to a child wanting to wear the costume of a character of a different race, perhaps these emotions are your responsibility to reconcile. Our culture is, after all, a large melting pot, where people will have different values and expectations. Best not to be too sensitive.

As comedian Bill Maher explains, "I call these people emotional hemophiliacs . . . . Their answer is not to (avoid) a room full of sharp objects. The answer is to make all of us wear bubble wrap, so nothing we ever do makes them have a moment of discomfort. It's very narcissistic." As damaging as it is to the social climate, this woke agenda is most destructive to those who embrace it. It is the mark of a dysfunctional mind to search for things to be offended by.

We need to be conscious of what we're telling people to look for because they will find it whether it is there or not. Self-esteem culture is training our kids to look for every balloon-deflating moment. Generations have now grown up on children's books, television shows, and movies where it is normal for kids to hold adults responsible for their ails—nine-year-olds storm away from dinners, slam doors, and pepper their parents with criticism. These themes are then reinforced in school. We teach our children to find every hardship and wallow in self-pity. The result is a creepy trend where many kids wear their afflictions like a badge of honor.

It is wonderful that we are fighting the stigma of talking about mental health and more wonderful still that society promotes empathy. But we should be clearer about drawing the lines. Empathy is admirable. Self-pity is ignoble and self-defeating. As we saw in chapter 3, by obsessing on hurt feelings, pretending life should be painless, and conflating hardships with *trauma*, mainstream society is programming far more pathologies than it is solving.

According to Haidt and Lukianoff, the social justice movement that has taken over college campuses is now training younger generations to adopt the exact same mental distortions that Cognitive

Behavior Therapy (CBT) works to untrain. By training students to see the world through these mental distortions, we are indoctrinating them in a self-destructive worldview that breeds mental dysfunction.

Think of distortions as purple dots that people have been conditioned to see as blue. Here are a few common examples you may recognize:

- **Mental Filtering Toward the Negative:** Framing everything in the worst light. People become very efficient at identifying how the world has conspired against them, which trains them to miss opportunities and overlook what is good.
- **Emotional Reasoning:** Determining that your personal emotions constitute objective truth. People are being told to believe whatever their individual feelings tell them is true, just because they feel it. Combine this with a negative filter and you get . . .
- **Fortune Telling:** Assuming certainty of other people's bad motives. From this assumption, any statement you don't like can be determined as a purposeful attack. This is also used to project the offense people *should* feel.
- **Labeling:** Taking complex people and defining them based on one negative label, which usually communicates their bigotry or irreconcilable ignorance. Once labeled an opponent's arguments can be entirely disregarded. After all, you wouldn't consider the opinion of a Nazi. Labels work the other way as well, creating a shield around those pre-determined to be in the in-group.
- **Catastrophizing:** Interpreting events in the most devastating way possible. Being awarded a promotion can be framed as an awful burden or even the bosses trying to make you look bad. Every challenge triggers an elaborate negative domino effect. Thus, every harm is traumatic and words can be deemed violence.

These distorted patterns of thought are actively indoctrinated by universities and overzealous human resource departments. The social justice narrative has come to define public schools, youth development norms, and all public dialogue. It is the prevailing mainstream narrative—the authority on what ideas and beliefs are fair game for public discourse. As political commentator Andrew Sullivan contends, "we all live on campus now."

> *"Tyranny is the deliberate removal of nuance."*
> —*Albert Maysles*

The core of this narrative is that hierarchy is evil. The world is split up into a continuum from most to least privileged and the goal of organized society must be to somehow account for every injustice and equalize them across all variables. The goal is not equal rules for all, but creating a game board where one group's advantages are quantified and then offset by an enlightened policy. Of course, one could fit into millions of different categories and subcategories other than those we've been programmed to filter people into. Rather than judging individuals on the content of their character, society learns to obsess upon social categories. Equality of outcome is deemed the highest possible good.

In education, the process of redistributing resources and adjusting standards in pursuit of equal outcomes is called equity. Equity starts with a wise insight: some people have more advantages than others and we should try to help those whose experience less adequately promotes success. But then it leaps to the assertion that any discrepancy in outcomes must wholly result from prejudiced systems and, based on that faulty premise, that the only solution is to amplify the importance of identity categories. The systems must make it their primary focus to engineer equal outcomes, regardless of how well individuals fit into the narrative of the group they are assigned.

The reality is that you cannot assume that a difference in group outcomes derives from systemic bigotry rather than culture or individual values. You cannot extrapolate that each isolated incident is indicative of culturally ingrained bigotry. Most importantly, you cannot assume that the best way to correct inequality is through identity-group based interventions.

Any meritocracy leads to a hierarchy. This is the beauty of merit-based societies. There is an incentive for people to work hard and become more capable. You want a surgeon who is most qualified. You want teachers who know how to read, write, speak, and think critically. We need meritocracy. It promotes personal responsibility and a society that judges people based on their actions.

Like freedom of speech and the marketplace of ideas, meritocracy was a beautiful enlightenment tenant that threw off the shackles of extremely unfair royal hierarchies. Meritocracy eliminated errone-ous, dogmatically enforced caste separations based on birth. It set the rules of the game and allowed people to strive and prosper.

Our meritocracy comes with flaws that are worth limiting. Many that reach the top of any hierarchy will seek to game the system to advantage themselves. History is littered with abuses of power that demand intervention. When your rent doubles or Purdue pharma-ceuticals stokes an opioid crisis for their own profit, it's time to rally the troops and kick ass. But those obvious examples don't warrant the belief that all of history can be reduced to a story of the powerful exploiting the weak, or that the only virtuous pursuit is identifying and dismantling power.

We can continue to improve the rules and identify more effective interventions without the fiction that a world without hierarchy is possible, or desirable. This simplistic delusion forgets that we need incentives. It forgets that people will be far better off if they don't per-ceive themselves as helpless; if they don't expect some force to level the playing field; and if they don't pretend that we can create such a sophisticated rule book as to account for desirable regulatory leveling without larger cobra effects.

Rather, people thrive when they develop nuanced beliefs—when they appreciate that life isn't fair, and, thus, that they should be em-pathetic to others, perhaps even working to eliminate injustice and help those less fortunate, while feeling empowered as individuals to overcome their own obstacles. A person's circumstances are the result of many factors outside of their own control. The lottery of birth is unequal, giving each of us talents, mentors, and a complex cocktail of nature and nurture that we've done nothing to earn. Still, the greatest advantages are an inclination to learn and the belief that you are the primary determinant of your own success and fulfillment. These advantages are available to all of us at any time. Demonizing the successful while reducing the world into victim and oppressor narratives does far more harm than good.

As author, doctor, and former prison psychiatrist Theodore Dalrymple explains:

> The historiography that a person is taught and grows up with has, in my view, an underestimated effect on his psychology. The danger of too optimistic an historiography is that a person will become complacent, self-satisfied and indifferent to the remediable sufferings around him; but too pessimistic an historiography will embitter him and stimulate the resentment that is never very far from the human heart . . . . Of the two deformations, I prefer the former, which at least is likely to encourage a desire to contribute something constructive rather than destructive: but need we have a deformation at all?
>
> Preferable to either deformation is an historiography that is capable of recognising defects and even horrors in a tradition, but also strengths and glories, such that the tradition can survive without remaining obdurately stuck in its worst grooves. This requires a certain sophistication, that is to say, an ability to hold in the mind more than one thought at a time. It also requires the recognition that . . . perfection is not of this world and cannot be demanded of the past, however glorious aspects of it might be. Suffice it to say that the encouragement of such sophistication hardly seems to be the order of the day in our educational institutions.

In addition to self-destructive resentments, utopian driven societies create too many avenues for excuse-making. Their efforts to eliminate pain and unfairness also eliminates the need for ingenuity and grit. When victim-hood and safety are trump cards, the majority of individuals will, consciously or subconsciously, learn to manipulate the concerns of well-meaning people. They'll be able to evoke sympathy that breeds learned helplessness. It is natural.

At age three, my son Ace would do this to any adult who let him. When he didn't want to do something, he'd say he had to pee. When he didn't want to eat something, he'd say his stomach hurt. I'd say put your shoes on and he'd walk by Grandpa with the shoes that he put on every day and begin grunting and grimacing as if he couldn't. He wanted to see if he could get Grandpa to do it for him.

In a youth development culture like ours, children are trained to find whatever disadvantages they face. They naturally learn to exploit well-meaning authorities. This breeds entitlement and prolonged dependency. It teaches them to hold other people responsible for their emotions and their outcomes. And most devastatingly for them, it creates a social apparatus that promotes socially-destructive behavior.

ANTISOCIAL NETWORKS

"That which isn't good for the hive isn't good for the bee."
—*Marcus Aurelius*

In chapter 4, we saw how the attempt to make the American legal system capable of righting every wrong created the modern lawsuit culture. As we expanded the number of offenses that people could be sued for, we muddied our shared expectations of personal responsibility. We legitimized every grievance and, in the process, created a liability-obsessed world, saturated in dehumanizing regulations.

As author Philip K. Howard explains in *The Lost Art of Drawing the Line*, "Law serves a social function as well as an individual . . . . When working properly, justice is like the liver. You never notice it. People go through their entire lives comfortable with their instincts of right and wrong."

Those instincts are what make community possible. They create a space that promotes constructive behavior. When legal confidence erodes, however, we atomize and lose any sense of duty to the common good. For example:

> A new medical school graduate, one week away from getting her license to practice, was recently driving in suburban New York when she came upon a motorcycle accident with the rider sprawled on the side of the road, obviously badly injured. After a brief discussion with her mother, she decided not to stop because she might be liable for practicing without a license. At first blink, her logic seems perfectly reasonable. But this only shows how warped we've become. How about helping out because you're a human being who happens to have the skills to save a life?

Howard's books are littered with true stories like this one. When you can sue for anything, freedom is reduced. An environment of hypersensitivity and neurotic overanalysis takes root. You can no longer expect people to assume that coffee will be hot or to accept that accidents may happen while children play. Every misfortune becomes an opportunity to assign blame. We begin to look at each other with suspicion wondering: *Is he the type of person who is going to try to twist this?*

The same has happened with social media callout culture. Where it once would have been reasonable to confront perceived insensitivities privately and with a tone of mutual respect (we have all spoken thoughtlessly, after all), we now award status for making confrontations as embarrassing and public as possible. Unintentional offenses that once might have prompted a polite, private conversation where both parties could grow, are now opportunities for social promotion. You get prestige for publicly humiliating people.

Thus, even though a nationally representative 2018 study found that 80% of Americans believe political correctness is a problem in American society, public discourse is subject to the constant anxiety of an attack from the lowest common denominator. We now feel the need to censor ourselves to appease the most sensitive and mentally distorted, whose pathology is reinforced by social media narratives and the trolling power that social media offers. Most devastatingly, our public institutions, from our schools to the governing bodies of every organization, tend to be the first to cast aside any sense of standards and join in so that they can avoid controversy. We now have a society that fears honesty—where having the type of conversations necessary to counter utopian delusions is seen as too risky.

Callout culture and lawsuit culture are spurred by the same utopian mindset. As Philip K. Howard explains:

> We got into this legal quicksand, because we woke up in the 1960's to all these really bad values. Racism, gender discrimination, pollution—they were bad values, and we wanted to create a legal system where no one could have bad values anymore. The problem is we created a system where we eliminated the right to have good values.

This is the problem with utopian delusions. Society aims its microscope at all that is wrong, deluding people into the expectation that systems can and should fix everything. But the world is not perfectible. And the quest to eliminate every ill produces a world that discourages heroism and authenticity. When the only safe thing to do is to keep your head down and go with the flow, good people become apathetic about the possibilities of making any sort of difference.

Our original legal mindset, which Howard proposes restoring, encourages judges to filter out cases that don't merit a trial or which set precedents that would harm society. We entrust judges to do their job. They are still held accountable to the collective voice of the people. The difference, as Howard explains, is that "The accountability is up the line, judging the decision against the effect on everybody, not just on the disgruntled person. You can't run a society by the lowest common denominator."

The same is the case for teachers, schools, and the entire social apparatus. Human judgment must reign over protocol, regulation, and standardization. When we try to eliminate any opportunity for bad things to happen, we stifle the organic energy that communities depend on. We weaken social trust and fracture the parts of society that pull us to be greater.

At its core this is about mediating the tension that lies at the center of every culture. As Jonathan Haidt explains in his book, *The Righteous Mind:*

> . . . all societies must resolve a small set of questions about how to order society, the most important being how to balance the needs of individuals and groups. There seem to be just two primary ways of answering this question. Most societies have chosen the sociocentric answer, placing the needs of groups and institutions first, and subordinating the needs of individuals. In contrast, the individualistic answer places individuals at the center and makes society a servant of the individual. The sociocentric answer dominated most of the ancient world, but the individualistic answer became a powerful rival during the Enlightenment. The individualistic answer largely vanquished the sociocentric approach in the twentieth century as individual rights expanded rapidly, consumer culture spread, and the Western world reacted with horror to the evils perpetrated by the ultra-sociocentric fascist and communist empires.

The sociocentric-individualistic debate should not be seen as an either-or dichotomy but a delicate interplay of competing values that each society must balance. Placing too much emphasis on the community stifles innovation and opens the door to oppression. But by trying to appease each individual you create tyranny by sensitivity. You fracture the social fabric that individuals depend upon for connection.

The overprovide and overprotect parenting paradigm and victimhood culture are the result of extreme, unchecked individualism. We've gone so far in our desire to make society the servant of the individual that society itself holds little value. There is nothing to bind us—nothing to rally around—no evident meaning. Society only exists to make everything infinitely safe and fair—to placate each individual's feelings.

Today's parents came of age in this very individualistic world. After years of aimless self-concern, children arrive and parents feel a sense of meaning. They once were lost, but now are found. This can be wonderful, but without any other deeply held values, it often creates a sort of child worship where the point of parenting becomes pleasing one's child-god and dreaming up evermore extravagant offerings. Youth culture grows more hollow and more individualistic as parents put the immediate desires of their children above any higher ideals.

This creates a phenomenon where today's parents often operate as a pseudo public relations firm for their children. When Junior throws tantrums, he's far more likely to be rewarded than disciplined. When he cheats or doesn't do his work at school, his parents are more likely to defend his behavior than to encourage the school's consequences while adding, "I can assure you, he will answer for this when he gets home."

Likewise, sports lose their focus on discipline, physical vitality, and learning to sacrifice for a team. They become an arena for individual self-promotion. Rather than helping kids understand that they need to play the position where their team needs them, parents lobby coaches to meet the child's wants. They work to ensure that he gets the number he wants, the position he wants, sufficient playing time, and ample individual recognition at the banquet. The team becomes an elaborate presentation, bent to satisfy the individual desires of each of its participants and their parents.

We have developed societies of more comfort, convenience, and efficiency than the world has ever seen, but this only seems to deter authenticity, connection, and the sense that kids should contribute to something beyond than themselves. No amount of abundance can fill the spiritual void. For humans to thrive, we must engage with individual human psychology as it is and understand that a person's well-being cannot be divorced from the society they live within. Culture and psychology are interwoven. As Jonathan Haidt explains:

> . . . you can't study the mind while ignoring culture, as psychologists usually do, because minds function only once they've been filled out by a particular culture. And you can't study culture while ignoring psychology, as anthropologists usually do, because social practices and institutions . . . are to some extent shaped by concepts and desires rooted deep within the human mind, which explains why they often take similar forms on different continents.

We are homo-duplex, the animal with a deep need to transcend ourselves through our relationship with society. We cannot thrive as individuals if we don't feel connected to a community. We need something greater to believe in. We need social forces that pull us to live better.

CHAPTER 8

THE BEAUTY OF
THE IDEAL

"Philosophy is a study of the part in the light of the whole, and its first lesson is that we are very small parts of a very large whole. The harmony of the part with the whole may be the best definition of health, beauty, truth, wisdom, morality, and happiness."
—*Will Durant*

As I prepared to pour into my final edits for this book, the 2020 COVID-19 pandemic began picking up steam. Early on, Americans watched the virus spread from China's Wuhan province with little more than a passive awareness. Oblivious of what was to come, my family and I sought a reprieve from the hustle and bustle of modern life, escaping to the hills of Broken Bow, Oklahoma for a spring break vacation. But things changed quickly. By that weekend, grocery store shelves were empty and schools and "non-essential" businesses had shut down all in-person operations indefinitely. An odd stillness settled in as everyone stayed home wondering when life would be normal again.

Other countries responded with even more caution. Germany banned gatherings of two or more non-family members. France required residents to fill out a form every time they left their homes. And India repeatedly turned to violence against its citizens to enforce aggressive lockdown mandates. All around the world, governments told people to stay home so the virus wouldn't spread. But not Sweden.

Sweden kept its schools open as well as its borders, restaurants, and even its pubs. People were encouraged to respect social-distancing recommendations and limit contact with at-risk populations, but life continued without forced closures and without ever subjecting kindergartners to screen-centered virtual schooling. State Epidemiologist Anders Tegnell explained the thinking behind Sweden's light-touch in a late March interview: "Closing borders at this stage of the pandemic, when almost all countries have cases, to me does not really make sense. This is not a disease that is going to go away in the short term or long term. We are not in the containment phase. We are in the mitigation phase."

That spring, deaths per million were higher in Sweden than its heavy-handed neighbors like Norway and Denmark. International ridicule poured in, but Sweden maintained their laissez-faire policy. It wasn't that the Swedes didn't take the virus seriously. They just took other things seriously as well, such as enjoyment of life, freedom to roam, and a commitment to measured response. As journalist and half-Swede Freddie Sayers explained, "To rip up a long-prepared pandemic plan and impose unprecedented measures just because everybody else was would be considered reckless; to close schools would have been considered morally unacceptable."

Back in America, conversations surrounding the coronavirus response were far more divisive. By August of 2020, as communities tried to make plans for a new school year, two staunch camps dominated the mainstream dialogue (even as the quiet majority yearned for a balanced conversation). People seemed to either believe that returning to in-person schooling was recklessly irresponsible, or that the mere suggestion of social-distancing was an infringement on personal liberties and that this whole thing might just be a hoax. You either drove around with a mask on in your car or you made a point of shaking as many hands as possible before eating.

On the surface, Swedes would appear to fall into the latter camp—evidence-averse individualists who rebelled against anyone who might want to tell them how to live. But Sayers argued the opposite, or the middle, anyway. According to him, the reason Sweden kept society open was because they had a stronger sense of shared values and a stronger commitment to the common good. Their debate wasn't between two sides who held each other in contempt. It was a conversation between a unified people who could appeal to unifying ideals. They trusted each other to respect social-distancing recommendations without legal mandates, but also shared a common sense that there were moral concerns that could rival safety.

The response to coronavirus is just one example of how clear ideals allow Swedish society to operate differently. With low obesity rates and a life expectancy over 80, Swedes routinely rank among the healthiest people in the world. This starts when they are young. The average preschooler in Stockholm spends six-hours outside each day during good weather and 90 minutes throughout the frigid Swedish winter. Kids have access to free preschool, outdoor classrooms, and an abundance of open space to explore. In fact, the Swedes maintain a Right of Public Access that allows people to walk anywhere they like, including the expansive acreage of millionaires, provided they respect the cultural edict "disturb not, destroy not." This ethos of respectful, communal freedom lies at the heart of Swedish values.

I don't highlight Sweden to make a statement about pandemic response policy or tax-payer funded pre-school. The point is that Swedes thrive because they live in a community with clear ideals. The Swedes wouldn't accept a lawsuit culture that discouraged kids from climbing trees just as they wouldn't accept the reduction of recess or a scarcity of public recreation space because these so obviously violate their sense of what is morally good for society. Lacking this unifying moral sense, American conversations about coronavirus (and society in general) have tended to be more selfish and combative. As Sayers put it:

The fragmented and highly individualistic culture of the UK and US, without much by way of universally shared values to fall back on, is a big part of why the response in those countries has been so uncertain and the debate so poisonous. Without habits and values that are commonly deemed morally good and too precious to give up, what remains when a new threat such as Covid-19 arrives? If the only unassailable moral good is saving lives, the "precautionary principle" becomes almost impossible to argue against. Well-meaning people find they have surrendered their whole way of life to its dubious authority.

CONNECTION VIA RUGGED INDIVIDUALISM

"Freedom is something that dies unless it is used."
                                        —*Hunter Thompson*

The French aristocrat, Alexis de Tocqueville, travelled around America in 1831 and marveled at the distinct American spirit, which he saw as both a by-product of and requirement for representative democracy. This was an adventurous, self-organizing spirit that he found most natural. It has often been labeled rugged individualism, but this individualism was also a proxy for strong community connection. Citizens looked at one another with a sense of recognition. All were participants in this bold new way of life. They saw in each other a common desire to live unencumbered by coercion and stagnant hierarchies.

That spirit led to a proliferation of self-governing groups where people united around shared interests. Tocqueville noted the abundance of voluntary organizations that characterized American life. As Matthew Crawford says in his book, *Why We Drive*, Tocqueville regarded these groups as the "nursery of democratic virtue." Just as children learn to socialize through play and freedom, Americans learned citizenship by governing their own communities.

Around 1960, the organizations that had become the bedrock of our social lives—the PTA, Kiwanis, Shriners, Elks, Boy Scouts, Girl Scouts, etc.—began losing energy and significance. Simultaneously, voter turnout, grass roots political activism, reading groups, and participation in adult sports leagues began a consistent decline. The demise of these self-organized groups is evidence of a collective social disinterest that had profound implications on our culture. If anything is responsible for the erosion of American cohesion, it is the loss of these self-organized groups and the shared experiences they facilitated. As we spent less time interacting with neighbors, our communities grew more isolated and untrusting. Norms and bonds, once fostered through shared projects, withered.

In his groundbreaking 2000 book, *Bowling Alone*, political scientist Robert Putnam addresses this decline in community involvement and identifies its causes. Among them one stands out as the most impactful. Television.

Between 1950 and 1959 the number of U.S. homes that had a television rose from about 10% to 90%. By the late 80s over 75% of homes had more than one television and as of 2001, the average American watched four hours of television per day, not including times where the TV was used as background noise (a stark contrast to the outdoor-dominated lifestyles of Sweden). But television didn't just fill the void, it helped create it. As Putnam wrote, "Nothing—not low education, not full-time work, not long commutes in urban agglomerations, not poverty or financial distress—is more broadly associated with civic disengagement and social disconnection than is dependence on television for entertainment." Social disconnection has only been exacerbated by smartphone ubiquity and mass data processing algorithms.

Putnam found that as community engagement declined so did social capital—a measure of the connection and trust within a community. Just as the properties, machines, employees, and inventories that businesses hold are forms of capital that facilitate production, societies work best when there is a high degree of social capital. For example, ultra-Orthodox Jews, have cornered New York City's diamond market, because their exceptional trust in one another allows them to operate without expensive security systems. As Jonathan Haidt explains in, *The Righteous Mind*, "If a rival market were to open up across town composed of ethnically and religiously diverse merchants, they'd have to spend a lot more money on lawyers and security guards, given how easy it is to commit fraud or theft when sending diamonds out for inspection by other merchants."

Social capital boils down to the trust and intimacy felt between members in a community. In places where social capital is high, people live unencumbered by worries that their cars will be broken into or that children will be lured into a van on their way to school. They are confident in the basic norms of society. One way to look at it is that law and order exist to fill the gaps in social capital. If social capital were infinite—everyone respected the same values, trusted their community, and felt capable of mediating whatever disputes arose—then there would be no reason for a legal code or justice system. As social capital wanes, however, bureaucratic features are called upon to coerce harmony.

Some loss of social capital is inevitable as communities increase in cultural diversity and size. After observing social connections in other primates and noting the number of close relationships they held in comparison to the size of their neocortex (the part of the brain responsible for cognition and language), the British anthropologist, Robin Dunbar, hypothesized that brain size dictated the number of close relationships a species could have. Based on the size of the human neocortex and the ratio he'd determined, he speculated that human brains are only evolved to maintain about 150 relationships. This has proved remarkably accurate. But societies have adapted by creating many of their own Dunbar-sized community organizations. When organized around a larger cultural myth structure (anything from Greek Mythology to Manifest Destiny) these subcultures stoke connection in both the immediate environment and the larger national structure. People see each other as similar comrades, with similar competencies, hopes, and dreams. Mild regional variations stoke friendly rivalries that bring dynamism and growth in each community. But when we lose trust in the myths and institutions that bond different communities, divisions grow hostile.

Social trust is built upon confidence that people and systems will operate predictably and that vital information will be presented accurately. As people lose faith in their news, their politicians, the intentions of their police departments, or what they can be held liable for in the legal system, they tend to atomize and draw into their tribes. Today those tribes are often virtual, having no bearing on the connection one feels in their immediate environment.

All of this is interrelated. Social groups once fostered a standard that drove people to be competent, community-oriented citizens and to face the sort of challenging experiences that promoted deeper connection and self-understanding. But, with the explosion of marketing, our societies grew more disconnected and self-centered. We increasingly looked to material items and diversions to fill the spiritual void in our lives. And as consumerism was embedded deeper into our culture, a milieu of industrial complexes (military, safety, prison, etc.) expanded their dominion, incentivizing our institutions to become less trustworthy. The development of cable news, the internet, and smartphones created a battle for attention that led to the devolution of traditional media sources and a culture fixated on outrage.

Neighbors now populate entirely different mental worlds. Each can turn to a different source, which spouts different *facts*. Disagreements no longer stem from different perspectives on the best way to solve problems, but a fundamental disagreement about what is true and, therefore, what is a problem. Thoughtful citizens struggle to know what to believe. Apathy blooms. The only thing we all seem to agree on is that corruption is widespread and the bulk of our news untrustworthy.

PARENTING WITHOUT A VILLAGE

"No nation deserves to exist if it permits itself to lose the stern and virile virtues; and this without regard to whether the loss is due to the growth of a heartless and all-absorbing commercialism, to prolonged indulgence in luxury and soft, effortless ease, or to the deification of a warped and twisted sentimentality."
—*Theodore Roosevelt*

Today's parents are children of the 80's and 90's when, for the first time in collective memory, there was no grand national mission. Each previous generation experienced a monumental test: World War I, the Great Depression, World War II, the space race, Korea, and Vietnam. But following the Soviet Union's implosion, children grew up without a unifying national challenge.

All of a sudden, the Cold War was ending and we celebrated how amazing we were just because we're American. To what did we attribute this inherent awesomeness? Consumerism. Those pinko commies couldn't keep up with our prosperity. We became kings of the world because we buy more stuff and create more stuff to buy. Add to this the Watergate scandal and post-Vietnam era disenchantment and we had all the ingredients for public distrust and boundless self-interest.

With no great cause and few shared missions, our nation lost that essential sense of being a part of something bigger than ourselves. We came to believe that we were insulated from the sort of disruptive challenges that have defined all of human history—to expect that our lives should persist without any major problems. And without that collective sense of an impending trial that our children should be capable of weathering, adulthood could be delayed indefinitely.

Over the past few generations, we have watched a culture of bulldozer parents reduce expectations of personal responsibility and remove the challenge from every rite of passage. This has created increasing ambiguity around the question of when children become adults and what adulthood even means. Our 18-year-olds are increasingly less capable of self-governance. Even more, they are less interested in going out into the world and becoming independent adults. This is to the liking of many parents.

Last year my wife's class read an article about the ways technology intentionally creates addiction. In the post-reading discussion, students began asking about how Neely and I handle technology with our own kids (who were two and three at the time). They couldn't believe that our kids never played on tablets or phones, and they accused us of being too controlling after hearing that we planned to limit our kids to a flip-phone until high school. Neely then explained our desire to give the kids symmetrical increases in freedom and responsibility. We want them biking all over town in elementary school and driving, dating, and becoming free and self-sufficient in high school.

Suddenly, the class was hailing our philosophy as they recounted how stifling their own childhoods had been. Over and over, students reported a bizarre phenomenon where their parents actively encouraged them to spend more time on their screens for the explicit purpose of keeping them at home. *I don't want you biking to the park, why don't you guys just play some live video games.* Parents preferred their kids seated and entertained to active and seeking independence.

The dominant parenting culture seems to have lost any sense of duty to make children capable of standing on their own or any sense that this power is an essential part of living a good life. Absent of any other purpose, parents try to hold on to the sense of purpose they've found through their children's dependency on them. Safetyism becomes justification for perpetuating an unhealthy codependency.

Today, there is tremendous pressure to give outcomes to our children, while neglecting the original purpose behind those outcomes. Rites of passage have become automatic upon the passage of time. If you don't quit high school, you will graduate. At age 18, we call you an adult even while your parents continue to pay your bills and fight your battles. When are you an actual adult? When do you feel that sense of self-worth, confidence, and freedom?

If we don't demand a standard of competency and unsterilized life experience from our children, they won't have the tools to thrive in our dynamic world. Even more, we must promote these experiences so they are capable of understanding that there are worthwhile values that aren't compatible with the infinite expansion of safety and convenience. As Matthew Crawford writes in *Why We Drive*:

> Safety is obviously very important. But it is also a principle that, absent countervailing considerations, admits no limits to its expanding dominion. It tends to swallow everything before it . . . . one must venture beyond the mental universe of risk reduction . . . . That universe takes its bearing from the least competent among us. This is an egalitarian principle that is entirely fitting in many settings, a touchstone of humane society that we rightly take pride in . . . . But if left unchallenged, the pursuit of risk reduction tends to create a society based on an unrealistically low view of human capacities. Infantilization slips in, under cover of democratic ideals. I will insist on the contrary, that democracy remains viable only if we are willing to extend to one another a presumption of individual competence. This is what social trust is built on. Together they are the minimal endowments for a free, responsible, fully awake people.

A society without the expectation that citizens meet certain standards of competency is no society at all. The dream of progress is to remove any need for competency and any risk of harm. It's time we challenge that dehumanizing ideal.

WHO ARE WE BECOMING?

In the 2007 comedy, *Idiocracy*, Joe Bauers is selected for a one-year hibernation experiment after a battery of tests indicates that he is the most average person in the entire armed forces. Bauers is cryogenically frozen, but soon thereafter the officer in charge of the experiment is arrested and Bauers forgotten. He remains frozen until 2505 when the collapse of a gigantic garbage pile awakens him to a world he hardly recognizes. People named after corporate brands spend their days in plastic homes, seated on chairs that have built-in toilets, watching television programs that would make *Beavis and Butthead* look refined. Bauers assumes that he must be experiencing hallucinogenic effects from the hibernation experiment so he checks into a hospital. This eventually leads him to take a 2505-style IQ test, which reveals that the once-average Joe is now, by far, the smartest person alive.

Similarly, the 2008 Disney and Pixar film *Wall-E* features a robot garbage compactor of the imagined future. Wall-E patrols the now-toxic earth centuries after humans have been evacuated by Buy-N-Large (the corporate giant who came to own everything). Wall-E eventually finds his way onto a "starliner" where we see the devolved, morbidly obese human population of the 29th century. People are conveyed across the spaceship on loungers. Screens hover in their faces, prompting them to consume, as robots zoom around to meet their every need.

Light-hearted as these films are, they convey something about the trajectory of civilization that we've all felt. Humanity en masse is growing less capable of an increasing number of basic human skills—from navigating, to running and climbing, building shelter, adding numbers in our head, and dealing with boredom or pain. Technological progress is creating a level of convenience, security, and distraction that seems to be making us less human. And if this lack of development makes us less human, the indication is that some level of skill-development is fundamental to our humanity. Without something pulling us up, we become a lesser version of ourselves—less capable, less activated, less engaged, and less likely to pursue the transformative experiences that might change us. This all might somehow be palatable if it wasn't also killing our spirits.

There is a vitality that comes from being totally immersed in a mission and seeing our efforts change the environment. This is especially evident in young kids. Children are hellbent on accumulating experiences and testing their skills in the world. They want to manipulate their environment just to see if they can. They want to make a fort and then climb on top of it. They want to take their toys from their organized baskets and hide them in small crevices throughout the house. They want to climb that bench, step onto the window-sill and traverse across it as far as they can. Even after finding themselves stuck in a precarious position, yelling *"Daddy!"* in order to be saved from falling, they remain undeterred. Three minutes later they are back on their perch. Life is doing.

Throughout human history the pursuit of competency has been essential to human survival and the survival of our communities. Civilizations had to develop a social apparatus that pulled people to a baseline level of competency or they would not last. Usefulness was a requirement of life and, consequently, humans evolved a deep yearning to be useful. But modernity, with its attention-hacking algorithms, automated processes, and rampant safetyism seems to be specifically designed to stamp out our basic inclinations for self-expansion. Advanced technology makes it possible for society to "progress" even while a majority of individuals never reach a baseline competency. People can now go their whole lives without being useful except as scrollers, eaters, and buyers. But this need not be the case.

When we talk about progress, we tend to think in terms of increasing technological capability. Progress is the development of technology like map apps and driverless cars that eliminate the need for human competency. This honors one or both of the chief values of modernity—safety and convenience—but runs contrary to the goal of human flourishing. We need a new definition of progress.

The imagined future of Star Trek is far brighter than that of Idiocracy or Wall-E. Extreme technological progress frees people to pursue growth. Culture drives people towards expanding their minds and personal capacities. Technology works with humanity, scaffolding us to greater heights. This isn't impossible. History shows that our social species can be quite adept at creating mechanisms to pull people to overcome impulse on behalf of some grander ideal. These mechanisms and that ideal are more necessary than ever.

CHAPTER 9

JUDGE THY NEIGHBOR

"Education is the most powerful weapon which you can use to change the world."
—*Nelson Mandela*

When you're seated at a restaurant and see an entire family sitting at the table staring at their phones—be honest—do you nudge your spouse and share a look of disapproval? Do you begin to discuss where and when screen time is acceptable, or how parents these days are dropping the ball? When you're walking down a grocery aisle and see a five-year-old playing phone games as he walks behind his mother—his toddler sister strapped in the top compartment of the grocery cart, entranced by a tablet—do you shake your head in dismay? On a hunch, do you peer into the grocery cart and, yep. No surprise. Cinnamon Toast Crunch, Coke, Hot Pockets, and frozen pizzas. Based on this experience, alone, do you presume a general haphazard impulsiveness defines their lives? Do you feel a certain superiority? *Reader. How could you?*

This is where we remind ourselves that it is not right to judge. First, take the log out of your own eye and all that jazz. But wise as these aphorisms are for our own personal development, they can't be applied at the group level. Judging other people is the very backbone of humanity's success. Gossip helped groups determine who was loyal, capable, and trustworthy. It helped society determine which behaviors were fruitful and discouraged those that were destructive to the long-term success of the community. In fact, the fear of social judgment is what lets us know that we are not supposed to publicly discuss condescending internal monologues like those mentioned in the previous paragraph. Fear of being labeled smug helps discourage pettiness and condescension.

We'd all do well to stay humble and focus our judgments on actions rather than people. But group success is predicated on a capacity to discern between better and worse paths and to create norms that influence productive behavior. When there aren't enough people judging parents for letting their kids stare at phones at the dinner table, then behaviors like this become common. And this makes it far harder on all those parents who want to set healthy boundaries.

In *The Happiness Hypothesis*, Jonathan Haidt, argues that the deterioration of a shared moral sense has removed much of the judgment from daily life, but, rather than make us happier, the result has been alienation and anxiety—what Durkheim (the sociologist who called humans *homo-duplex*) called anomie. Anomic societies lack a sense of norms, standards, or shared values. Their institutions lack gravitas. People get to behave however they want to, but they feel disconnected and struggle to find purpose. Durkheim found that as anomie increases, so do suicides and antisocial behaviors.

It sounds nice to live in a judgment free world, but this is devastating to the human spirit. As Haidt explains:

> One of the best predictors of the health of an American neighborhood is the degree to which adults respond to the misdeeds of other people's children, rather than look the other way. When community standards are enforced, there is constraint and cooperation. When everyone minds his or her own business, there is freedom and anomie.

The failed parenting paradigm is defined by parents who put no virtue above their child's immediate wants and who frequently question school authority in an effort to make their children's lives easier.

Schools have exacerbated this trend by prioritizing parental appeasement over any sense of standards. But, despite their failings, schools are the institution best positioned to reverse anomie-producing trends. As our cultural nucleus, schools have the opportunity to clarify standards and shape what we deem acceptable. Just as the food giants changed the nation's eating habits by targeting schools, we could use schools to intentionally craft more fruitful societal habits.

WHERE IS YOUR HONOR?

"High-purpose environments are filled with small, vivid signals designed to create a link between the present moment and a future ideal. They provide the two simple locators that every navigation process requires: Here is where we are and Here is where we want to go."
—Dan Coyle

Until the enlightenment, all cultures were what we would now call honor cultures. There was little room for interpretation about the best way to live your life. In an honor culture, loyalty, duty, and societal roles are everything. Failing to meet standards came with significant social costs.

A Mongol who couldn't do gymnastics on his horse was no Mongol at all. A Lakota Sioux youth who complained about his ice baths would be mocked. And a Spartan who lost his shield in battle would be disgraced and possibly put to death. Honor cultures value displays of excellence and put the group over the individual. They demand courage and are often rife with turf wars and *Hatfield and McCoy* style feuds. Today, honor subcultures survive and thrive in gangs, the military, and sports teams, but are typically seen as barbaric, antiquated, and the antithesis of "woke."

Since the Enlightenment, most civilizations have been moving away from cultures of honor and towards dignity. Dignity cultures believe in the rule of law and universal human dignity. There is no avalanche of shame for behavior deemed "disgraceful" and no vigilante justice or *Burr-Hamilton* duels. Crimes are seen as an attack on human dignity rather than on any individual person or group's honor. We see this in the wording of legal cases. It was OJ Simpson v. California, not Simpson v. Nicole Brown, Ron Goldman, or their *kin*. Justice is handled by impartial third parties and the law is absent of emotion. As legal scholar, Orit Kamir, explains, "dignity follows no norms of conduct and is measured against no standards of achievement. It involves no competition and no rivalry. Nothing a person does or refrains from doing can enhance or endanger his or her human dignity."

Honor cultures value capability, loyalty, and commitment to purpose. Dignity cultures value rising above emotion, learning to tolerate differences, and taking care of those who are less fortunate. Combined, these two value structures promote emotionally intelligent leaders. But without honor, dignity culture devolves into the newest social value system: victimhood culture. In a victimhood culture the ideals of dignity are discarded because they are hard to uphold. Prestige is awarded for being more sensitive and getting more offended.

Ideally, we'd strike a balance between honor and dignity frameworks. Dignity cultures are good in the macro but insufficient for the micro. They provide great guiding principles for governments to protect human rights and can offer necessary confines for subcultures of honor to work within. Yet without the good of honor culture, they leave a society with no reason to strive and nothing to bind them.

At its worst, honor cultures are excessively violent, misogynistic, xenophobic, and resistant to innovation. Their worst is obviously bad, yet their foundational tools—honor and shame—are indispensable.

We've been taught to see shame as a social ill, but it is a natural and powerful mechanism for helping a community dissuade destructive behaviors. We want to live in a society where racism, child molestation, and drunk driving are shameful. Shame is an adaptable and sophisticated behavioral modifier. Notions of shame change and mature as the people do. And with shame comes a reciprocal notion of honor.

To promote specific behaviors, dignity cultures have to squelch personal freedoms and create policies that are full of unintended consequences. But in honor cultures, people achieve honor by displaying admirable behavior. Honor cultures offer both carrots and sticks, while dignity cultures only have a stick (law). As philosopher Tamler Sommers explains, in his book, *Why Honor Matters*:

> Honor frameworks recognize that it's not easy to be virtuous, to take risks and act with integrity and solidarity. We need motivation—what evolutionary biologists and behavioral economists have called commitment devices—to overcome our natural impulse towards comfort and safety.

We see examples of commitment devices in the martial arts belt systems and the military's ranking system. In *Why We Drive*, Matthew Crawford muses about doing the same with our driver's licensing system to promote better driving (and create a market for lighter, cheaper, more eco-friendly vehicles):

> Consider, as a thought experiment, a regime of graduated driver's licenses, pegged to both the competence and the involvement of the driver . . . . The restrictions and permissions you enjoy as a driver would be based on certain competencies . . . and tied as well to certain characteristics of your car. First among these would be weight. A car that weighs a thousand pounds less than the cars surrounding it accomplishes three things: it is more maneuverable, it poses less threat to the occupants of its more massive neighbors should they collide and most important the driver of the lighter vehicle has more skin in the game, for the same Newtonian reasons . . . .
>
> The next consideration . . . would be the "ecology of attention" the car supports. The fewer the distractions, the more permissive the license granted to the driver-car combination. At the upper limit if you are willing to drive, a fully

shielded car from which no communication is possible, with no stereo or navigation system, and you are able to put said car into a controlled four-wheel drift at will, and that car is three standard deviations lighter than the median car, then you would enjoy the highest grade of license, and the greatest latitude in doing whatever seems best to you in getting from point A to point B.

Further, let's make the licensure of any driver-vehicle combination visible to other drivers at a glance, perhaps on license plates of different colors. This would enlist vanity and social comparison, those powerful aids to virtue. It would make visible a rank order of drivers.

The mere existence of such a system would communicate that driving is a skill worth valuing and incentivize a population to see driver competency through a more nuanced lens.

Critics will say that we should be creating a society where people transcend competition, rivalry, and merit-based honors, but that is not realistic, particularly for those under 30 (or 60). Honor and shame have been a feature of every successful culture because humans are wired for them. We yearn for significance and connection. As Crawford explains, "Our aspiring nature connects us to other people through emulation. What (you) might be capable of is something you have to discover, and the whole process is set in motion by watching other people and feeling the sting of rank."

We want our children to develop the courage to act with integrity even when it goes against what is popular. But that doesn't mean we should ignore the immense power of social comparison and neglect to use it as all effective social orders do—to clarify desirable ideals and pull people toward them.

When societies don't take the time to do this, other forces will. In the absence of a competency-based tier system, marketers have exploited the immense power of social comparison to create an environment where driver status is based on how expensive a driver's car is. Social pressure pulls us to go into debt, rather than to aspire towards greater skill or a demonstrated commitment to reduce our cost on others. To ignore competitive instincts under the delusion that we can overcome such *"divisive"* competitive tendencies, leaves our culture to the whims of the marketer.

What is more, rather than divisive, such competitions are fundamental to both individual maturation and community solidarity. As Crawford explains:

> The contest for honor gives rise to deference and trust among players . . . . Contests and games require rules, after all. Unlike the simple lust for power, they require that participants recognize the legitimacy of standards that aren't simply emanations of their own will.
>
> The sense of a world that is indifferent to you, and a capacity to accommodate yourself to it, is precisely what an infant lacks. The world revolves around him, and he experiences his mother as an omnipotent extension of his own will. Anything that thwarts his will is enraging. This is called infantile narcissism . . . .
>
> ... there can be no well-founded pride without a corresponding capacity for self-disgust, and it is other people (and their rules of play) who provide the marks on this vertical scale.
>
> To efface the scale or deny that it exists in the name of egalitarian scruples, is to guarantee arrested development on a mass scale.

Tier systems establish a clear path to continual self-development. They create a legacy of skill acquisition that encourages the community to support its youngest members as they try to master fundamental competencies and overcome common rites of passage.

But these systems are only effective in relation to the integrity of their standard—the degree of veracity between what honors indicate and what is reality. By giving everyone a trophy, a juice box, and an all-conference award, we distort and diminish real excellence. When everyone gets an A, the grades are meaningless. Kids are less likely to invest the amount of effort required for real impact and access to deeper lessons. Traditions of excellence devolve into collections of individuals who feel entitled to the outcomes their "program" is supposed to guarantee.

In an effort to appease all, we've demonized most of the standards that would pull people to a higher level of personal conduct. A guiding dogma of the modern youth development paradigm is that any standard of personal conduct is insensitive to those who do not achieve it. Physical proficiency standards could make people feel bad. Educational standards are mechanisms of disenfranchisement. Thus, we should celebrate everyone while eliminating standards. All those adaptable, natural methods for establishing productive values and social cohesion are now deemed insensitive.

In his book *12 Rules for Life,* psychologist Jordan Peterson details the standards blue-collar working crews (and most effective teams) have always enforced among one another:

> Do your work. Pull your weight. Stay awake and pay attention. Don't whine or be touchy. Stand up for your friends. Don't suck up and don't snitch. Don't be a slave to stupid rules. . . . Don't be dependent. At all. Ever. Period. The harassment that is part of acceptance on a working crew is a test: are you tough, entertaining, competent and reliable?

Natural social orders, such as these, produce strong social cohesion and high productivity. They turn hard work environments into places of laughter and connection. Most of all, they pull behavior up. Being tough, entertaining, competent, and reliable is a good thing both for society and for each individual. You will be happier if you are tough. You'll laugh more, be more industrious, and enter challenging experiences that breed authentic connection. By contrast, being oversensitive guarantees that you will feel more afflicted by each inevitable hardship. It saps energy and honesty from every room—insisting others walk on egg shells to protect your fragile ego.

In an oversensitive and shameless society, we lack the positive peer pressure pushing people to exercise, read, stop scrolling social media, or even to be courteous. But even more, such a standardless society breeds alienation. Individuals have the comfort of standardlessness but at the cost of the shared passions, sacrifices, and trials that foster deep connections. This is far more devastating to our social species than most pains could ever be.

THE BABY AND THE BATHWATER

"If you want to make a society work, then you don't keep under-scoring the places where you're different—you underscore your shared humanity."
                                                    —*Sebastian Junger*

Following World War II, consumerism grew and shared notions of virtue gave way to a more morally relativistic ethos. Community-driven, producer-virtues were gradually replaced by an emphasis on seeking individual preferences and personal happiness.

At the same time, the counterculture movement gained steam and Americans began a long overdue interrogation of its misogynist and racist norms. The need was undeniable. But, as so often happens, the pendulum swung to a new extreme. Increasing diversity and toler-ance became indisputable trump cards, on the same level as safety. Suddenly, presuming to teach character education reeked of intoler-ance. Schools began to intentionally avoid promoting values, instead encouraging students to discover their own sense of right and wrong.

This "values clarification" movement, which still reigns today, was another case of utopian delusions gone awry. As Haidt explains:

> " . . . it cut children off from the soil of tradition, history, and religion that nourished older conceptions of vir-tue . . . . Asking children to grow virtues . . . looking only

within themselves for guidance, is like asking them each to invent their own language. Even if they could do it, the resulting isolation would be crippling."

Haidt argues that there are two distinctly different types of diversity—a good diversity and a socially destructive form—and that the failure to make distinctions between the two has had dire results. Good diversity (demographic diversity) is best thought of as justice or equality. This means working to include and respect previously excluded groups. By contrast, bad diversity (moral diversity) emphasizes differences between groups and aims to delegitimize value norms so that every other lifestyle is more viable. It effectively neuters the power of a common moral realm, which is the glue that binds people into a community. Lacking any unifying values, society devolves into tribalism and anomie.

We are right in wanting to resist oppression and keep our society open to new ideas, but that can't come at the expense of the social cohesion we all depend upon. For a society to work, we have to be bonded by more than space and legal codes. There has to be a shared moral sense that transcends race or any other identity categories. The genius of Martin Luther King Jr., Frederick Douglass, and Nelson Mandela was that they embraced a common legacy and pointed to a common future. King studied the same classical rhetoricians that the founders did and found some of his greatest inspiration in the American Transcendentalist, Henry David Thoreau. Despite their flaws, King saw genius in our founders' work and made the fight for equal rights a movement about fulfilling the founding promise, rather than an inquisition of past hypocrisies.

Likewise, in his 1894 speech at the dedication of the Manassas Industrial School, Frederick Douglass encouraged African Americans to embrace education by highlighting its power to promote equality and greater freedom. He then acknowledged the great wrongs done to African Americans but called on his audience to transcend their preferences for "race pride . . . race men, and the like." As he explained:

. . . at the risk of being deficient in the quality of love and loyalty to race and color, I confess that in my advocacy of the colored man's cause, whether in the name of education or freedom, I have had more to say of manhood and of what is comprehended in manhood and in womanhood, than of the mere accident of race and color; and, if this is disloyalty to race and color, I am guilty. I insist upon it that the lesson which colored people, not less than white people, ought now to learn, is, that there is no moral or intellectual quality in the color of a man's cuticle; that color, in itself, is neither good nor bad; that to be black or white is neither a proper source of pride or of shame.

Our culture has no future if we can't restore this shared common-sense and work to redefine values that pull us together. Pride and shame are essential social mechanisms that must be at the center of our efforts, but to elevate and bond us, these efforts have to focus on shared expectations of conduct irrespective of identity groups. *I don't care what you look like. What do you value? What will you stand for? Can we come together to rally towards an ideal of human thriving?*

WHAT IS RIGHT?

". . .when people thought the earth was flat, they were wrong. When people thought the earth was spherical, they were wrong. But if you think that thinking the earth is spherical is just as wrong as thinking the earth is flat, then your view is wronger than both of them put together."
—*Isaac Asimov in his Relativity of Wrong Essay*

Tucked away in the American heartland there is a community standing up against the norms of this crazy world. They are hard-working, educated people, deeply committed to their families and their faith.

They take time for the things too often overlooked in American society like family dinners, book-study, and community service. In
fact, they are deeply committed to their own unique service projects.
Specifically, picketing soldier's funerals and community events with
signs like: "Thank God for Dead Soldiers" and "God Hates Fags."

The town is Topeka, Kansas and this is the Westboro Baptist
Church. Many would conclude that each of these members is evil but,
from their distorted lens, they are the last vestige of human morality.
They and everyone that matters in their life are certain that they have
the right interpretation of the Bible—that they hold the irrefutable
truth about the origins of the universe, the meaning of life, and what
happens when we die. From Westboro's worldview, the only ethical
path is to get the word out that if everyone else doesn't change, they
are destined to burn eternally in a lake of fire. Staying quiet would be
tantamount to watching a child climb into a furnace.

Members of Westboro Baptist Church are certain of what is right
and wrong. They are not open to considering different perspectives.
This highlights the danger of uncompromising moral certitude—of
dogma. But it also highlights the flaws of the opposite extreme, moral
relativism, where people maintain that no behaviors or beliefs are
better than any others. *To each their own. Who am I to judge?* On the
contrary. Westboro's behaviors are evidence that there is a better and
worse. Call me old-fashioned but I say picketing soldiers' funerals is
worse than not picketing them, just as punching infants in the face
is worse than not punching infants in the face. I don't need divine
counsel to confidently condemn baby punchers.

Many people today fixate on the flaws in every person and ethical
code and conclude that there is no objective right or wrong—that
all blemishes are equally damning and, therefore, society should not
favor one path over another. In fact, it should discredit "dominant"
values (thereby reducing their power to unify) and consider them
mechanisms of tyranny. This, of course, becomes its own dogma—
one opposed to standards.

But we need standards. They have the power to rally people toward better living. We also need the ability to question and amend

standards so they remain relevant and constructive. Modern citizenship requires this middle ground between dogma and relativism.

Determining right and wrong (or better and worse) paths usually won't be as obvious as with Westboro. When it comes to complex values, we never reach an absolute true *best*. Yet our earnest desire to move in that direction is fruitful.

Any value system you develop will be incomplete. However, that doesn't mean all opinions are equal. Just as all basketball players are not equal. Lebron James can learn from practicing with Kevin Durant and vice versa. Playing each other leads both of them to pinpoint weaknesses and improve. They are close enough in value that you can debate who is better. Similarly, Kobe Bryant, Michael Jordan, and Lebron James are all close enough in value that you can argue who is the greatest of all time. And even if you say it is Michael, a reasonable person will still concede that the other two have elements of their game where they exceed him. But these conversations are only interesting because all three parties are so good. You can't make the argument that Lonzo Ball is as good of a basketball player as Lebron James or that I am as good as Lonzo Ball. That's just silly.

Likewise, when comparing thoughtful opinions, it will be hard to prove which is best. There will be merits to many different ways of thinking and each time a person honestly engages the merits of a different value system they will subtly refine their own. But that doesn't mean every path is equal. There are still better and worse understandings, better and worse goals, and better and worse applications of the various values that people might hold.

Wisdom is the bull's-eye and, though we will always miss, we're far better off for having defined a target. Societies need this shared target. They need both a revulsion to dogma and a commitment to standards that they hold sacred. They need humility and an open mind, but also a clear sense of better and worse.

In its consumptive, self-serving fervor, our modern culture has failed to clarify such a vision. Progress is reduced to the expansion of convenience, efficiency, and comfort. Morality is reduced to whether a person believes the right thing or not—whether that is traditional religious dogmas or new political ones (disbelief in climate change for the far right; the moral imperative to manufacture equal outcomes for the far left). Virtue now requires nothing more than a Like button. It is completely divorced from standards that require self-development—ideals like endurance, toughness, adaptability, courage, honesty, prudence, stewardship, health, vigor, or thoughtfulness. We oscillate between relativism and dogma, employing each as it serves us, while neglecting the essential conversations: What do we stand for? What capabilities should we expect of ourselves and others? How ought we live?

These questions were at the center of ancient Greek culture. To them, philosophy (which literally translates as *love of wisdom*) was not a subject but a way of living that all citizens were called to embody. They knew that to honestly engage in the pursuit of wisdom would only create more questions—that they would never perfectly embody the ideal—but that the process itself was required for individual and societal flourishing. By putting human flourishing at the center of their culture, the Greeks defined high standards that pulled the entire population up.

THE IDEAL

In his transcendent book, *Zen and the Art of Motorcycle Maintenance*, Robert Pirsig develops a philosophy of living that seeks to solve the growing alienation and meaninglessness he saw in society. He posits that in exchange for the progress of science, we compartmentalized every facet of life. Science (rationality) and art (human intuition) were siloed to their respective corners never to cross-pollinate. Virtue was divorced from shared myths and from daily living.

In Pirsig's story, the character Phaedrus, a professor of rhetoric, begins to believe that the solution lay in a cultural reorientation toward pursuing quality. *Quality,* in Phaedrus' view, should lie at the heart of society. But there is a stigma among rational people against notions like quality which cannot be explicitly defined and proven. Therein lies our problem today. If there is no argument for better tastes, how do you combat the ever-expanding drive for comfort, convenience, efficiency, and safety? Perceptions of quality are subjective and intuitive, but that does not mean quality isn't a real thing that we can move closer to.

In his search for a defense of quality, Phaedrus comes across "*The Greeks,*" by H.D.F. Kitto, and is swept away by how much their heroic ideal matches his *Quality*:

> What moves the Greek warrior to deeds of heroism," Kitto comments, "is not a sense of duty as we understand it . . . duty towards others: it is rather duty towards himself. He strives after that which we translate 'virtue' but is in Greek arête, 'excellence' . . ."
>
> Kitto had more to say about this arête of the ancient Greeks. "When we meet arête in Plato," he said, "we translate it 'virtue' and consequently miss all the flavour of it. 'Virtue,' at least in modern English, is almost entirely a moral word; arête, on the other hand, is used indifferently in all the categories, and simply means excellence."
>
> Thus the hero of the Odyssey is a great fighter, a wily schemer, a ready speaker, a man of stout heart and broad wisdom who knows that he must endure without too much complaining what the gods send; and he can both build and sail a boat, drive a furrow as straight as anyone, beat a young braggart at throwing the discus, challenge the Phaeacian youth at boxing, wrestling or running; flay, skin, cut up and cook an ox, and be moved to tears by song. He is in fact an excellent all-rounder; he has surpassing arête.

The Greek ideal was not embodied by some solitary, monastic elder who lived cast away from society. It wasn't the contemplative philosopher who spent his days coming up with ethical proofs to systematize right and wrong. The Greek ideal was accessible to all and required from all.

As Matthew Crawford explains: "In ancient Greek, one doesn't speak of "morality" as an external demand laid upon us (and therefore always difficult to know, requiring guidance from priests), but of "virtues" in the plural, meaning particular excellences that are manifested in action. Here the ethical and practical are inseparable, and remain close to experience."

Those Greek excellences were the standards that all people were expected to pursue. These ranged from courage and physical vitality to justness and balance. At the root of all of them was a fervor for human excellence. The ancient Greeks were obsessed with living to the fullest. They wanted to explore the bounds of human potential— to play, laugh, love, fight, think, and live with as much energy, life, and excellence as possible.

And there it is. Arête. The pursuit of excellences—of the life-well-lived. A standards-driven ideal durable enough to maintain what is best in humanity regardless of competency-replacing technological advances, while adaptable enough to improve with us as our moral intuitions mature. It's time that our norms pull us to this ideal.

A NEW NORM

The most influential forces in modern society are billion-dollar industries whose primary objectives are to increase the number of things we want and the amount of time spent consuming. Our data is tracked and sold. Biochemical dependencies and evermore sophisticated marketing strategies funnel us towards consumption and away from the pursuits that would foster purpose and growth. No major cultural force is standing against unhealthy trends and giving us the tools to overcome mass propaganda. Consequently, enormous momentum pulls even the most well-intentioned away from best practices.

Just as ubiquitous industrial food makes it difficult for parents to instill healthy eating patterns, the smartphone problem is made infinitely more challenging when most kids begin using social media before Junior High. Teens and tweens feel excluded when all their friends are pinging away on their smartphones without them. Parents often feel forced to make compromises between what they think is best and what a standardless culture has deemed normal.

To meet the challenges of our time, schools must make it their mission to be an authority in human development. Guided by a pursuit of arête, they must make judgments and intentionally offset pernicious cultural developments—everything from Pop Tarts at breakfast to bulldozer parenting. This starts with controlling what is acceptable at schools, but it also requires actively guiding community norms through explicit parental education.

Schools have the ability to clarify expectations for how parents introduce and control new technology. They should explicitly tell parents to delay giving their kids smartphones, to keep kids off of social media until high school, and to ask parents to keep smartphones out of the bedroom at night. They have the power to teach a new set of healthy tech manners. Imagine if everyone was taught that it was rude to have their phone out while eating with others or disrespectful to scroll through their phone while talking with others. But it shouldn't stop there.

Schools could help re-establish fruitful norms in everything from tech and eating habits to the way we interact with each other. It isn't just stuffy traditionalism to expect kids to say "yes ma'am," hold doors, give up their seats for the elderly, throw trash away, or show respect to authority figures (barring rare circumstances). Such norms establish an environment that pulls the best out of us and fosters connection through shared ideals. In the age of distraction, dependency, and entitlement, we must establish strong norms that pull people to better pursuits. First among these norms is to teach people to think about the complex interplay between individuals and society.

Whether in regards to ubiquitous industrial food or a clickbait information ecosystem, over and over, pernicious forces have exploited the impulses of the masses for their own profits. "It is just business", we are told. But that is what we must change. In a healthy culture, most people would get pissed off by such ploys. Manipulation would earn our revulsion. Diminish the culture and you'd see the public turn on you. That instinct has to be taught, however. The costs of not doing so are larger than most recognize.

I'll address these costs more in Chapter 10, but first I want to identify a few practical parenting directives. This is the sort of parent education that schools should be leading. Through the majority of this book, I focus on fundamental principles, because these can be applied across contexts. But there are also many specific practices, resources, and tips that most parents would find helpful.

CHAPTER 9B

PARENTING MENTALLY & PHYSICALLY HEALTHY KIDS

"A child educated only at school is an uneducated child."
—*George Santayana*

MODEL

First and foremost, your model is the most powerful gift you can give your children. Everything you say pales in comparison. This is why it is important for parents to have a sense of purpose that goes beyond serving their children's needs. Having your own interests helps you avoid smothering your kids and teaches them to find the world interesting. Passionate kids almost always have passionate parents. Thus, taking the time to work on yourself is one of the best gifts you can give your children.

The power of the parental model extends into every area of your life, especially health:

- Want your kids to value nutrition and eat well? Start by eating well.

- Want your kids to value their physical health and to grow up moving and exercising regularly? Start by moving and exercising regularly.
- Want your kids to read more and spend less time on their phones? Read more. And spend less time on your phone.
- Want your kids to speak well? Speak well.
- Want your kids to drink responsibly when they get older? Drink responsibly.
- Want your kids to value sleep? Go to bed at a consistent time and keep screens out of your bedroom.
- Want your kids to develop the belief that they can improve through practice? Let them see you learning, improving, and overcoming obstacles.
- Want your kids to play outside and enjoy time in nature? Play outside and enjoy time in nature. Figure out what you like best and find a way to do more of it. Exercise outside. Read outside. Go on walks and bike rides. Visit local parks. Hike. Camp. Fish. Hunt. Play outdoor sports. Too cold? In Sweden, the average preschooler spends six hours outside each day in good weather and 90-minutes throughout their notoriously cold, wet, and frigid winters. Throwing on the rain boots is a great way of modeling the belief that external conditions don't have to determine your life.

Kids won't do everything you do just because you do it, ESPECIALLY, while they live under your roof. But there is no better way to influence their long-term behavior and values than modeling what you want to see.

OWN THE ENVIRONMENT

Control what you can control. Design an environment that promotes success:

- Want your kids to eat nutritious foods? Serve nutritious meals and don't keep heavily processed, industrial convenience snacks available at home.
- Keep juice, soda, Gatorade, and other sugary beverages out of the home.
- Video game systems are very addictive. They tend to be less problematic than smartphones, however, because they are social. For many kids, they provided an invaluable social outlet during the coronavirus lockdowns. But during normal conditions, I'd say either keep them out of the house, or restricted to a specific schedule.
- Keep screens out of the kids' bedroom. That means television, computers, tablets, and phones. This goes a long way to helping keep the family together and helps everyone sleep better. Try having one central phone charging station where phones go each evening and keep computers and televisions in a central family area.

Controlling the home environment is essential, but there is a tension we have to make peace with. Currently, most of the world will not value your kids' health as much as you do, but your kids need to go out and experience the world free from your supervision. Soccer games will end with sweets. School classes will have too many occasions that call for pizza, donuts, or cupcakes. Kids will have sleepovers and go to friends' houses where they have nothing but candy, pizza, and soda. It will happen. Trust that your model and the foods you make available on a daily basis will win out in the long run.

Still, you may be able to make choices and investments that make it more likely that your kids experience better environments when they are not in your home. For example:

- Some schools value health, movement, and nature far more than others. The first preschool my wife and I looked at for our kids

had a minuscule playground and wanted them to eat the breakfast (French toast sticks), lunch (pizza, tater tots, apple slices),
and snack (chips, gummies) that the school provided. We chose
another place that had them bring their own snacks and lunch
and had wonderful, loving teachers. Still, it lacked sunlight, the
playground wasn't great, and they spent most of the day in their
very small classrooms. The next year we found an outdoor based
preschool with great teachers and an emphasis on active learning, free play, and learning outside whenever possible.

- Camps, camps, camps. When summer comes around get them
  up, out, and moving.
- Prioritize active vacations and mini-excursions like skiing,
  fishing, hiking, camping, kayaking, horseback riding, surfing,
  paintball, etc.
- Some purchases, like smartphones, iPads, and video game systems guarantee less movement and more time in passive entertainment. Other purchases promote more engagement and
  activity. Prioritize the latter. Things like bikes, skateboards,
  playsets, monkey bars, a basketball hoop, Slamball, a trampoline, sprinklers, water guns, and ping pong (the greatest indoor
  game ever).
- Ask yourself, does our environment promote play and movement?

SCREEN TIME AND OTHER
HELPFUL BOUNDARIES

One of the greatest parenting misconceptions is that it isn't a big deal
to leave kids on the iPad or watching TV programs all day if they
are digesting educational content. The reality, as Victoria Prooday
explains, is that:

Nothing can replace human interaction, playing live games,
spending time in nature, and involving children in household chores. The harm of exposing children early to technology outweighs its benefits. Today, we know that the key

to success in life is emotional intelligence. While playing on computers and watching TV as their primary free time activity, kids don't have the opportunity to develop and use their social skills.

Screen-based entertainment can be great, provided that you set limits. The American Association of Pediatricians (AAP) Recommends:

- 18 months and less: Avoid use of screen media other than video chatting.
- 18- 24 months: Adding any is your choice, but limit and co-view.
- 2-5 years: Limit screen time to 1 hour per day of high-quality programs.
- For older kids, create a family media plan with consistent rules and enforce them.

According to the AAP, "The reality is that most families will go through periods of heavy and light media use, but, so long as there's a balance, kids should be just fine." That means you can let four-year-olds watch Toy Story, Mulan, or The Sandlot. Just consider that if they are watching a movie after dinner, they should probably be active and outside during the day. Do an internet search for "AAP family media plan" for some fantastic resources.

SMARTPHONE-SPECIFIC SUGGESTIONS

"This is a global problem. It is eroding the core foundations of how people behave by and between each other. I can control my decision, which is that I don't use that shit. I can control my kids' decisions, which is that they're not allowed to use that shit."
—Chamath Palihapitiya, Facebook's former
Vice-President of User Growth

I use my smartphone all the time. For podcasts, audio books, web searches, maps, weather, pictures, chess, scheduling trips, reading articles, Uber, Airbnb, fantasy football, video, text messaging, and even for phone calls. It is probably the most essential tool in my daily life. But, despite the convenience and entertainment these devices bring, smartphones have had a negative net effect on most people. Children will clamor for the day they get a smartphone, but this could be their undoing. Without clear boundaries, we cannot expect our children to have a healthy relationship with their devices.

It may be best to begin looking at smartphones and similar technology as controlled substances. Not that smartphone use should be legislated, but we need to approach our devices with a respect for their addictive nature and the disruption they present to optimal mental health. Within clearly defined boundaries, smartphones can enhance our lives. Yet, just as you wouldn't allow your 11-year-old carte blanche of the liquor cabinet, it is unwise to give them free reign of an infinite device. If you leave a 13-year-old girl to use her smartphone however she likes, she will scroll, post, and "like" from sun-up to sun-down, breaking only to stage clever selfies and eat meals (after she has photographed them, of course). Her grasp of reality will grow distorted, her expectations unrealistic, and her desire to live in the real world will erode.

So how do parents best manage the challenges associated with smartphones and social media? This is the parenting question of our time. There are no easy answers. Strategies will have to continue evolving as the technologies do. But all solutions boil down to creating a boundary between our kids and the cues that would tantalize them. This might look different for different people.

Shark Tank's Barbara Corcoran turns her phone off when she gets home from work each day. Similarly, I put my phone on a charger in the kitchen before dinner each night and give it one last check at 7 p.m. before winding down for the evening. I wait to look at it again until after my morning routine the next day. To help me maintain these desired phone free times, I've changed my phone settings so that between 7 p.m. and 6 a.m. notifications for calls and texts will only come through from people I've selected as favorites.

I talk to my students about charging the phone outside their room and not looking at screens in bed, but it is insane to expect status-obsessed high school students to maintain such seemingly extreme boundaries simply because they are better for them. Parents have to insist upon these boundaries.

There are many apps that can help. The Screentime app allows parents to lock their kids' phones during certain hours and limit what the phone can be used for. The Lifesaver app allows parents to disable their teen's phone when their car is in motion. But it can be hard to keep up with the ever-growing assortment of popular apps and technology threats so it is best to rely on a group of experts who have made responsible tech use their life mission. Tristan Harris's Center for Humane Technology maintains a list of helpful apps and easy changes you can make to your phone's settings to promote more intentional use and less susceptibility to mindless pulls. For more information, go to: http://humanetech.com.

Other helpful directives:

- Charge phones each evening at a family charging station. You may need to purchase a few good old-fashioned alarm clocks.
- Go to phone settings and turn off all phone notifications other than real-time phone calls and texts.
- Explore apps like Bark or Screentime that can help you block inappropriate media sites and restrict media use to the parameters you prefer.
- Have young adults take on one social media platform at a time. There is no reason to go from no social media to juggling Instagram, Twitter, TikTok, Facebook, Vine, and Snapchat plus 14 group chats. Let teen's pick one or none to start with.
- Device-free dinners.
- Other suggested no phone zones include:

- In bed
- While reading or doing homework
- While watching television (one screen at a time)
- While outside (exceptions for music and pictures)
- And consider it good manners to make social time phone free, except as the phone contributes to in-person social activity

The most powerful step you can take is to delay giving your child a smartphone. At some point, you'll want to give him or her access to a phone for calling, but I recommend a call and text only flip-phone until kids are in 8th or 9th grade (search the *Wait Until 8th Initiative*).

Even in 9th grade, there will inevitably be negative effects from having a smartphone, but we should also remember that the smartphone is central to how teens conduct their social lives. The problems it invites have to be balanced against the emotional costs of feeling left out of an entire world. Much of that is mitigated by a flip-phone that allows text-messaging, but around the time they are entering high school it is probably time for a smartphone. Look at it like an extended learner's permit where you can teach and enforce healthy boundaries and help young adults learn to manage this power before they are full-fledged adults.

It may sound like a contradiction to critique safetyism and then claim that schools and parents should take greater steps to protect kids from social media, but the goal is to spur the greatest possible long-term human flourishing. From that lens, it makes perfect sense to not allow your 13-year-old to have a Snapchat or Instagram account, just as you wouldn't allow them to spend their evenings in the red-light district. Social media is Pandora's box. Once opened, it will promote unhealthy beliefs and be an ever-present drain on your kid's psyche. To handle this well, young adults will need healthy interests, good models, and education in self-mastery. Now, more than ever, we need to be getting better at being human.

INFLUENCE

As seen with the "preacher's kid phenomenon," restriction can bring resentment and eventually rebellion. We have to be careful not to set boundaries that feel too stifling. Often the most important factor is how we present things. Emphasize the advantage of your unique path—how doing things different than most is making your kids special in specific ways. Kids will respond better if you talk to them like adults and trust them to understand where you are coming from. You can foster a sense of pride in them for their creativity, curiosity, and ability to focus. Tell them how much you appreciate their maturity and encourage their passions.

But we also have to let go of the reins and make peace with some typical teen smartphone behavior. If you demonize everything while appearing stressed and angry, then kids just see your approach as crazy. Try to get a sense of what battles are worth fighting. There is no harm in kids using a phone to set plans with friends or enjoying a fun new app when not much else is going on. In fact, these are wonderful perks of the smartphone. Note the difference between phone patterns that enhance your kids' lives and negative propensities—like feeling the need to check social media constantly.

If we want more active, physically and mentally healthy kids, we should create barriers to the things that pull them to sit by themselves and do nothing. But more than that, we should think about how we can create an environment that begs them to move, explore, and connect with the world.

There is nothing worse than feeling bound up. We are best off de-emphasizing what is being limited and putting our attention on all those things that we are freeing ourselves to do. We set boundaries so that we are freed from manipulation and can experience a broader, richer life. Boundaries create more opportunities to master ping-pong, learn to backflip on a trampoline, build a hidden talent for chess, and develop a passion for the guitar. This is not about deprivation, but being intentional about how we spend our lives.

CULTURE:

"It's no sign of health to be well adjusted to a sick society."
—*Jiddu Krishnamurti*

It is one thing to notice problems and understand that modern norms regarding technology, nutrition, and our broader youth development paradigm have grown dysfunctional. It is quite another for busy parents, feeling alone in their values, to figure out how to mediate the gap between what is and what should be. We live in this world and, as much as any other need, we need to feel connected with our community. This is why finding, or creating, like-valued communities or subcultures will be among the most important things we can do in our lives. My greatest hope is that this book helps people do that.

CHAPTER 10

ENLIGHTENMENT OR BUST: THE ROLE OF SCHOOL IN THE 21ST CENTURY

"Democracy remains viable only if we are willing to extend to one another a presumption of individual competence."
—Matthew Crawford

In an interview between political commentator Dave Rubin and evolutionary biologist, Bret Weinstein, the two discussed some of the enormous challenges facing our world—the pace of economic change, the social effects of social media, weaponry that can end all life—that sort of thing. Weinstein argued that the greatest existential threat to humanity was the rate of technological progress, to which Rubin asked:

> "But can it be slowed down? . . . What force could slow down progress?"
>
> "Wisdom," Weinstein responded. "And that's the problem. We are children in this landscape . . . The key to raising children properly is to back off the things that protect

them enough that they actually get burned without being burned so severely that they're crippled. In other words, you have to experience the places that your notions are naive in order to become less naive. We are now in a situation in which we are behaving . . . like children running around in a foundry. There is molten metal and things we need to figure out how to recognize and we're just running around pressing buttons."

As Weinstein suggests, the law of unintended consequences does not just apply to bureaucratic interventions like dead cobra policies, but also every new invention. The pace and power of today's inventions are on a scale we've never seen and that will only increase. Exponential increases in technological power now allow each decision to have infinitely greater effects. The most depraved, axe-wielding Viking could never hope to kill as many people in a lifetime as a terrorist with an atomic weapon could in one afternoon. Likewise, a confused teenager who has been influenced by racist dogmas can go online and find millions of people eager to support his radicalization. The confusion of growing up is now accompanied by instant access to the world's most misguided ideas and people.

There is no precedent for these challenges. History provides some insightful trends but the scope of our issues leaves us in entirely new territory. It's like we've taken the birth of television, the industrial revolution, the internet revolution, mixed them all together and then multiplied the result by 100. There is no utopia here. No system will be adaptable enough. To successfully navigate this world, we must prioritize the pursuit of maturity and wisdom.

Dan Carlin says it more bluntly. While talking to historian Danielle Bolelli about the complexity of modern challenges, Carlin asked the question most of us have thought but never uttered: "What if we need better people?"

To a large extent, that's what I've been arguing in this book. It is harder than ever to avoid manipulation and create a fulfilling life. Because of the complexity of our issues and the power of our decisions, today's citizens need to be better than ever at exploring hard truths, thinking critically, and learning from failure. They need to be capable of rising to a vast array of occasions. To thrive individually and survive collectively, we need to produce better people.

But, in most respects, the opposite is happening. We're more comfortable, but less likely than ever to have our human needs met. We have more information, but are less likely to pursue wisdom and less capable of making sense of the world. We have more opportunity to hear a diversity of perspectives, but we seem to be growing less likely to adapt our opinions.

Two-time presidential candidate, Adlai Stevenson, once claimed that in a representative democracy people tend to "get the type of government they deserve." The last U.S. presidential election took place eight months into the COVID-19 pandemic, after a summer of widespread social hostility, and economic uncertainty. To meet these challenges, we were given a choice between a 78-year-old, Joe Biden, who made no campaign promises other than that he would continue to not be Donald Trump, and a 74-year-old Trump who, among other things, made it clear that he would not honor election results if they weren't in his favor (apparently some people took that seriously). I don't know if we *deserve* this but we are getting a mirror effect where our politics and news reflect our cultural failings.

If we somehow upgraded our values and became a savvy, less easily duped population, then our news and politics would shift in kind. If we could somehow improve the quality of our people, then we may see a positive snowball effect where more avenues of the consumptive complex came to reinforce more fulfilling pursuits. We'd have the collective bandwidth to rally around a necessary third-party candidate, to demand reforms that end lobby-centric political corruption, and to stand against technology platforms that incite animosity and sell our attention.

WHAT WOULD YOU DO?

"Only a virtuous people are capable of freedom."
—Ben Franklin

Following the Holocaust many questioned how such atrocities were possible. How could a vast network of people orchestrate such evil? Why weren't there refusals all throughout the chain? The soldiers who did the dirty work weren't the only people culpable. Entire countries watched as Jewish citizens were forced out of jobs, into ghettos, and then repeatedly subjected to attacks. It would be impossible not to notice as former friends and colleagues were shipped away. Many people would have witnessed Jews being treated like animals along their path to the concentration camps, and the towns next to these death camps surely witnessed plenty of evidence. This was simply too large of a concerted effort not to require the acquiescence of millions.

The defense offered over and over by Nazi officials at the Nuremburg War Trials was that they were just following orders. But who could follow such orders? Surely, most people in most times and places would have never been party to such an atrocity.

Yale psychologist Stanley Milgram set out to test this in his famous 1963 Obedience Experiments. Milgram took a random sample of people and told them that he was conducting studies on learning. Each participant was led to believe that they were being paired with another willing study participant, just like them. In fact, they met this person and drew lots to see who would be the "teacher" and who would be the "learner." This was fixed, however. The "learner" was always the same man, a Mr. Wallace. The teacher then watched as the learner was put in a back room where many electrodes were attached

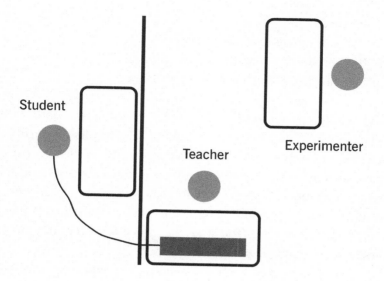

to his arms. The experimenter, a gentleman in a gray lab coat, then directed the teacher to a separate room (as seen below).

The teacher was sat in front of long switchboard, like a piano. The far-left switch specified "15 volts (slight shock)." A little past half-way came a switch indicating "375 volts (Danger: Severe Shock)" and the final of 30 switches simply read "450 volts (XXX)." The teacher was instructed to ask Mr. Wallace questions and administer a pro-gressively higher shock for each incorrect answer. Unbeknownst to this teacher, Mr. Wallace was not actually receiving the shocks. His responses, most of which were incorrect, had been tape recorded so that all "teachers" heard the exact same response.

As the teachers administered progressively higher-level shocks, they heard Mr. Wallace begin to respond in pain. By 150 volts he yells, "Ouch! That's all! Get me out of here! Get me out of here, please! I refuse to go on. Let me out!" At 180 volts, he interjects, "I can't stand the pain! Get me out!" Teachers usually got uncomfortable and turned to the experimenter for direction. Each time the experimenter gave one of four consistent prods:

1. Please continue.
2. The experiment requires you to continue.
3. It is absolutely essential that you continue.
4. You have no other choice but to continue.

Eventually, the terrified voice on the recording is begging the teacher to stop the torturous experiment. At 375 volts the shrilling cries cease altogether leaving one to assume Mr. Wallace is either dead or unconscious. Still, most continue administering shocks. The absence of a reply is treated as a wrong answer and the experiment continues. In 65% of experiments the teacher shocked Mr. Wallace through all 30 switches. The study has since been repeated many times with similar results.

Most are horrified to see that a majority of people may be capable of participating in the most heinous acts when they can defer responsibility to a norm or an authority. As we've seen on countless occasions, from the Atlantic slave trade to McCarthyism, humanity is capable of terrible collective behavior when social proof or authority figures deem them acceptable.

As a teacher, I used to show all my students the Milgram Obedience Experiment early in the year. I wanted students to be shaken from their passivity and to begin cultivating a sense of a higher standard. It is easy to focus on the majority who deliver lethal shocks, but what about the other third or so? What gave them the moral courage to overcome their social discomfort and to say "No More!"?

Likewise, how did Miep Gies develop the conviction and bravery to hide Anne Frank and her family for years in Nazi occupied Amsterdam? And where did a Pakistani teen named Malala Yousafzai get the courage to defy the Taliban—to insist that women should be educated and to create such an influential example that the Taliban felt they must kill her? She survived a gunshot to the head and has become the spiritual leader of a movement to give equal educational access to all women around the globe. How do we empower more Malala's?

Schools should be intentionally determining how to increase the percentage of people who stop delivering shocks from 35% to 85%, or more. Our environment has the power to pull people towards excellence and moral courage. Even more, our world demands it. To meet future challenges and find fulfillment our children must develop the capacity to stand for something.

WHAT DO YOU STAND FOR?

"What would you risk dying for—and for whom—is perhaps the most profound question a person can ask themselves. The vast majority of people in modern society are able to pass their whole lives without ever having to answer that question, which is both an enormous blessing and a significant loss."

—Sebastian Junger

On October 26, 1967, U.S. Navy Lieutenant Commander John McCain was shot out of the sky as he flew over Hanoi, Vietnam. The North Vietnamese quickly captured him as he lay stranded in enemy territory with both arms and his right leg shattered. They took him to one of history's most brutal and infamous prison camps, the "Hanoi Hilton." Within a year of his capture, McCain's father was promoted to Commander of all U.S. forces in the Pacific. McCain was offered his freedom in an attempt to demoralize the other prisoners. But he refused, later explaining:

> I knew that every prisoner the Vietnamese tried to break, those who had arrived before me and those who would come after me, would be taunted with the story of how an admiral's son had gone home early, a lucky beneficiary of America's class-conscious society.

As McCain undoubtedly expected, his angry captors intensified their torment to levels of pain scarcely imaginable. Over the next half decade, he faced frequent torture and even two full years of solitary confinement in a windowless 10-by-10-foot cell. It wasn't until March of 1973, after 1,966 days, that McCain was released along with the other Hanoi prisoners. If he'd only accepted the freedom he was offered, he would have avoided over four and a half years in the most brutal conditions imaginable. But he chose to endure hell because he thought it was the right thing to do.

It is easy to write off McCain's tremendous integrity as the consequence of some rare, innate courage—to say he was just born with better stuff. As with Nelson Mandela's capacity to forgive or Kyle Maynard's tenacity, we look on in awe before categorizing these behaviors as superhuman—the stuff of heroes—irrelevant for comparison. But that lets us off the hook too easily.

Even if McCain displayed character at a level surpassing our immediate grasp, he is still a mere human. His example demonstrates the untapped strength that lies somewhere within us all. McCain was able to make hard choices because he built his life around clear values. He was the product of an environment that promoted discipline and integrity. These standards were forged through intentional experiences and rigorous self-reflection.

When it comes to heroism, this is almost always the case. Whether we are talking about McCain, Mandela, Malala, Maynard or any other hero, these are people who held themselves to a standard that required them to make judgments about what path was better or worse. It is important for a society to have heroes. They bond us over common values, common stories, and a common sense of who we are and what we stand for—what we value and what our children will aspire to be like.

GOING WITH THE FLOW

"Bad men need nothing more to compass their ends, than that good men should look on and do nothing."   —*John Stuart Mill*

On August 6, 2000, 15-year-old Nicholas Markowitz was walking along the side of a road in his affluent hometown, West Hills, Los Angeles, when a van stopped. Out popped three men in their early 20's. They kicked and punched Markowitz before blindfolding him and throwing him in the van.

Nicholas's older brother, Ben, owed drug-dealer Jesse James Hollywood $1,200. Hollywood and his crew were on their way to confront Ben when they saw Nicholas walking along the road and made an impromptu decision to take him hostage. After blindfolding Nicholas, they sped off to Santa Barbara, about 70 miles up the coast. Despite his initial terror, Nicholas soon settled in after the gang explained the situation. He was brought along to various parties where they encouraged him to enjoy booze, drugs and "the good life." Two days of debauchery culminated at a motel pool party where Nicholas cozied up to a 17-year-old girl. As many as 32 partiers later acknowledged they knew Nicholas had been kidnapped but did nothing because it appeared he was having fun.

Markowitz looked up to his captors and their fast, carefree lifestyle. He was assured that he'd be returned home soon and was confident that this would soon all be an exciting memory. The smalltime pawns he hung out with probably believed that too. They seemed to welcome Markowitz and celebrate the novelty of partying with their hostage. For a bunch of spoiled kids turned amateur criminals, this stunt substantiated their desire to be perceived as hardcore, edgy deviants. While his crew basked in their narcissism, Hollywood met with a lawyer who made it clear that Hollywood could face life in prison for this kidnapping. Realizing the magnitude of his mistake, he called Ryan Hoyt, his most eager "whipping boy" who also owed him money. He had a way for Hoyt to pay off his debt.

Hollywood gave Hoyt a modified, fully automatic TEC-9 pistol. After two days of partying and fun, Hollywood's posse now followed Hoyt's lead. They bound and gagged Nicholas as Hoyt drove him up the scenic Santa Ynez Mountains overlooking Santa Barbara. They dug a shallow grave and shot Nicholas Markowitz 9 times.

The 2007 movie, *Alpha Dog,* is based on this true story. I remember seeing the film in theaters on opening night. You could feel the audience won over by these seemingly harmless young adults and their wild lifestyle. Justin Timberlake plays Frankie Ballenbacher who is based on Hollywood's confidant, Jesse Rugge. Timberlake's charismatic fun-natured spirit makes him especially endearing. The whole thing feels like just another party movie with the twist of a light-hearted kidnapping. Hollywood's crew seems cool and immature enough that the kidnapping is laughed off as a harmless stunt. As they party with him, Nicholas Markowitz's character is affectionately dubbed "stolen boy."

You could feel the audience cheering on the party scenes, the crude dialogue, and the innocent fun of a few young adults who just want to drink and do drugs. The movie brilliantly creates a subtle subtext of *"What's the big deal? This is what young people do."* If, like me, you didn't know the story ahead of time, you're still expecting everything to end up okay, until boom. Timberlake hits this kid over the head with a shovel and then he's shot to death. You could hear a pin drop in that theater. It hardly seemed real. Did that really just happen?

The kidnapping and murder of Nicholas Markowitz is a tragedy. It should not have happened. As witnesses testified in the trial, he could have escaped on many occasions. He was 15 and fooled by the illusion that this was all no big deal. Most of Hollywood's flunkies were just overgrown children. They wanted to believe they could be cool and do whatever they want and that this was all just fun. They wanted to believe they could kidnap a kid and it was no big deal because *we're treating him nice and partying with him.* Likewise, any of the many witnesses could have gone to the police at almost any point. These weren't hardened criminals. They did drugs, partied, and were seduced by the desire to be cool.

While exaggerated, this is the world most of our kids are pulled towards. Standing for anything is considered *"extra."* People are empowered to voice their indignation behind a keyboard, but that is easy. It costs nothing to say that bullies and racists suck. But what does it cost to fight a more nuanced battle? What does it cost to take a stand against scapegoating or straw-man arguments? It is hard to act according to values. If you do not stand for something, you can avoid making anyone mad. If you live according to your convictions, you'll upset those who'd prefer you *"be cool."*

A few years ago, the high school football program where I work kicked a young man out of the program after he was found with a bag full of smartphones, headphones, and shoes he'd stolen from his teammates unlocked lockers. A year later, he showed up at the JV game and walked onto the field into the north endzone where the Varsity team watches sub-varsity games. Other than coaches and players, no one else is allowed onto this section of the field. Still, like a conquering hero, he walked through the entire row of athletes giving handshakes and bro-hugs. Over 50 young adults who had either been robbed or had friends who were robbed, shook his hand and acted like his presence was acceptable. Not one man thought to say, "Hey, this tradition is reserved for members of the team. You can watch from the stands." So, I did.

After he left, I played dumb and asked some of the athletes to refresh my memory about what he'd done. They eagerly reminded me and filled me in on many other disturbing transgressions that had forced him to move to a different school. The athletes clearly understood how inappropriate it was for this young man to come down on that field, but they were all unwilling to take the hard stand.

What you stand for defines you. I'm glad you are nice and agreeable, but so is any coward. What are you willing to be unpopular for? What would you fight for?

I fear that, now, more than ever we are creating a passive generation who will not develop convictions much less stand for them. Kids grow up in the age of social media where everyone is great at putting on masks of bravado, but living up to values requires more than tough tweeting.

Recently, a teacher told me about a class discussion where students began to defend how common cheating had become. To universal support, one student exclaimed, "What else are you supposed to do if you don't know the answers?"

This sentiment speaks to a far greater society-wide problem: the rationalization of shortcuts at the expense of any more worthwhile ideal. There is hardly a concept of integrity, truth, or of the value of your word. And in the age of Google, there is scarcely a sense that education should be about more than finding answers and regurgitating them.

MEETING THE MOMENT

"A primary object should be the education of our youth in the science of government. In a republic, what species of knowledge can be equally important? And what duty more pressing than communicating it to those who are to be the future guardians of the liberties of the country."   —*George Washington*

Stacy is an intelligent and social high school junior. She plays soccer, works on the student council, and does well on her classwork. This week she learned how to solve equations with two square roots, created a PowerPoint on urban tenement living conditions in late 19th century America, was quizzed on how inertia and friction affect movement, and demonstrated her understanding of short-story elements by writing about the flat tire she got on her way to see Taylor Swift in concert. Her generic coursework is completely unsurprising, at least until you stop to think about the world we are preparing her for.

Stacy's teachers have never mentioned deep fake technologies and how they will soon allow anyone to take a person's image and voice recording and make them appear to do and say anything. There has been no class or faculty discussion about the needs of workers in an increasingly automated job force or the instability that is likely to characterize future employment. Stacy's classes have never mentioned the potential of genome editing to create enhancements in future humans or 3D bioprinters and how they could soon allow an average citizen to print off the next global pandemic. Her teachers don't seem to know or care about Dr. Nick Bostrom's Vulnerable Earth Hypothesis or its assertion that a "black ball" technology could be discovered at any time allowing one unskilled madman to wipe out an entire city. As Bostrum explains:

> ... suppose it had turned out that there was some technological technique that allowed you to make a nuclear weapon by baking sand in a microwave oven or something like that . . . . Presumably once that discovery had been made civilization would have been doomed. Each time we make one of these new discoveries we are putting our hand into a big urn of balls and pulling up a new ball—so far we've pulled up white balls and grey balls, but maybe next time we will pull out a black ball, a discovery that spells disaster. At the moment we have no good way of putting the ball back into the urn if we don't like it. Once a discovery has been published there is no way of un-publishing it.

I don't really think it matters whether or not we discuss 3D bioprinters and "black ball" technologies. But, given the volatility of the world our children are inheriting, perhaps safe spaces and superficial curriculums aren't such a good idea. Maybe we are looking at education with too much apathy and naivety. Students who have not mastered basic logic and dialectical principles—who have no sense of how the world works, no grasp of history's deeper lessons, and no experience discussing uncomfortable ideas—will not have the means to solve complex challenges.

We've hardly begun to imagine the challenges future generations will inherit. College has grown nonsensically expensive, the national debt defies comprehension, and our biggest technological companies collect and sell all of our data. They exert super-governmental control while repeatedly demonstrating a disregard for any legal or sovereign power who would try to limit them. Their unchecked influence is only poised to grow.

There is a fundamental disconnect in education where the status quo reigns without any appreciation for the needs of our time or the responsibility of education to adequately prepare youth for a volatile world. Most of us won't be enlisted in creating specific solutions, but we have to understand the scale of these issues in order to have any sense of proper societal prioritization—to be the type of informed citizen democracy requires. We have to be educating in a way that gives our students the best opportunity to thrive.

As technology grows, it increasingly appears as if our only options are a descent into either mass chaos and anomie or Orwellian oppression. The polymath, Daniel Schmachtenberger, explains his view on the only path out of this dilemma (which gives my thesis a beautiful framework):

> The only answer out of the oppression or chaos is the comprehensive education of everyone and the capacity to understand at least three things: They have to increase their first person, second person and third person epistemics.
>
> Their third person epistemics is the easiest—philosophy of science, formal logic, their ability to actually make sense of base reality through appropriate methodology, and find appropriate confidence margins.
>
> Second person is my ability to make sense of your perspective. Can I steel-man where you're coming from? Can I inhabit your position well? And if I'm not oriented to do that, then I'm not going to find the synthesis of a dialectic. I'm going to be . . . harming something that will actually harm the thing I care about in the long run.
>
> And then first person. Can I notice my own biases and my own susceptibilities and my own group identity issues

and whatever well enough that those aren't the things that run me . . .?

We need a new cultural enlightenment now where everyone values good sense-making about themselves, about others, about base reality, and good quality dialogue with other people that are also sense-making to emerge to a collective consciousness and collective intelligence that is more than our individual intelligence . . . . it's cultural enlightenment or bust as far as I'm concerned.

Unfortunately, only a very few great high schools do a good job covering third person epistemics. None, to my knowledge, have a program for developing first and second person epistemics. And here we see the most glaring and immediate failure of our schools. Amid a mental and physical health epidemic, we have not considered the duty of education to prepare its citizens to live healthy, fulfilling lives. Drug overdoses, suicides, obesity, depression, anxiety, and mass shootings are all at never-before-seen peaks and each of our efforts to reverse these trends ignore the underlying causes.

By all appearances, most of our educational leadership has no idea about the significant challenges they should have at the forefront of their minds. There seems to be little concept of mass marketer manipulation or the challenges of infinite technology, no collective understanding of the psychology behind learning, and no sense of duty to model self-mastery and lifelong learning. They show little awareness of what the smartphone is doing to society and have not offered even the most basic steps to empower its users. It seems that most never even read a book outside of pop-educational pseudoscience. In short, it never occurs to most educational leaders that they should be fighting negative trends, because they lack the fundamental knowledge necessary to understand and combat them.

Schools are the cultural nucleus of society, having more potential for society-wide impact than any other institution. They are our greatest opportunity to course correct and create a citizenry more capable of thriving. But only if they develop a sense of duty to become an authority in human development. In the absence of this standard, our schools have become breeding grounds for many of our most self-destructive trends.

EDUCATION AND REFORM

"If your plan is for 1 year, plant rice. If your plan is for 10 years, plant trees. If your plan is for 100 years, educate children."
                                                    —Confucius

"If you do not change direction, you may end up where you are heading."
                                                    —Lao Tzu

As far back as 1982 the famed educator Marva Collins, who was twice asked to be the U.S. Secretary of Education, wrote a book contending that public schools were in a state of crisis. As she asserted, "What I once assumed to be inferior education for the poor and underprivileged has become a nationwide malady that afflicts the middle and upper classes as well. I have found bad education in the places I least expected to find it."

As with all generalizations, Collins' statement does not tell the whole story. But that does not negate her conclusions or their long-term implications. For generations now, public education has not sufficiently met the needs of the moment. After decades of lowered standards, we are reaping what we sow. The students Collins observed are now our parents, teachers, and administrators, and what Collins perceived as "bad education" is the only system most of them have ever known.

In light of Collins' opinion, I want to invite you to question your own educational experience. What would education need to look like to prepare students for our complex world? If, as I contend, education is the best route for challenging a culture of human degradation, what should it look like?

CHAPTER 11

MODERN EDUCATION— THE LAND OF SMOKE AND MIRRORS

"If you see fraud and do not say fraud, you are a fraud."
—Nassim Taleb

Ten years ago, I showed up for my first day as a high school teacher. I had landed a job in the best school of what is often called a "destination district." Still, I knew I was facing an uphill battle. Warnings abounded of an American public school system in decline. But I was undeterred. I had that youthful sense that education needed change and I was just the one to change it.

Throughout that first year I worked incessantly—creating lessons, grading, and making myself available to students an hour before school each day. I ran around the room joking with students, telling stories, creating relevant analogies, and turning pop-culture songs into lesson reviews that I'd sing for the class:

The classic Outkast song *Hey Ya,* became, *Pay Y'all,* outlining the flaws of the Treaty of Versailles:

> *My country didn't get to Paris, the trenches slowed us down*
> *and now we Owe for Suure.*

But iiiis it really right to put the blame on us for the Entire Waaaar.

Katy Perry's *Firework* became the story of the Constitutional Convention:

Cause baby we're America!
General George Washington
Made them go Bye, Bye, Bye
So now it's time we got it Right, Right, Right

And Carly Rae Jepsen's *Call Me Maybe* became a review of all the ancient river valley civilizations:

Hey! I'm Sumerian. We made the Wheel.
But life is tough here. These Rivers are Crazy.
It's hard to grow crops, when it's not raining.
But here's a flood. Dang there goes Jimmy.

If you're trying to picture me singing, most would describe my voice as a combination of Fergie and Mike Ditka.

My students looked forward to my energy and I enjoyed their sense of humor. Still, I couldn't have predicted how unprepared my students would be. These students had never taken notes. They were shocked that my test reviews weren't a list of the questions on the test. They couldn't understand why I didn't allow 20 minutes of review before the test or why a history exam would have sections requiring written responses. In fact, many would just skip the entire short answer and essay sections, despite being given these topics in advance. Those who did respond often wrote single words or incoherent run-ons.

I'd spend entire classes explaining what I wanted to see in the short answer responses. We'd practice writing the "who, what, where, when, and why this concept is important." But little changed. After their years of schooling in which writing never extended beyond filling in a blank, my expectations were analogous to asking high schoolers to solve algebraic equations when they had not yet learned to multiply and divide. They were capable, but it was going to take a lot of effort to fill in the gaps. Which raises the question, why would a student be willing to put in that much work?

I was fighting the overwhelming tide of a system intent upon handing over diplomas. Half of my students would have failed if I gave them the grade they earned. But the unwritten, yet well-communicated, rule was that teachers should never fail a student if it could be helped. The onus was on the teacher to hound students for late assignments and find a way to bump them to a C.

As much as I wanted to fight every battle, I eventually caved to the exhaustion of a demanding Texas high school coaching schedule (which seemed to be the job I was really hired for). I compromised more times than I would have ever thought possible. I eliminated homework, allowed test retakes, gave fill-in-the blank notes, graded essays at a 5th grade level, gave test reviews that were basically the test, and intentionally made tests easy. When there were still too many students failing at the end of a grading period, I went above and beyond to manufacture easy routes to a passing grade so that only a handful of incomprehensibly effort-averse students failed.

Disillusioned, I worked to create a position as the campus Strength and Conditioning Coordinator where I ran the training programs for each sport. At least there, I thought, I could still uphold a standard of excellence. After five years of teaching, I was out of the classroom, but my heart remained committed to creating better education.

The failures that brought us to this state are deeply entrenched and are only getting worse. We can't afford to keep entertaining the notion that *education is not so bad*. This is not an attack on the individuals involved in public education, but the institutional operating system that handicaps all educators. What is to follow should be welcomed by anyone who earnestly wants public education to approach its tremendous potential. We can only reach that potential by first being honest about where we are. But I should also make it clear that I am only drawing on my own experiences and that of the teachers I've spoken with over the years. Experiences may vary. Still, the more I speak with teachers from other cities and states, the more I'm convinced that the trends I note are typical across public education today.

AND HOW WOULD YOU LIKE YOUR A?

"Never, ever, think about something else when you should be thinking about the power of incentives."   —*Charlie Munger*

While intrinsic motivation can be cultivated on an individual basis, humans, en masse, tend to respond to two things: impulse and incentives. The most reliable ways for a system to shape behavior are by eliminating temptations and by paying attention to the consequences, good or bad, that their incentives produce.

For example, Congressional approval is almost always below 25%, yet congressional reelection rates are consistently above 90%. At first glance that makes no sense. But when you understand the incentives, the picture becomes clear. Each representative is only accountable to the voters of their own local district. They almost always forsake the common good when it benefits their constituency because this is the surest path to re-election. You can claim that we should want politicians to be intrinsically motivated to do the right thing (and I'd agree), but that hope won't fix Congressional performance. Similarly, the most fundamental cause of educational failures is a faulty incentive structure.

The two primary metrics used to evaluate teachers are how frequently they use technology and how high their passing rates are. Sure, there are an ever-changing array of buzzwords used to describe ideal teaching practices—*staying in the "power zone," differentiating instruction, calibrating assessments*—but these are mostly a distraction. You can fill tests with as many level-two, three, and four questions as you want, but that doesn't matter when your study guide gives the answers and your grading policy hides the high number of test failures. Schools may want higher level learning, but they want low failure rates and immaculate graduation rates more.

Our school boards and district administrators are politicians trying to appease the loudest groups of parents. While they almost certainly care about kids, most are long past a conscious or subconscious acceptance that the system is broken beyond repair. In order to climb the educational ranks, they tow the party line.

Emails and staff meetings make it very clear that failing kids should be avoided if at all possible. Administrators acknowledge that some students will make it impossible to pass them, but if the grade is anywhere close: *"Don't write the kid off. Were you a perfect teacher every day? I don't think so. Maybe that was the difference."* Such sentiments ignore the obvious: if not for a healthy dose of lifelines these borderline students would be failing by at least 10 more points.

For those few students who still fail a course, teachers have to submit a failure report to their administrators documenting all the times that the high schooler's parents were contacted. Teachers can't help but feel a degree of self-doubt as they invite this audit. *Did I contact parents too late? Was there enough documentation?* Many teachers have been reprimanded for high failure rates or failing a student with "involved" parents, but I've never heard of a teacher being scrutinized for passing everyone.

One of the biggest challenges for teachers in their quest to give good grades is that test grades tend to be very low. To offset this, teachers give assignments that will raise everyone's grade (presuming students do them). This usually takes the form of elementary task work where teachers award full credit to everyone who turns the assignment in. Such grades are known as "warranty work." Like the warranty on your car, they guarantee anything broken is fixed for you. They mitigate bombed tests and ensure that in most on-level classes, any student can get a B without the inconvenience of learning anything.

The best demonstration of this system at work is the final week of any grading period. Teachers schedule a couple of guaranteed 100's early in the week—sometimes just giving a grade for class discussion (warranty work at its finest). Then they show a movie or give some other busywork at the end of the week, so they have time to call all the failing students up to their desk, tell them what they are missing, and give them time to work on it. A handful of students from every class never turn in assignments until the last week of the grading period.

Then, teachers will spend the afternoon calling the parents of these students to try to make sure that they pressure their student to complete the assignment. Despite the fact that grading systems allow parents and students to see every assignment grade at any time of any day and despite the fact that obsessive parents can turn on a messaging ding every time their child's teachers put a grade in, parents are often upset that they are just now being contacted about their 16-year-old's failing geometry grade. To reduce such headaches, most teachers slowly lower their expectations. Some teachers have even made it a personal policy to never fail any student. There is no excusing this behavior, but it is unsurprising given the incentives.

Higher passing rates do not indicate better teaching but lower standards. These students might have learned more if they'd been allowed to fail. When grading periods are saturated with warranty work and students have learned to expect test retakes, late work, and the teacher's cyclical one-on-one pep talk—*"I'm going to bump your grade this time, but you have to promise me you'll work harder next grading period."*—why would the student work hard? Education is full of *Kumbaya* answers to this question, but the reality is, without incentives we all give less effort. Even Tom Brady turns it up a notch on game day.

Keeping with the football theme, there is a football coach at a nearby school who is well known for his by-the-book, politically-appeasing style. One day I met with one of his assistants to discuss my football off-season training program. I explained how I expected players to run down from the school building, get dressed, and be in their designated place on the field by exactly five minutes after the bell each day. Anyone late had an automatic 200 yards of air-raids (an undesirable punishment).

As you'd expect, these athletes were impressively punctual. Still, over time I became frustrated by a few groups who continued chatting after I blew my whistle to begin warm-ups. So, I initiated another policy where the last person down in a push-up position plank had 200 yards of air-raids. Every day there would be a last man down and you did not want to be him.

My message was clear: great teams move with a sense of urgency and in a group of over 100 athletes, you should not be last to anything. While this may sound harsh, my athletes loved it. It brought competition, enthusiasm, and a sense of connection. Whoever was last always laughed and took their consequences well, because I had explained how these policies pull up the entire group. I always talk through my thought-process with students and invite them to think from my perspective.

As I explained my policies, the coach expressed frustration with his situation: *"I couldn't dream of suggesting standards like that,"* he said. *"Our head coach puts it on us when kids are late. He says 'we have to find out why an athlete is late and make him want to show up on time.'"*

While this prevailing educational attitude may sound very progressive, it is complete insanity. We are dealing with hundreds of high school students. I can tell you why they are late. They aren't incentivized to be on time. They'd rather talk longer with their girlfriend, joke longer with their buddy in the halls, check social media, and walk slowly rather than jog. If they think they can get away with something they will.

These expectations, or lack thereof, are the complete opposite of the world our students are about to enter. Try telling your boss he needs to *make you want to show up on time.* What poses as grace and understanding is really a veiled form of cruelty that sets students up for failure. You hold students to a standard because you know they are capable of reaching it and they will be better off for their efforts. We must develop the proclivity in youth to do the hard things that ultimately make their lives better.

THE CONFUSION OF FLEXIBLE STANDARDS

"When people lose the connection between their actions and their consequences, they lose their hold on reality and the further this goes the more it looks like madness." —Robert Greene

Every class has students who work hard and look around the class mystified by how incompetent most peers are. But there are many more who think they are working hard because the standards have always been so low. They are doing all that has ever been asked of them. Whenever college freshman come back to visit, I always ask how the transition to a four-year university went. Without fail I hear a variant of, *"I wasn't ready. College professors expect you to learn the material. You have to read, write, and study a lot and they never hand out note packets. Why don't y'all do more of that in high school?"* Good question.

A recent study conducted on students at the Naval Academy convincingly showed that, teachers who tend to give out easier grades "dramatically hurt subsequent student performance." That is, students were less successful in their future because the course was made easy. This will be obvious to anyone who has ever been around schools or kids. If students don't have to learn well to earn a grade, then they will not.

Perhaps the most powerful incentive for lowering standards is social proof. The large number of very bad schools (typically in low-income areas) lowers the expectations of every other school by manner of comparison. Students transfer in from these schools and are amazed to see teachers even attempting to teach lessons. Teachers transfer from these schools and are shocked that most students turn in their work. This creates an atmosphere where any comment about low standards is met with a dismissive, *"Try working where I used to work. These kids are a teacher's dream."*

The saving grace for education is a high-achieving sub-culture driven by the College Board's Advanced Placement (AP) Programs. I was fortunate enough to teach both AP and regular level courses. AP classes are often leveled down to meet the school population where they are, but they are still by far the best route for anyone who desires an impactful education. AP teachers compete for higher test scores and are able to challenge their students with less pushback. These programs aren't perfect, but they are courses for people actually concerned with learning. A growing gulf separates the general population from AP students.

Critics will say that I need to recognize that everyone isn't a high achiever. *Some students just need to get through high school so they can move on to the next thing.* I'll concede that many students will never use most of what they are taught in high school and that we should re-think our educational approach, but allow me to posit a radical hypothesis:

What if grades were directly tied to quality? What if the "A" represented a standard of excellence and people knew they had to work to earn whatever grade they received? What if there were no test retakes, warranty work assignments, and online credit recovery classes? Would students work harder? Would they—realizing they would not be passed along just for showing up—develop some gumption, invest more, and pay attention more? Would these behaviors become more normal, thus driving the campus culture up? Would teachers, then, work harder and find a renewed desire to improve? Would they feel more inspired in a class culture that was engaging with the content? Would students who had invested enough to cultivate more refined interests begin to speak and see the world through a more mature lens? Could this then bleed into the way they spent their free time, the quality of the entertainment they consumed, and the level of our national discourse?

Upholding a higher standard would, unfortunately, leave a small sub-population who did not rise to the occasion. But we have that right now, too. Rather than insisting on social promotion that gives students no sense of where they actually stand, honest grading would provide honest feedback. By refusing to confront reality, we preclude adaptation by students and the educational system at large. Honest grading would lead us to develop far more relevant alternate paths—vocational schools, apprenticeships, and legitimate course re-take options that don't just hand over the grade. A more realistic grading system would prompt a more appropriate response.

Accountability won't solve all of our problems. As I'll explain in the coming chapters, our core curriculum and basic educational philosophy are completely archaic. But even this broken system would have some merit if there were real standards and student accountability.

The Yin-Yang

We should be careful to avoid running to the opposite extreme, where standards are used to excuse rigidity and callousness. There are kernels of truth in the educational dogmas. Many students really do have terrible personal lives. You'd be amazed how many students deal with abuse, drug-addicted parents, hunger, sexual-abuse, and more. They need compassionate, caring adults who can exercise common sense. Furthermore, students really do prefer to learn from people who connect and genuinely care about them. Greet kids enthusiastically. Call them by name. Take an interest in who they are. Catch kids doing right and praise those efforts. All of these positive behaviors are magic when working with youth, but only if they are accompanied by clear expectations and consistent accountability.

Student accountability is the missing keystone whose absence allows the entire educational structure to fall. Teachers have more incentive than ever to pass students and students have less incentive than ever to monitor their own progress, to listen, study, revise, and do the hard work of higher-level thinking. Why would they when there are four social media apps beckoning and someone is going to pass them along anyway?

LOWERING THE BAR

"The truth will set you free, but first it's going to piss you off."
—*Unknown*

While the system itself bears much responsibility, we cannot, in good faith, pretend that subpar teachers don't contribute to this problem. Far too many people get into teaching because they don't know what else they'd do. They don't value learning and are wholly unimpressive employees. There are teachers on every campus who speak poorly, write poorly, display no initiative, bumble through lessons without a plan, and can't complete the simplest of tasks. They just want to get by while doing as little as possible and it's very hard to get rid of them once they've been hired. This archetype is certainly not the majority of teachers, but they are a reality that are too often ignored.

The U.S. Department of Education's 2001 Baccalaureate and Beyond Longitudinal Survey looked at all the 1999 college graduates who were employed as teachers by 2001 and found that *nearly half had been in the bottom third of all graduates*. 47% of teachers were from the bottom third, 29% from the middle third, and, an unfortunately low, 23% from the top third. These rankings were based on SAT and ACT scores (an imperfect while informative criteria). By contrast, Finland, South Korea, and Singapore recruit their teachers almost exclusively from the top third and routinely rank amongst the best educational systems in the world.

These numbers shouldn't diminish the exceptional teachers that can be found on every campus, but they do raise the question, why is the bar so low? Shouldn't we want the vast majority of our educators to have been successful educating themselves?

To be sure, teaching is more than content mastery. The smartest guy or gal in the room often wouldn't make a great teacher. But that is true of most people. Most people wouldn't make great teachers, just as most would not make great CEOs, lawyers, or accountants. That doesn't negate the obvious: education would be better off if the majority of teachers came from the top third of their graduating class rather than the bottom.

We should be finding better ways to attract and identify the most hardworking, passionate, and creative candidates. We need to bring in a larger, more qualified pool of applicants to infuse competition and innovation into education. As educational innovator, Sir Ken Robinson has said, "There is no school in the country that is better than its teachers." All those expensive initiatives can't hold a candle to great teaching.

But getting the right people in the door doesn't solve the teaching problem. Once hired, teachers are engulfed in a culture of complacency. With few incentives for continued education and a stagnant salary scale, the best usually move out of the classroom and into administration, or they leave education altogether. There is a passionate subset of top-tier teachers, who never leave the classroom setting. Many come to mind. Still, the least dedicated educators are likely to keep teaching throughout their entire career. They are far more accepting of the status quo and usually have no problem remaining employed. In the rare event that a school does remove a subpar teacher, they'll usually ask him to resign in exchange for keeping his record clean so he can find another job more easily. This practice is common enough to warrant the saying: *Passing the Trash*.

My personal experience is in Texas where teachers' unions are exceptionally weak. It is even harder to remove bad teachers in places with powerful unions, like California and New York. Because of influential unions, New York City's un-hirable teachers are placed in the Absent Teacher Reserve where they do menial tasks or fill sub jobs while continuing to collect full salary, benefits, and yearly gains in seniority pay. But even worse than paying these teachers is putting them back in the classroom. In 2017, Mayor de Blasio began placing them back in a full-time role against the desires of campus principals.

And then there are New York's infamous "rubber rooms". Teachers accused of misconduct (like intoxication or improper relations with a student) are paid full salary to clock-in and bide their time for however many years it takes for their case to be resolved. Often, they find their way back into the classroom, because the system makes it near impossible to get rid of them. According to the Wall Street Journal, firing an incompetent teacher takes an average of 830 days and costs the taxpayers $313,000. We must remind ourselves that being for teachers' unions is not necessarily being pro-education. These policies are anything but good for kids.

CHARTER SCHOOLS

"It is difficult to get a man to understand something, when his salary depends on his not understanding it."   —*Upton Sinclair*

Given the failings of public education it would be easy to conclude that school choice, and in particular, public charter schools will be an essential part of the solution. I argued against this conclusion in my initial draft, claiming that school choice dilutes resources, community support, and the potential for education to make a broad impact.

Working in public schools, I've been subjected to a healthy dose of anti-charter propaganda, which led me to believe that charter schools typically had less qualified teachers and were even more prone to appeasing parents, because they had to lure them away from public schools.

My initial argument was that, with few notable exceptions like KIPP Schools and the Ron Clark Academy, charter schools are less effective and their mere existence is a major cause for lowered standards in public schools. Public schools receive funding for every student in their enrollment. When a student leaves, the school district loses thousands of dollars. Thus, the fear of losing students to charter schools has made public education more prone to appeasing parents. I believed that we should focus public energy and resources on fixing public schools.

But my feelings began to shift throughout 2020, as I watched state legislators sabotage school districts at every turn as they tried to adapt to the challenges of educating children during a pandemic. Too much state oversight appeared to be most of the problem. At least charter schools had the flexibility to innovate and do what was best for their specific students.

Then I read Thomas Sowell's 2020 book, *Charter Schools and Their Enemies,* where he explains how misrepresented and dishonest the rhetoric around charter schools has been. We cannot compare charter schools, en masse, to public schools because scores are skewed by the vast differences in the educational pedigrees of students at each school. To give an idea of how this can happen, Sowell references a comparison of state test scores from 2018, which found that students in Iowa scored higher on average than students in Texas. However, " . . . whites in Texas scored higher than whites in Iowa; blacks in Texas scored higher than blacks in Iowa; Asians in Texas scored higher than Asians in Iowa; and Hispanics in Texas scored higher than Hispanics in Iowa." Iowa's higher total score is only possible because Texas has many more low-income students and far more cultural diversity.

The majority of charter schools serve low-income, majority black and Hispanic communities. When comparing charter schools with the awful public schools these students would have gone to, it becomes clear that charters are almost always better, often drastically so. They are a beacon of hope for poor families desperate to give their children better options. But, as Sowell explains, "Even the most successful charter schools have been bitterly attacked by teachers' unions, by politicians, by the civil rights establishment, and assorted others."

The hostility has nothing to do with educating students and giving them the best opportunities to succeed. It is rooted in a fear that the status quo will be threatened and money will be lost. It costs money to educate a student, so it makes sense that when a student leaves one school to attend another, the money goes with her. No one has ever contested this when a student moves from a Dallas public school to a Fort Worth public school or a public school in the Bronx to one in Harlem. It only becomes a point of contention when these students move to a charter school.

Anyone concerned with giving low-income students access to better education and more opportunities to improve their circumstances, should be critical of anti-charter rhetoric. I'd encourage all public education teachers who have been similarly propagandized to read Sowell's carefully researched book.

If we could turn down the animosity and look at charter schools on a case-by-case basis (as their strength lies in their individuality), we may find that these schools have a lot to teach us. They have the flexibility to try different strategies that, when effective, should make their way into public schools. Perhaps we should look at charters as an essential piece of the educational puzzle—as laboratories to investigate possible improvements. This would allow us to continue to empower those charter schools whose ideas prove successful, while also focusing on bringing these improvements to public schools.

The educational emphasis needs to be on honesty, not confirming preconceived narratives. As Sowell says:

> . . . schools exist for the education of children. Schools do not exist to provide iron clad jobs for teachers, billions of dollars in union dues for teachers unions, monopolies for educational bureaucracies, a guaranteed market for teacher's college degrees, or a captive audience for indoctrinators.

Any honest look at public schools will invite a lot of change. This is scary and may be painful for many who have profited from the educational status quo. But it is necessary. Educational reform has to be a top priority for everyone concerned about the future. We can't allow this conversation to be dictated by special interest groups who are far more concerned with themselves than the education of our children.

CHAPTER 12

SIX PRACTICES THAT ARE RUINING EDUCATION

"If you need large groups to pretend not to understand something obvious, you'll need to tie employability to never acknowledging it."
                                                        —Unknown

Public education, like any profession, is full of all manner of professionals. The bulk of them do their best, but too often are pulled down by a failing culture. In this chapter, I'll identify seven common educational practices that are most disruptive to student development. Some are universal. Some are just common. All are evidence of the deeper issues.

PRACTICE ONE: I.E.P. AND 504 ACCOMMODATIONS

Classrooms today are a collection of many different students at many different levels.

There are special education students who, typically, have a learning or behavioral disability. They receive an Individualized Education Plan (IEP) that outlines the required changes that teachers are expected to make for all of their assignments and daily experiences. Then there are the many students who qualify for 504 accommodations due to a similar need. For practical purposes, 504s are basically the same as IEPs, but tend to be easier to get (IEPs are required by the Individuals with Disabilities Act and 504s by a federal civil rights law—Section 504 of the Rehabilitation Act of 1973). Many schools also have a number of English as a second language (ESL) students who have access to needed support. And, finally, there are the students who walk into class without any legal document requiring special circumstances.

IEPs and 504s require teachers to make accommodations like reduced answer choices on assessments, preferential seating, extra time for assignments, and for teachers to provide copies of notes for the student. Some students also have the option to leave class in order to work in a resource room where they can have individual help. While the idea of providing extra support is wonderful and individualization is often necessary to best serve varying needs, the complexities presented by this system create many unfortunate costs, which educators are not allowed to openly discuss, lest they be viewed as blasphemers.

The well-meaning attempt to accommodate a student's disadvantages can quickly blur into a perpetual "get out of jail free" pass. More often than not, the line between support and learned helplessness is crossed and then left miles behind. As one teacher of twenty years expressed: "All we've ever taught these students is what they can't do. You'll give a 17-year-old an assignment and she'll panic:

"There are four answer choices! I'm supposed to only have three."

"It's just a brief review of today's lesson. I think you can do this. Try."

"No, I need fewer choices. I can't do this."

"Can you just try? Let's see how you do and I can adjust if we need."

"That's not fair. I get reduced choices.""

Over and over, we protect students from having to try, experiment, overcome, or adapt from failure. Schools will tell you that their goal is to wean students off their accommodations, but this rarely happens because it runs contrary with the school's primary mission: higher graduation rates.

Teachers are expected to track every assignment they give to IEP and 504 students and document each specific assignment modification and accommodation. But as teachers become busy trying to plan and teach well, they overlook documentation. To cover their bases, they usually just commit to never giving a failing grade to one of these students.

Failing a student with an IEP or 504 is an institutional no-no. Rewarding good grades with sensuous back massages wouldn't invite reprimand any quicker. Students and parents alike learn that all they have to do is claim one accommodation wasn't followed to the letter and they'll be able to demand whatever they want.

I attended one faculty meeting that outlined teacher expectations for documenting each student's accommodations. Amidst the many handouts was an actual student's 504 (his or her name was blocked out so it could be used as a model). The accommodation stated that this student: *"can use their earbuds to listen to music during all assignments."* What is the condition where distracting music helps a student learn? How does listening to Drake or Taylor Swift help a student better understand algebraic equations or clarify thoughts as he writes an essay?

The exploitation of these well-meaning accommodations has done as much to lower standards for all students as any other school initiative. A disproportionate amount of each teacher's time is spent catering to those whose assignments require covert individualization, often far below any measure of reason. With an ever-growing list of responsibilities, teachers often opt to simplify the entire class's work to these legally required lower standards. A third of the class is required to have notes printed and handed to them prior to a lesson. So, rather than deal with the headache of trying to keep dozens of accommodations straight, teachers simply lower the bar for all. All students receive fill-in-the-blank notes and all students receive a study guide that is basically the test.

Whether people want it to be this way or not, teachers will adjust their focus, attention, and style to the lowest common denominator because this is what their incentives pull them to do. Even if teachers wanted to track every accommodation while still pushing every student to the full extent legally allowed, they are handicapped by the lack of skills students come to them with after years of lowered expectations by other teachers.

We must make a system for accommodating student disabilities, but we can't build it at the expense of the rest of the system and it can't be based on a willing ignorance of reality.

PRACTICE TWO: LATE POLICIES AND TEST RETAKES

As tests are being handed out, students invariably call out: *"Mr. Smith! When are retakes!?!"*

Most districts require teachers to accept late work and allow partial credit retakes for any test a kid fails. Students never feel the urgency to perform. They can always blow off school and decide to bail themselves out if and when they need to. The cost of not caring is simply too low.

The narrative is that without allowing retakes and late work, students would never learn the content they neglected to learn. But we've always known that students would miss or forget some of the curriculum. No individual unit can replace the profound lessons learned from natural consequences. You failed. Now you're in a hole. Time to focus, get a planner, do your classwork, and learn how to study. These meta-lessons are among the most important.

You could dramatically increase student effort if you required teachers to:

1. Assign grades exclusively according to the student's performance. Grade each assignment based purely on the quality of the content (while continuing to place almost all the emphasis on effort).

2. Never offer retakes or accept late work. Keep a sick/emergency policy where students have a day for every day they miss, but nothing more.

The lessons endeared through such policies would be more valuable and long lasting than most of what is taught in class. Students would naturally begin to take steps to remember their assignments, persist beyond initial resistance, and learn.

PRACTICE THREE: EXEMPTIONS

Because state dollars are allocated based on attendance, many schools allow students who have good attendance and no disciplinary referrals to opt out of a few final exams. This offers many students a path to graduation where they never have to take a challenging final exam. Students who get exemptions tend to be your college going crowd—the ones who need practice taking these exams the most. College bound students will graduate and enter courses made up of nothing but research papers and challenging tests. In college, their grades will be entirely determined by one very foreign concept: mastery.

Teachers prepare final exams for a group of students that predominantly consists of their lowest achieving students—the ones they are desperately trying to pass. Out of necessity, teachers make the exam painfully easy in hopes of keeping kids from failing.

In any school with an exemption policy, AP courses are even more essential for those serious about succeeding in college.

PRACTICE FOUR: ONLINE CREDIT RECOVERY

Despite the district's best efforts, sometimes students fail. Some students just won't do anything for multiple semesters and they fall far behind. How, then, is the district to ensure that everyone graduates? Online Credit Recovery classes.

In these courses, students can make up credit for a course in a matter of weeks. An entire semester can be distilled into a few easily gamed online modules where each test offers infinite retakes.

PRACTICE FIVE: SMARTPHONE AND TECHNOLOGY POLICIES

"You're not early adapting. In fact, quite the opposite. You're taking too long to catch on."   *—Bill Maher*

Technology looks good. It makes schools appear to be on the cutting edge. Districts invest grand sums to be able to give each student a tablet or laptop, but they never clarify a system for using these devices well. There is just a succession of technology posing as progress even as basic competencies erode.

While smart technology makes life easy, it often precludes skill development. We've all noticed how we've lost our intuitive sense of direction following the rise of map apps. Likewise, my athletes are constantly trying to use the calculator app on their phones to figure out how much weight they are lifting. It isn't as if they are Atlas lifting the entire gym. The bar is 45 pounds and they have a 25 and 5 on each side. 45+60=105 pounds. This is simple arithmetic, yet immersed in a lifetime of tech dependency, many have never cultivated these skills. Sure, the calculator will usually be available, but we don't allow children to use a walker their whole life just because the technology exists. Parents prompt them to walk unaided so that they gain this fundamental capacity.

The smartphone is the most pernicious threat to our younger generation's learning and future fulfillment. This is why Silicon Valley attention engineers have made it standard practice to either restrict or completely prohibit these devices for their children. Moguls like Bill Gates and current Apple CEO Tim Cook limit the use of their own products. Cook doesn't allow his nephew to use any social media.

Before him, Steve Jobs was outlawing the iPad in his house. Tech insiders understand that iPads and smartphones present an overwhelming obstacle to creating the qualities that matter most—focus, depth, empathy, and an active, intentional life. As Taewoo Kim, the Chief Artificial Intelligence Engineer at One Smart Lab put it, "You can't put your face in a device and expect to build a long-term attention span."

"Deep Work," defined by Cal Newport as "the ability to focus without distraction on a cognitively demanding task," is where we should focus. As technology progresses, tasks that don't require significant skill, or that are repetitive, are quickly being made obsolete. But schools have made technology their sacred cow, convincing themselves that any lesson is ineffective without flashing screens and the latest apps. They assume there is an inherent value to any new technology. Instead of working to correct unhealthy trends, constant partial attention is accepted as the new norm. Teachers are told to stop expecting focus or a capacity to read because modern students *don't learn that way.* They need quick, flashy, and superficial.

In order to use modern technologies for good, apps and internet sources should be restricted to a *white list* of approved applications. Creating a *black list* does not work because the catalog of disruptive applications grows far faster than overseers can possibly keep up with. Tablet learning becomes impossible as every student has a bouquet of distracting games and multiple messenger group conversations constantly popping up on their screen. Students become masters at quickly toggling from their apps back to class work any time a teacher approaches.

These issues are compounded by Bring Your Own Device (BYOD) policies that allow students to use smartphones in class. Most schools have symbolic *acceptable use guidelines,* but students usually feel entitled to take their phones out at any moment. A culture develops where students constantly text, tweet, snap, and Instagram. Their games and chats constantly beckon.

After one training session, a student stayed after to ask me a question. We talked while walking from the weight room back to the main school building. Then I saw him hit his phone's home screen to check what he had missed. He had dozens of missed alerts. Texts, snaps, tweets, and more had been pinging away incessantly during our one-hour training session. Since then, I've noticed the same message overload in student after student.

Imagine being 16, completely absorbed with your social life and knowing all your friends were engaging in this behavior. How could you possibly focus? Even if students wanted to use their phone for schoolwork, they'd be doing so through the constant interruption of message alerts. Do we really believe this temptation is possible to resist or that learning is improved by making the smartphone available?

Some teachers fight the good fight, but the majority cave to the overwhelming tide of modern culture. The smartphone is a great babysitter, after all. As teachers move away from homework, dead time at the end of class is more common. Students will rush through their assignments so they can get back to their game or check how their social media posts are doing. Many teachers even allow students to put earphones in and listen to music while they work (a tribute to the absence of rigor). In fact, if you talk to modern students, the majority will claim that they can't focus without music (and I don't mean classical instrumentals). This is simply not how the brain works.

Our kids have been so immersed in constant distraction that the single-tasking necessary for deep flow is too uncomfortable for them to handle. After years of constant partial attention, they lack the capacity for focus to such a degree that attempting to do only one thing is unbearably boring.

The smartphone simply does not offer any benefits that justify its infinite distraction. Allowing any classroom use invites far more harm than help. Cheating becomes infinitely easier, focus dwindles, and in those moments where phones aren't allowed, student's anxiously sneak peaks. You can't base a system on intrinsic motivation when infinite temptation beckons.

PRACTICE SIX: TEACHING TO THE TEST

"Teaching is about learning. If there is no learning going on, there is no education going on. People can talk a long time about education without ever talking about learning."
—*Sir Ken Robinson*

Nothing defines American public education quite like its obsession with standardized curriculums and standardized testing. Each core course has a long list of requirements that teachers must cover so their students are ready for standardized tests. Curriculums expand in order to placate every interest group. Rather than seeking mastery of principles and high-level thinking skills, schools focus on long, arbitrarily arranged lists of information.

Standardization should not be conflated with the standards I have been advocating. State standards have nothing to do with pulling students up to a standard. They push all the attention to the lowest achieving students and perform sleight of hand to make it appear that these students have learned.

For example, Texas's Freshman Biology STAAR Test has 54 multiple-choice questions. Rather than producing a score based on the percentage a student gets correct (e.g., getting 50 of 54 correct would be a 93%), scores are subjected to a bizarre formula. Missing every single question results in a score of 1418. Getting just one correct jumps the score to a 1972. To pass the STAAR Biology Test, students only need to get 19 of 54 questions correct—a 35%, or as the state reports it, a 3550. Schools will celebrate that over 90% of their students passed the Biology STAAR exam, while hiding this insulting passing standard.

Standardized tests can be a relevant diagnostic tool, but they shouldn't be the driving force in educational culture. When that happens, schools forget the purpose of education and testing becomes much more about manipulating a desired perception than ensuring that our students are well educated.

The primacy of standardized testing in schools has opened the door to standardized curriculums, which are becoming more common. Parents complain that one Biology teacher is harder or one English teacher gives more homework and before long administrators require all teachers to teach each subject identically—with the same assignments graded the same way. There are now entire city districts following a single curriculum program. If a teacher creates a great new assignment, they have to get every teacher of that subject to agree to use it. This usually negates any assignment that takes time, effort, and skill to grade. And as teachers assign fewer essay tests, presentations, and assignments that require subjective grading skills, both student and teacher lose the capacity to discern between degrees of quality.

As we saw from Phillip K. Howard, systematically removing situations that require judgment cripple people's capacity to judge. The point of education is to build our student's capacity for judgment—to give students the tools to analyze their environment, turn over its components, come to conclusions, and then, from that judgment attempt, to live better. Google can't help you there.

The move to standardized curriculums is based on that old utopian delusion that we can systematize every concept and make sure everything is perfectly fair. Each student gets the same "perfect" lesson that yields the same "correct" final understanding and no one can claim to be more or less advantaged. Have no fear, robo-curriculum is here. And since everyone passes, everyone must have learned what they needed.

We pretend we can all roll out the same plan and get the same results for everyone, but for most subjects, once a student surpasses the simple knowledge level, there is rarely a perfect answer. Learning is about developing nuanced skills, confronting faulty assumptions, and cultivating an ability and inclination to pursue deeper understanding.

In an effort to ensure optimal appeasement, schools have placed lessons into the most bland, superficial, and impossibly inoffensive package. They have lost any concept of pursuing an ever-elusory truth. Instead, students are told what to think so they can check the box and consider themselves learned.

Sir Ken Robinson takes on standardization in his Ted Talk, *Escaping Education's "Death Valley"*:

> One of the effects of the current culture has been to de-professionalize teachers. . . . the dominant culture of education has come to focus on, not teaching and learning, but testing . . . . in place of curiosity, what we have is a culture of compliance. Our children and teachers are encouraged to follow routine algorithms, rather than to excite that power of imagination and curiosity.

This has bred education's low quality professional culture where schools focus more on grades than learning and more on feel-good strategies than developmental psychology. High school teacher trainings promote elementary school activities and "niceness," but they never mention critical research about best developmental methods. We never discuss the terrifying trends in mental and physical health. We don't talk about the cognitive skills necessary for a future job force or the effects of smartphone distraction on the mind. No one seems to have any sense that education has a duty to be an authority in human development.

By contrast, Robinson identifies three things that all the highest performing education systems—Finland, Singapore, Australia, Canada, South Korea, etc.—focus on:

1. They individualize teaching and learning. They recognize that for optimal student learning, the system has to engage students' curiosity, individuality, and creativity.

2. They attribute a very high status to teachers and acknowl-edge the investment required in high quality professional development.
3. They devolve responsibility to the school level to get the job done, rather than putting control over educational practices into the hands of state governments. As Robinson explains, "The thing is, education doesn't go on in the committee rooms of our legislative buildings. It happens in classrooms and schools and the people who do it are the teachers and their students. And if you remove their discretion, it stops working."

Teachers must have the authority to select lessons, teach, give fail-ing grades, punish those who cheat, and determine that behavior is unacceptable without themselves being subject to a courtroom in-quisition. School administrations must be empowered to determine that students need skills not required on state tests. They must be able to remove incompetent teachers and tell insubordinate parents that their child's individual demand is not in the best interest of all. Education can only become what society needs it to become when we empower every school, teacher, and student to actively participate in the educational process. We don't need extensive rule books or broad state mandated curriculums. We need talented teachers who are ex-pected to be an authority in human development and are empowered to utilize their judgment to create an energized, challenging learning experience.

CHAPTER 13

TOWARDS A BETTER EDUCATIONAL PHILOSOPHY

"The dogmas of the quiet past are inadequate to the stormy present. The occasion is piled high with difficulty, and we must rise with the occasion. As our case is new, so we must think anew and act anew."
—Abraham Lincoln

During the 2020 coronavirus pandemic, my wife and I took the ice cube trays out of our freezer to make room for more frozen food. Like many of you, we stocked up in case there were any food shortages and, with limited freezer space, ice was not a priority. There were times, however, when we wanted ice for an evening drink. I kept suggesting that we run up to the gas station to get a bag that we could keep in a cooler, but it never happened. Then one day it finally occurred to me: we have many small cups and containers. Why not fill a couple with water, and stick them in a small opening on the freezer door? Boom! Ice. It was as if I had forgotten that ice didn't have to come from an ice cube tray.

We often have trouble finding solutions because our minds are clouded by *the way we've always done it*. Even the most passionate educators don't realize the full extent to which education falls short of its potential. Their vision is limited by the fog of their own experience.

Educational reforms fail over and over because they are built from the same pieces as our broken cultural model. We've added a little technology to each class, replaced high-demand life skill trades like woodshop with computer labs, and de-valued former keystones like physical education and home-economics. We've lowered standards, inflated grades, and demonized direct instruction. But other than that, our core curriculums and basic school structure has hardly changed in over a century.

Of course, we should explore history for bright spots and pull together the ideas of our wisest and most innovative. But we, also, need to step away from these old models and think unclouded by past assumptions.

FIRST PRINCIPLES

First principles are the fundamental components we work with to solve any problem. First principle thinking seeks to break systems down to their most basic elements so they can be reassembled in new ways.

Imagine that you want to build an electric car in hopes of creating a new automobile company. Most people would read books on how to build cars. They'd follow the step-by-step model provided to them and they'd build their car in the same form and fashion as the other market competitors. Inevitably, their product and costs would be relatively similar to everyone else's.

Elon Musk took a very different approach. He went back to the fundamentals of powering machinery. He looked at each necessary component and even broke down the constituent parts of those components—*an electric car battery is made from cobalt, nickel, aluminum, carbon, some polymers for separation, and a seal can.* By attaining a complete understanding of the form and function of all the car's ingredients, he was able to create a better electric automobile for far less than any competitor. This approach requires an understanding of the underlying principles. This is the difference between following a recipe and being a chef.

Musk describes the way most people think as "reasoning by analogy." They work with the forms they are given—a compilation of blocks someone put together long before, rather than the actual building blocks. If we can leave behind our conditioned assumptions about how schools operate, a world of opportunity opens up.

The purpose of education is to learn. Many problems arise when we forget this obvious directive. Many solutions arise from remembering it. Later, we'll look at what we should learn, but first we need to explore how we learn and make sense of the world.

SENSE-MAKING AND THE HUMAN MIND

Humans experience the world through flawed senses. Optical illusions, magicians, and marketers repeatedly take advantage of our imperfect perceptions. We've all been dazzled and mystified by the Necker cube, Andrus' Impossible Box Illusion, or that YouTube video of the moonwalking bear we missed because we were busy counting basketball passes.

There are also many things we simply cannot detect. Human eyes don't see ultra-violet (UV) light, the electromagnetic wave responsible for sunburns. Bumblebees, ants, and some lizards can see UV light, but humans can't unless their cornea is removed. This is an advantageous protection, but it also limits our capacity to see reality.

Likewise, we can detect some gases like methane (men love to remind each other of this) but we can't see or smell oxygen. Still, if all oxygen suddenly vacated your premises, reading this chapter would be the last thing on your mind. Our ability to perceive something does not always predict its importance. Despite the fact that humanity had no way of seeing germs, these microorganisms have caused illness and death since the beginning of human history. All of us use an incomplete sensory set to interpret the world. And all we have to make sense of our senses is our own narrow set of experiences.

Most Americans assume that everyone needs a car, that prescription drug advertisements are normal, and that people in third world countries are less happy than us. A couple centuries ago, most people were raised to believe women should not work and that slavery was part of the natural human order. Growing up, I assumed no one talked during football games and everyone lived to debate political theory. Before I was married, I assumed a 1:1 pillow-to-person ratio was sufficient. When I adopted two black children, I assumed our hair care needs would be similar and that babies would sleep at night. The list of faulty assumptions is endless.

In addition to the biases that stem from our past experience, each of us are subject to a vast number of cognitive biases inherent to human thought. Warren Buffet's business partner, Charlie Munger, famously outlined several important cognitive biases in his Harvard speech on the psychology of human misjudgment. A few examples:

- **Social Proof Bias**: Our tendency to believe local norms are correct. Social proof has allowed humans to adopt bizarre beliefs and oversimplifications even against overwhelming evidence. Hello, Westboro Baptist Church. Hello, Pop Tarts for breakfast. Similarly, we see from the Stanley Milgram obedience experiments that people tend to yield to authority. Social proof bias and our bias to trust authority combine to explain how the Holocaust was possible.
- **Reciprocation Tendency**: The Marketing professor and author, Dr. Robert Cialdini went around a college campus asking people to take young children to the zoo. One in six said yes. Then, he went around asking different people if they would devote two afternoons a week to watching young children. One hundred percent said no, but when he followed that question up by asking, "Well, would you at least take them to the zoo once?" half the respondents said yes. By starting with a big-ask,

he tripled the likelihood that people would agree to his original proposition to take children to the zoo.

- **Contrast-Caused Distortion**: We are easily fooled by contrast. Put a hand in hot water and a hand in cold water, then plunge them both into room temperature water. One hand perceives that water as cold and the other hot, yet it's the same water. Likewise, a mediocre home seems like a dream after the real-estate agent shows you a few overpriced dumps.
- **The Paradox of Choice**: We assume that having more choices is better. But with more choices, our decisions become increasingly irrational and we are less satisfied with every decision. Each choice is subject to far greater buyer's remorse as we obsess on all the other options that we could have chosen. Also, as our choices grow, we are more likely to never make a decision. Paralysis by analysis.
- **Prevalence Induced Concept Change**: The Blue-Dot effect. The mind finds what it sets out to find.

It is with flawed senses, shrouded in cognitive bias and limited by a narrow set of experiences, that we humans try to make sense of the world and make decisions about the best ways to conduct our lives.

Education is the process of improving our capacity to interpret the world so that we are better able to respond wisely to events and live a more fulfilling life. If you are still reading this book, you've probably encountered ideas that will change the way you perceive and respond to future experiences. That is why we read, question, and seek knowledge.

With all this in mind, I'd like to expand our original premise, that the point of education is to learn. The primary role of education is to promote:

1. More accurate interpretation of the world by acquiring vital knowledge and logic-driven critical thinking skills. Let's call this **sense-making.**

2. A greater capacity to make good choices and to adapt one's situation to produce desirable outcomes. Let's call this **wisdom**.
3. The above two points should be driven by a master goal of enriching the human experience. This requires a basic understanding of how humans thrive but also an emphasis on creating citizens inclined to form the sort of cohesive social unit that people thrive within. Let's call this **human flourishing**.

The best path for meeting these goals varies drastically depending upon the time and situation. For most of human history and for most early civilizations, there was no need for an education system. If you were a hunter-gather on the African savannah or even a young Sumerian farmer, the intimate adults in your life would convey all the necessary skills. Life was your school.

Certain inventions necessitate education, however. Representative democracy is one. Voters must be well-educated in the principles of government and have a means of obtaining and interpreting new information. Add the printing press and suddenly it is clear that society can't function well unless everyone learns to read. You need schools to ensure mass literacy, teach the science of government, and to inculcate a sense of community obligation.

What new competencies must we give people to make them capable of sense-making, wisdom, and flourishing in a world of mass information. What lessons do the internet and the smartphone necessitate? How about the industrial food complex?

As outlined by Daniel Schmachtenberger at the end of chapter 10, we must train all of our citizens in three levels of sense-making. Students need to master:

1. First-person epistemics: Can I recognize my own biases and how they are impacting me? Can I recognize impulses that are not serving me and become better at mastering myself?
2. Second-person epistemics: Can I take on other peoples' perspectives and find what drives them? Can I see the many

viable long-term considerations that are weighed in every group choice? And can I communicate in a way that makes my message most likely to be received well by others?

3. Third-person epistemics: Can I more accurately make sense of reality? Can I understand the world better and train myself to come to better interpretations? This is logic, science, and philosophical inquiry.

   – Combining 1st, 2nd, and 3rd person epistemics, can I make the best possible case for your opinion (steel-manning) so that we are debating from agreeable premises while not succumbing to emotional outbursts, low blows, or fallacies.

Beyond these fundamental skills, human flourishing also requires that our schools focus on providing an environment that promotes community and breeds a culture committed to optimizing physical and mental health. Much more on this in chapter 16.

With these broad goals in mind, we can finally turn to determining how we learn best.

HOW DO WE LEARN BEST?

Learning is built upon both *direct experience* and different forms of *direct instruction*, which give us conceptual models for deeper understanding. As I'll show, both are necessary.

In 1982, philosopher Frank Jackson created the Mary's Room thought experiment to color the learning discussion:

Mary has lived her entire life in a room that only contains black and white. Despite her limited experience with colors, she is an expert on the science of color and how it is perceived by the human brain. She has read scores of black and white texts, watched countless hours of black and white educational documentaries, and enjoyed many days

contemplating the physics and biology of color with colleagues over the phone. Mary knows everything language
can communicate about color. One day, she leaves this room
and is exposed to all the colors of the world. Does she learn
anything?

Undoubtedly, red now has much more meaning to Mary after she
leaves the room, even though she already knew every physical fact
about the color red. Similarly, you may know the flu is an undesirable sickness, but you have a new level of understanding after a week
in bed. There are some properties of knowledge only available to us
through experience.

Experience is especially powerful to the young mind. Hot doesn't
mean much to children, until they burn their hand on the stove.
Children learn the nuances of degree by also experiencing a hot summer day. Both stoves and summer heat are hot, but the latter is toler-
able. If they experience a summer day in Tucson, Arizona and then
visit Tampa, Florida they'll learn the difference between dry heat and
humid heat. More experience creates more capacity for nuance.

But we can't expect students to construct essential higher-level
lessons from only self-discovered experiences, as many progressive-
sounding educators argue. There are essential skills like reading that
cannot be freely constructed. Furthermore, even if Mary never left
her black and white room, I'd still think Mary is better equipped to
build color enhancing goggles than that guy cheering on the Bears at
Buffalo Wild Wings.

It is not possible to learn everything through physical experience
and, as we've already seen, we couldn't entirely trust our senses to
do so anyway. Direct experience is what led humans to presume the
earth was the center of the universe. Your direct experience may lead
you to believe that the earth is flat, all red-haired people are loud
narcissists, and your softball team wins more games when you don't
wash your socks.

Learning requires us to confront our misunderstandings in order to build a more accurate interpretation of the world. If I'm explaining how airline control centers work to someone who believes the earth is flat, the flight patterns won't make sense. *Fly west from L.A. to get to Japan? But Japan is in the far east.* Yet, if they have a concept of roundness, they'll quickly be able to assimilate a workable model after being told that the earth is a giant rotating ball.

In his book, *The Power of Explicit Teaching and Direct Instruction,* Greg Ashman takes issue with the simplified, experience-focused view that predominates modern education. One prominent educational text perfectly illustrates the insanity that dominates the radical constructivist philosophy:

> The teacher's role is to facilitate learning . . . .The teacher must set the classroom in a way that allows pupils to enquire, by posing problems, creating a responsive environment and giving assistance to the pupils to achieve *autonomous discoveries.* This applies to all areas of education, from discovering prose and its meaning in English to design problems in technology.

Constructivism is a valid theory of learning which argues that new learning has to either fit or change past mental schemas (see my earth is round example). But the validity of constructivism as a learning theory in no way suggests that all education should focus on facilitating "autonomous discoveries." Constructivism applies to learning by listening to a lecture just as well as it explains how we'd learn from a direct experience.

This is all lost in the reigning educational perversion. As Ashman writes, "Plucked from its philosophical and scientific roots, constructivism in the classroom usually equates to asking students to find something out for themselves—to "construct" knowledge rather than passively receive it . . . . ", He contrasts this approach with Sir Isaac

Newton's famous proclamation that, "If I have seen further, it is by standing on ye sholders of giants." In modern education, Ashman jokes, "It is as if the giant is there, offering children his shoulders, but instead we are asking them to construct a ladder out of sticky tape and drinking straws."

I've advocated for more free play, autonomy, and room for discovery in childhood, but as kids mature, the skills they need to master require more direct instruction. There is something profound and essential about the ability to learn from others or to read text and derive complex meaning. If we are to learn above an elementary level and benefit from the hard lessons of others, our minds must become capable of these skills. Education must teach students how to listen, read critically, and learn from others. This will be a source of inspiration that gives them the capacity to imagine something and bring it into reality—to have an idea and bring it into existence.

All this is to say, we can learn and be inspired by experience, but experiences must be filtered through a well-trained mind and enhanced by explicit teaching. We need clumsy physical experience, illuminating direct instruction, and practice communicating and critiquing ideas. The more we use knowledge, break down its parts, manipulate it to fit new contexts, and subject it to critique, the more understanding we can have. This is best accomplished with depth, not breadth.

Many organizations, such as the Knowledge Matters campaign, argue that accumulating more knowledge brings many educational advantages and enhances students' lives. I couldn't agree more. Students do better when they know more history, geography, science, math, classic literature, and have a broader familiarity with how things work. These students tend to find school more interesting, because school subjects begin from familiar building blocks.

However, this familiarity comes best from an enriching home environment where knowledge is not shoved down children's throats but is a natural extension of parent interests, family dinners, vacations, and trips to the zoo or planetarium. It is fostered by homes that feature physical artifacts like globes, books, chessboards, and instruments. There is no substitute for an environment where learning is a part of living.

We can't ignore the vast differences between children's home experiences—the number of books they read, the number of different words they hear, the amount of time spent in passive vs. active entertainment, and the psychological connotations they've formed around learning. If a learning tradition does not come from home, then students may need to spend more time on basic knowledge accumulation in order to best close the substantial gaps by the end of high school. Unfortunately, this is an enormous challenge, which many students, particularly those whose families don't emphasize education, will not bridge. We will have to continue to adapt to make these gaps less common.

Still, it is foolish to suggest that all children need the same things or that teachers in one classroom can best facilitate extreme differences in students' home educational environments. Different school populations will have different predominant needs and charter schools can help provide for major differences. But the public education system and its prevailing educational culture should not be built upon an expectation of bookless homes, lest they continue making that a more likely reality.

Most schools would do well to break free of the heavily compartmentalized, knowledge-accumulation approach. Today's subjects are sanitized and separated from the real world. Students chase test scores on broad state tests. They craft essay responses for the simplified grading standards of a far-away reader but rarely learn to think critically or express themselves well.

What good does it do you to learn 20th century world history if, after three months, you have no idea what caused World War I or what contributed to the rise of totalitarian governments? What good is passing a geography course if you still refer to Muslims as Islams and have no clue where Vietnam is in relation to Somalia. What good is any class if it doesn't change how we interpret, experience, and act in the world? Students will always forget many specific details but, for a class to be worth it, it has to create understandings that last after the final exam. We don't learn in order to pass tests or achieve ceremonial outcomes. We learn to create a richer human experience. The goal of school is to promote long-term human flourishing.

Today, the number of possible future occupations far surpasses our ability to speculate. We can't possibly teach our children everything they will need to know. We have no idea what the future will look like, nor can we expect our students to remember every concept covered over the course of their education. What matters most is that youth cultivate higher order sense-making skills, learn how to learn, and feel inclined to do so. In addition, they need to build the antifragility to learn from failure and adapt as situations change. If they have these skills, regardless of their situation, they'll have the tools to improve their circumstances and guide their own future.

Make no mistake, these are skills. The culture and guiding philosophies of our schools will largely determine whether or not students develop these skills. With that in mind, we can turn to reimagining what education should look like. But, in doing so, we should be careful not to fall into what Nassim Taleb calls "neomania," where we presume anything new is progress. Neomania has created an education system that is obsessed with technology for its own sake and that immerses its teachers in pseudoscientific bunk. There is a big difference between dreaming of a perfect education and putting it into practice. For that reason, it will be helpful to temper our reformist zeal with the wisdom of past models.

CHAPTER 14

THE LOST TOOLS AND OTHER POSSIBLE REFORMS

"It is important to view knowledge as sort of a semantic tree. Make sure you understand the fundamental principles, i.e. the trunk and big branches, before you get into the leaves/details or there is nothing for them to hang on to."　　　　—*Elon Musk*

Perhaps the greatest critique of modern education was written over 70 years ago in 1947. In an essay titled, *The Lost Tools Learning*, Dorothy Sayers rejects the broad, "checklist" educational approach, focusing instead on creating self-reliance and the ability to learn. She writes:

> And today a great number—perhaps the majority—of the men and women who handle our affairs, write our books and our newspapers, carry out our research . . . and who educate our young people—have never, even in a lingering traditional memory, undergone the Scholastic discipline . . . We have lost the tools of learning—the axe and the wedge, the hammer and the saw, the chisel and the plane—that were so adaptable to all tasks. Instead of them, we have merely a set of complicated jigs, each of which will do but one task and no

more, and in using which eye and hand receive no training, so that no man ever sees the work as a whole or 'looks to the end of the work.'

What use is it to pile task on task and prolong the days of labor, if at the close the chief object is left unattained? It is not the fault of the teachers—they work only too hard already . . . . They are doing for their pupils the work which the pupils themselves ought to do. For the sole true end of education is simply this: to teach men how to learn for themselves; and whatever instruction fails to do this is effort spent in vain.

The *tools of learning* Dorothy Sayers refers to are the trivium—a model of three sequential parts of learning: grammar, dialectic, and rhetoric—that correspond with the child's developmental age.

There is very little good that comes from strapping 6-year-olds down to a desk for most of the day. Likewise, it would be futile to ask them to analyze different political theories and synthesize their best attributes into an optimal government. At this stage in a child's development, which Sayers calls the "Poll-Parrot" stage, students have less capacity for abstract reasoning, but enjoy accumulating and memorizing facts, particularly when done through song and activity. As Sayers says, "To know the name and properties of things is, at this age, a satisfaction in itself."

Elementary students are naturally inclined to observe and memorize. Thus, these years are for fostering children's natural sense of curiosity and mastering the basic building blocks—arithmetic, language, reading, geography, science, and a knowledge of prominent historical figures, events, and chronology.

As Sayers concedes, this is not a radical departure from the elementary standards of 1947. "The difference will be felt rather in the attitude of the teachers who must look upon all these activities less as 'subjects' in themselves than as a gathering-together of material for use in the next part of the trivium." More than anything else, teachers must develop new attitudes about learning and a firmer grasp of the type of education students require.

I would add to Sayers' suggestions that we must expect students to accumulate this baseline knowledge gradually as we keep our foremost emphasis on respecting children's developmental age and natural orientations. Young students need to be encouraged to explore and find pursuits that will later become portals to deeper understanding and thematic learning. They need multiple recesses and P.E. every day. These are essential needs, not luxuries to be shoved aside in the pursuit of knowledge accumulation. And we should foster, rather than squelch, kids' natural inclinations for competition and rough-housing in order to bring more passion and excitement to the school environment.

Matthew Crawford makes this point brilliantly, stating that:

> I think we confuse the will to distinguish yourself . . . with the will to dominate others. And so the thirst for distinction gets a bad rap because it looks like the will to tyranny. The irony here is that it is the effort to clamp down on play that is itself a kind of tyrannical need to control everything. And you see that in, for example, affluent, progressive schools where you have these playground minders who are on the lookout for signs of trauma to the fragile selves they're busy cultivating.

Teachers would do well to give young students more freedom to self-organize and mediate their own disputes whenever possible. These meta-skills are the foundation of future emotional health and antifragility.

> *"How can juvenile people be expected to self-govern or to navigate an advertising-saturated market economy full of propaganda and untruths? How can they determine fact from opinion or what's been proven from what might be possible?"*
> —*Ben Sasse*

The next stage, according to Sayers, begins around the age when students grow more argumentative and "pert"—probably starting sometime around 6th grade and extending throughout the awkward early adolescent years. Students' contrarian inclinations should be put to work learning formal logic and the foundations of dialectical reasoning—the dialectic. This is perhaps the most fundamental skill set of all, without which students will never be capable of critiquing claims or forming coherent opinions.

Sayers sees formal logic as the basis of all education at this stage. Having mastered vocabulary, language can focus on structure, arrangement, and analysis. Reading can shift from narrative to argument and criticism. Nearly every subject would feature dialectical debates and written argument. Social studies, in particular, should meld history, political theory, and current events so that students have a framework to ask hard questions like: "What form of government is best?" Or, "What recent movements most closely parallel the extremes that led to Robespierre's Reign of Terror?" And, finally, math and science instruction will turn to algebra, geometry, and how to apply the scientific method. These fields are a natural extension of logic as they are systems built for testing what is true.

"But above all," according to Sayers, "we must not neglect the material which is so abundant in the pupils' own daily life." All around us, from sports games, to politics and what's trending on Twitter, there are good and bad arguments to critique. The more we can apply lessons to their lives, the more students will enjoy their learning and take it into the world. This speaks to a whole range of subject-matter that Sayers neglects and which I will emphasize in my own educational framework (in chapter 16).

To Sayers, every subject is truly secondary to the mental skills that it aims to cultivate. As she puts it, "The 'subjects' supply material; but they are all to be regarded as mere grist for the mental mill to work upon. The pupils should be encouraged to go and forage for their own information . . . and shown how to tell which sources are authoritative and which are not." The primary goal is to create an environment where teachers and students are "ready to detect fallacy, slipshod reasoning, ambiguity, irrelevance, and redundancy, and to pounce upon them like rats." One can't help but note that the majority of college graduates today have nothing approaching the skills Sayers would expect us to master by high school.

According to Sayers, it is around high school that students' imaginations tend to reawaken as they become far less sure of their assumptions and more cognizant of the limitations of logic alone. With heightened cognitive abilities, students can approach old, rote subjects from exciting new angles. Without sacrificing expectations of quality, student learning should become increasingly self-directed and individualized. As Sayers explains:

> . . . each pupil should learn to do one, or two, subjects really well, while taking a few classes in subsidiary subjects to keep his mind open to the inter-relations of all knowledge. Indeed, at this stage, our difficulty will be to keep "subjects" apart; for Dialectic will have shown all branches of learning to be inter-related, so Rhetoric will tend to show that all knowledge is one.

When we dig deep into any subject we learn about ourselves and build a level of understanding that allows us to pull apart pieces, stitch them together creatively, and apply the themes to other fields. Depth is what is most important in the final stage. The deeper we learn anything the more we learn about everything.

Sayers thought that the entirety of public education should be finished by age 16. Thus, this final stage would last from ages 14 until 16. Her expectation says something about how much we have delayed maturation. Still, I'd argue that we should maintain our current system where senior year ends at age 17 or 18. It would be better to slow down and expand the length of the first stage (grammar) for a couple years, thereby giving more room to honor developmental exploration and pushing back the other phases a year or two as well. So many of the most important lessons are born from freedom and social experimentation, and so many brilliant people dismissed their schooling until later when someone brought it to life for them.

While Sayers' vision does a wonderful job of addressing third person epistemics, it mostly ignores first and second person epistemics, as well as the central role of health. Still, the basic trajectory and principles behind her vision should inform our thinking about an ideal educational approach. By the end of high school, students must have developed an earnest desire to learn and direct their own lives, as well as an ability to critique arguments and appreciate different perspectives. We must expect this of citizens as we head into a chaotic 21st century environment. As Sayers explains, this was even the case back in 1947:

> We who were scandalised in 1940 when men were sent to fight armoured tanks with rifles, are not scandalised when young men and women are sent into the world to fight massed propaganda with a smattering of "subjects"; and when whole classes and whole nations become hypnotised by the arts of the spellbinder, we have the impudence to be astonished. We dole out lip-service to the importance of education . . . we postpone the school leaving-age, and plan to build bigger and better schools; the teachers slave conscientiously in and out of school-hours, till responsibility becomes a burden and a nightmare; and yet, as I believe, all this devoted effort is largely frustrated, because we have lost the tools of learning, and in their absence can only make a botched and piecemeal job of it.

Our world is far more complex and dynamic than eighty years ago. To make a great future, we need to rediscover the lost tools.

STUDENT EXPECTATIONS

For any of this to happen, we must understand that education holds no merit if students do not invest in it for themselves. Passionate personalities can help awaken interests. Relevant curriculums can better tap into intrinsic motivation. Teachers who model a growth mindset will create a learning culture. Honest grading and appropriate expectations will help foster maturity and self-awareness. An environment with fewer distractions and better incentive structures will promote more focus. Still, no amount of teacher support will matter if there is not a clear understanding that students are ultimately responsible for their own learning.

Today's schools devote an inordinate amount of their energy into handing diplomas to the bottom tier of their students as if this will fix whatever disadvantages stood in the student's way. In the process, they've distorted the entire system. You will often hear comments from teachers like: *He doesn't need this class; he just needs to get through high school.* Or even the dubious claim that: *Nowadays students will need a high school diploma to work at McDonald's too, you know?*

This pervasive line of thought is the problem. No, you don't need a worthless piece of paper to do any job. The only reason a high school diploma or any ceremonial indicator could matter is if it truly demonstrated mastery of some level of competency. The paper is only ever as good as its requirements. If the high school diploma came to indicate that students had successfully completed a high school program like the one Sayers suggested, then the majority of occupations that currently require a bachelor's degree would only need a high school diploma.

In the process of making a world where the high school diploma means nothing, we have watered down the entire system and, subsequently, the baseline level of adult citizens. Students now have to pay tens or hundreds of thousands of dollars and attend four more years of school to learn the skills they should have mastered by the end of high school. We push high schoolers toward a college diploma even as it becomes more expensive and less valuable, and even as most students are less ready to determine a future path and less interested in the academic benefits of college.

Rampant grade inflation and social promotion place many students in classes they can't begin to understand. Learning builds upon prior learning. If a high school freshman can't do single digit multiplication in his head, why would we promote him to algebra? He isn't in a position to learn it, so why pretend to teach him? Unfair as a student's circumstances may be, we do him no favors by passing him along.

According to clinical psychologist Jordan Peterson, the best way to address social issues is through broadly emphasized individual interventions. In a 2010 study, a group of college students went through Peterson's online Future Authoring Program, which required them to vividly describe their ideal future and then contrast that to a less desirable future possibility. This group was then prompted to create a specific plan of action. Academic performance improved by 20% for students who went through the program. Additionally, the gender performance gap decreased by 98% within a year and the ethnic gap shrunk by 93% within two years. Peterson is often attacked for not accepting the social justice ideology which dominates college campuses, but his efforts do far more to promote equality than their dogmatic social agenda.

Peterson's study takes advantage of the power of environment while also mitigating the danger of teaching people they are victims. Regardless of what we teach students, they must leave school with a sense of responsibility for their lives and a sense that they can learn what is needed to adapt to their challenges.

BALANCING REFORMIST PHILOSOPHIES

"Philosophy is written in this grand book, the universe, which stands continually open to our gaze. But the book cannot be understood unless one first learns to comprehend the language and read the letters in which it is composed." —Galileo Galilei

Dr. Peter Gray (whose play research I referenced in chapter 4) advocates for a much freer and wide-open educational experience. He would argue that low expectations are not the problem—that, in fact, the problem is having any expectations at all. Gray is an advocate for the *unschooling movement* and often references the Sudbury Valley "non-school" School where children are encouraged to learn by spending their days however they want.

It is good that such laboratories exist to challenge conventional wisdom and provide opportunities for kids who can thrive in this environment. But such students tend to be gifted and have well-educated, involved parents. For the masses, this approach would be a chaotic mess leaving them ill-prepared for life.

By contrast, it appears that some students, particularly those in low-income environments with the least home support, might benefit most from a highly structured STEM-oriented environment where discipline is put at the forefront. In particular, the most successful charter schools, Success Academy and KIPP schools, have changed many students' lives with an approach that demands discipline and high standards of conduct. While I wouldn't build the entire system in this image either, these schools are perfect for the needs of their students, just as "un-schools" might best suit their students' needs.

There will always be those who thrive in non-conventional environments like Sudbury Valley, but society must be built upon a far more realistic framework. Social cohesion stems from a shared sense of standards that are far more likely to be the reason people thrive, rather than the reason they "shut down." In fact, for most students, shutting down only becomes an option because they live in a culture where it is such an obvious and appealing option—where so many adults are eager to make excuses for students and tell them how teachers aren't accommodating their unique needs.

Now, more than ever, we need standards that help build willpower and challenge the cultural momentum which pulls us to only ever do what feels good in the moment. It sounds very enlightened to call traditional schooling an archaic prison and claim that all students would love learning if it wasn't for all that discipline. *How would you feel if people were telling you what to do all day?* But standards are essential for creating an environment where students invest enough to cultivate rewarding interests and enjoy learning essential subjects.

Still, as silly as educational idealists sound, they highlight kernels of truth that are worth bearing in mind. Students have different interests, learning styles, and temperaments. They all can find a passion for learning, especially when nurtured well early on by teachers who care about them. And when possible, offering students flexibility, autonomy, and creativity in how they reach a learning goal can make subjects come to life. As Sayers pointed out, most subjects are mere "grist for the mental mill" to help train better sense-making skills.

The reality is that no matter how hard we strive, there will be no perfect education. I'll do my best to clarify an even better vision in chapter 16, but the most important thing to remember is that our students must create their own future. Learning and growth are messy and mistake-ridden, not linear. A teacher's greatest impact comes through creating depth and connection. Rather than giving students fish, they transform lives by teaching their pupils how to fish and helping them discover a passion for fishing.

Education's foremost focus should be to train the specific skills and understandings that are most fundamental for people to flourish in the modern world. This system must incorporate Sayers's lost tools of learning, but also give students a roadmap for self-mastery. Before I introduce my educational vision, we must explore some essential principles of human behavior that no student should graduate without.

CHAPTER 15

MASTER THY SELF

In the famed Stanford Marshmallow experiments, Dr. Walter Mischel put hundreds of four- and five-year-olds alone in a room with a single marshmallow. The children were instructed that they could eat the marshmallow or wait fifteen minutes for the researchers to return and be rewarded with two marshmallows for their patience. Imagine four-year-olds in a room trying to distract themselves for what seemed like an eternity. I'm sure the video is priceless.

These children were tracked over the next four decades and those who successfully delayed their gratification for fifteen minutes, tended to be healthier, wealthier, happier, and more successful by every metric. They had lower rates of addiction, lower incidence of divorce, and greater economic freedom.

Similarly, in the 1940's, Harvard conducted a study to see how long college sophomores would stay on a steeply inclined treadmill traveling at high speeds. Researchers believed test performance would indicate the "extent to which a subject is willing to push himself or has a tendency to quit before the punishment becomes too severe."

Some participants jumped off after little more than a minute. The majority made it about four minutes. Scientists contacted all the study participants every two years for the next 60 years to collect data and a lifestyle questionnaire. Just as in the Stanford experiments, they found that those who persisted longer were more successful and better psychologically adjusted.

FREE YOURSELF

"No man is free who is not master of himself."   —*Epictetus*

We love our freedom, but in light of the mass dependency characteristic of 21st Century America, can we really claim to be free? When
I felt compelled to stay in a shower until I thought of the name Mark
DeRosa, was I free? If that email alert dings at 8 p.m. on Friday night
and you just have to check it, are you free? How about when your
best intentions to eat well are sabotaged by the smell of your friend's
French fries? Are you free then? Or, when you are driving along feeling great and someone cuts you off in traffic. If you fly off the handle
and allow that to prompt an angry downward spiral, are you free?
The reckless driver is long gone, blissfully ignorant of your insults.
Yet you still suffer from the anger you *can't* seem to let go of.

To some degree, this is just part of being a warm-blooded mam-
mal. There is nothing desirable about becoming a passionless robot.
Still, most worthwhile pursuits are characterized by an ability to
overcome impulse for something greater. This doesn't mean that we
should numb ourselves from every feeling, but that we should work
to be able to feel an impulse, and objectively decide that we will be
better off if we ignore infantile emotions. This is maturity in a nut-
shell, and it is the secret to being who we would like to be.

There are differences in the values and mindset between disciplined people and those who are more controlled by the allure of instant gratification. But for the most part, both types of people would
choose similar outcomes if given the same choices.

- Would you like to have savings or debt?
- Would you like to have connected, reliable relationships or su-
  perficial relationships built on convenience and pleasure?
- Would you like to be healthy or sickly?
- Would you like to have projects you feel excited about or noth-
  ing to do?

Both the self-mastered person and the *instantly-gratified person* would choose the first option in each scenario. What all those preferable outcomes have in common is they are made possible by the discipline of delaying self-gratification. Millions of tiny impulses have to be overridden or ignored.

Where the fulfilled and impulsive differ most is in their ability to define what is most valuable, script the critical moves, and act upon them. Planning and acting are the secret to being who we want to be. Therefore, acting is where we should place our emphasis. Educators, coaches, and parents should go to great lengths to help develop kids' ability to overcome impulse.

DEVELOPING YOUR WILL

"Do not be afraid to exaggerate the role of willpower. It is an exaggeration with a purpose. It leads to a positive self-fulfilling dynamic, and that is all you care about." —Robert Greene

In the late 1990's the psychologist Roy Baumeister conducted a famous study on willpower. Participants were placed in a room with two plates of food—a plate of radishes and a plate of warm fresh cookies. He instructed half the participants to abstain from eating cookies and only eat radishes. The other half were told that they could eat whatever they wanted. Then the two groups were given a puzzle to work on. Unbeknownst to the subjects, this puzzle was impossible to finish. The experimenters wanted to see if the radish-only group, who had been fighting back their cookie cravings, would quit earlier. And they did. Radish-only participants lasted an average of eight-minutes while the eat-anything group and the control group both averaged 19-minutes.

After many similar studies, Baumeister concluded that willpower was like a muscle, which loses strength as it fatigues. Many have since taken this willpower depletion model to rationalize impulsive behavior as an inevitable consequence of circumstances. It provides us an easy cop-out after a work day when we'd rather plop on the couch than exercise. More broadly, it is a common justification for excusing low standards in schools and other developmental institutions: *It isn't fair to ask as much of her because she has disadvantages that drain her willpower.* What appears as compassion is actually subtle cruelty. We amplify the effect of people's disadvantages by seeking out rationalizations for every misstep, thereby removing the impetus for correction. Rather than instill the belief that if they try hard enough, then they can find a way, we program students to find an excuse.

This tendency is especially problematic in light of recent research indicating that past studies have overstated the willpower depletion effect and excluded findings that did not fit their desired conclusion. A more comprehensive meta-analysis of the willpower research revealed that the most significant factors in people's ability to persist are how committed they are to their goals and whether they believe they have the necessary willpower or not. The most important factor for people's success is whether or not they believe they have the power to be successful.

Still, willpower depletion can't be dismissed altogether. It is a relevant variable, but most people missed Baumeister's larger insight: willpower is indeed like a muscle. It grows stronger with exercise. Triathletes don't use the existence of fatigue as justification to demand a shorter race. They train their capacity to endure longer and go faster. Likewise, success in life will continue to require willpower and to reward those who build more of it. This is one of the few certainties we have about the future.

Thus, educators and parents should consistently put youth in situations that require them to develop willpower. *No, you don't get to put your head down now under the guise that you'll just do the assignment for homework. No, you don't get to watch TV before doing your homework. Yes, it is hot outside and I expect the lawn to be mowed as usual. Bring some water.* We must expect people to demonstrate willpower and train it through millions of tiny expectations. Willpower training is a staple of life and should be a central focus of every school and every parent's worldview.

But the implications of the radish study don't stop there. A large part of the challenge for the radish-eating group was smelling cookies and watching others eat them. Remove the cookies and you remove the willpower fatigue. Likewise, if you go to a school where there is no access to social media and phone games, where it is normal to study, and where all the available food options are nutritious, then it requires far less willpower to focus, study, and eat well. Rather than teaching our kids to expect safe spaces, second chances, and infinite accommodations, we should build our environments to support effort, focus, courage, toughness, perseverance, honesty, and the competition of ideas.

Further, we should explicitly teach students how to design their environment so that they are more likely to behave as they objectively want to. My experience with students is that they have vague goals, but don't know how to make a plan or adapt to the inevitable hiccups along the way. They feel helpless. We should explicitly teach and model environmental design throughout every school. This begins with setting smart boundaries for technology but, more than that, we must give our students a toolkit for creating behavior change that lasts.

THE RIDER, THE ELEPHANT, AND THE PATH

"It's time you realized that you have something in you more powerful and miraculous than the things that affect you and make you dance like a puppet." —*Marcus Aurelius*

In *The Happiness Hypothesis,* Jonathan Haidt explains that the mind is run by two separate, but often competing systems. He illustrates this with the metaphor of a man riding atop an elephant. Your logical mind is the rider, who sits atop an elephant (your emotion). When your emotional side is dispassionate, the rider can easily determine the best route. However, when your emotions are strong, the rider cannot muscle the reigns and get his way for long. If your rider decides to wake up at 4:30 am to work out, you may get your way for a few days, but the rider can only control an unruly elephant for so long. Eventually, emotion wins and you hit snooze . . .11 times. When we train willpower with small, daily disciplines, we develop our rider's ability to control a rebellious elephant while, simultaneously, teaching the elephant to crave a more fulfilling reward.

It is tempting to conclude that the elephant is the problem, but that would be like a CEO concluding that workers are the problem. The elephant has tremendous power and energy. Without emotion, we'd never decide to exercise or study in the first place. The elephant informs us about our larger dreams and fuels our creativity. We need to employ both the elephant and rider to achieve long-term success in any endeavor.

In their book, *Switch,* brothers Chip and Dan Heath introduce a third element to this analogy: the path. Even the unruliest elephant will walk straight and narrow on a cliffside path. Likewise, the most important variable for producing consistent action is to shape our environment.

If I want to be successful in my 4:30 a.m. training schedule I need to use my rider to construct an environment that promotes success by limiting my elephant's opportunities to pull me off course. Before beginning my new habit, I should consider my sleep needs and set up a sleep schedule so that I consistently get to bed at an earlier hour. Then I could set three alarms, each farther away from my bed. The furthest alarm might be right outside my bedroom door with my workout clothes staged right beside it. Or maybe there are other people in the house that I don't want to wake up. I could set a second alarm outside my daughter's bedroom door, but program it for one minute after the first alarm goes off so I know I have to hurry to disarm it before it wakes her. I could further strengthen the environmental pulls by challenging friends to do the same workout and to hold each other accountable with a daily check-in. For some people, this still might not be enough. However, if they joined a Marine boot camp, I'm certain they'd have no trouble finding the motivation to get up on time.

For four years, I trained a talented high school football player who showed little desire to grow up. He was dependent on his mother for everything from waking up on time, to knowing what assignments were overdue, to being reminded that his SAT was scheduled for the next day. But he was a good athlete and went on to play college football. On a visit home during his freshman year, I asked him how the transition went. He told me that he'd slept in and showed up late for his first 6 a.m. workout, but was proud to report that after an aggressive punishment, he had not been late since. The path has power.

Our schools and youth development culture should be obsessed with helping students learn to manipulate their environment and to train their willpower. These are the keys that unlock everything from health and grades, to lifelong hobbies and healthy savings habits. They underlie patience, focus, and every other positive interpersonal skill.

This is no secret. Nearly every philosophy, religion, or mythology professes the essentiality of self-mastery while offering their own unique training protocols. Yet, our youth development paradigm does not work to create it. Teachers are never given strategies to develop delayed gratification in their students, nor explicitly taught the value themselves. There are no district initiatives to train greater focus and no course that teaches habit formation and environmental design to students. In an age of more temptation than ever before, we must give our children a framework to free themselves from manipulation.

CREATING A GROWTH MINDSET

"It's not that I am smart. It's that I stay with problems longer."
—*Albert Einstein*

As essential as it is to learn how to design our environments, the most essential ingredient in creating capable youth may be to praise the right things. Or, just as important, to avoid praising the wrong things.

Stanford's renowned mindset psychologist, Carol Dweck examined over 400 students across six studies to look at the effects of different kinds of praise. One by one, fifth grade students were taken out of their class and into a testing room where they were given a set of "moderately difficult" problems. After completion, their test was scored. All students were told they'd done well. Some were praised for their ability: "Wow, you must be smart to get so many problems right." Others were praised for their effort: "Wow, you must have worked hard at these problems."

Then, the researchers gave students a far harder problem set. Each student was told that they had done poorly after they finished. Researchers then asked if they'd like to take this more challenging problem set home to practice. The kids praised for effort ("you must have worked hard") were far more likely to take these problems home than those praised for intelligence ("you must be smart"). Later, when students were given a third set of problems, those praised for effort outperformed those praised for intelligence. At the end, students had the option to choose between reading how they could improve their test performance in the future or seeing their peers' results. Those praised for effort were far more likely to want to learn how they could improve, while the ability-praised wanted to know how their peers had done.

The group praised for being smart had quickly learned to measure themselves based on what people said about their performance. They were considered intelligent when they easily solved problems, thus struggling to solve problems and needing to ask questions must mean they were dumb. Any increased challenge was a threat to their identity. Dweck calls this a fixed mindset.

Conversely, the group praised for effort overwhelmingly reported liking the harder problems just as much, if not more than, the previous task. Most of them were eager to take the problems home to practice. They were praised for giving effort and this hardworking identity freed them to enjoy a good challenge. Dweck calls this a growth mindset.

In his book, *The Art of Learning*, the chess prodigy turned world champion Tai Chi Push Hands fighter, Josh Waitzkin, compares the hazards of a fixed mindset to a hermit crab who starves itself to avoid outgrowing its shell. Hermit crabs take on a shell for protection early in life. At a certain point, however, they outgrow the shell and must discard it in order to find a larger, more suitable one. The crab has to journey out, completely exposed, in search for a new shell. As Waitzkin explains, "That learning phase in between shells is where our growth can spring from. Someone stuck with an entity (fixed) theory of intelligence is like an anorexic hermit crab, starving itself so it doesn't grow to have to find a new shell."

Without growth we are truly starving ourselves. Helping kids enjoy challenges is the best way to help them live fulfilling lives. As Dweck puts it:

> If parents want to give their children a gift, the best thing they can do is to teach their children to love challenges, be intrigued by mistakes, enjoy effort, and keep on learning. That way, their children don't have to be slaves of praise. They will have a lifelong way to build and repair their own confidence.

Dweck's research indicates that praising people for traits like "being smart" or "naturally athletic" creates a fixed mindset and promotes risk aversion. People avoid failures that might shatter their fragile self-image. They would rather look like they don't care than be seen to care and fail. By contrast, growth-minded people build true confidence. They are willing to risk failing because they are more focused on the doing. Thus, they learn to love the process.

"It is impossible to live without failing at something, unless you live so cautiously that you might as well not have lived at all - in which case you fail by default."
—*J.K. Rowling*

When we obsess on outcomes, it is easy to misinterpret feedback and never learn the nuanced lessons that come from raw experience. Failure might not warrant course correction. As professional poker player, Annie Duke explains, "If you define failure as merely losing, then you will think failure is just an outcome. And you might try to adjust your play to avoid losing even though your decisions were great."

Duke has a lot of experience learning to analyze failed poker hands. As she says:

> . . .just because I win doesn't mean I succeeded . . . . What matters is the decisions I made along the way, and every decision failure is an opportunity to learn and adjust my strategy going forward. By doing this, losing becomes a less emotional experience and more an opportunity to explore and learn.

Our children must learn to make this distinction. We and our children must learn to think much beyond immediate outcomes. If we are not failing, then we aren't putting ourselves in situations to learn and grow. When we can appreciate the lesson in each experience, then the world turns into a fascinating laboratory.

This isn't to suggest that we can't enjoy success and feel the pain of failure. Nor should it be misconstrued as a reason for inflating grades or not keeping score. Such developments reflect an environment where adults are so obsessed with outcomes that they are afraid to let kids deal with reality. Outcomes are a vital feedback mechanism. As we explored in our analysis of honor cultures and ranking systems, social comparison is an inevitable and essential tool to use for creating excellence-driven environments. But the only reason to recognize that outcomes matter is to give a measuring stick for the virtues—effort in particular—that make those outcomes possible.

Teachers and parents should emphasize student effort while maintaining the expectation that students continue working until they have created a high-quality result. Students need to learn to persevere until a project is done well and take pride in doing their work "the right way," but feedback should focus on effort because this is all anyone can control.

Likewise, it is essential to critique a lack of effort even if the outcomes are satisfactory. In my time as a Strength and Conditioning Coordinator, I've repeatedly watched coaches who allow their best athletes to give less effort and get away with far more. Many coaches fear upsetting their stars, so they protect these athletes from the constructive criticism that they desperately need. These players are destined to reach a level where their talent no longer fills the gaps for their lack of effort. But by this point, they will be years behind in developing the focus, antifragility, and emotional intelligence necessary for higher level performance.

Teachers often do the same in school. With incentive structures that pull their focus to the low-achieving students, the most intelligent students are rarely given the critique or challenge they need to grow. After years of being lauded for being smart, these students learn to give teachers exactly what they want, without ever daring to think differently.

There are some schools who pay lip-service to fostering a growth-mindset but they usually have not internalized what this means. They talk a lot about how everyone can grow, but these idle words don't translate to much difference in teacher or student behavior.

A study of 400,000 students co-authored by Michigan State and Western Case Reserve University purported to show that growth-mindset interventions had only a small effect on academic performance. This will come as no surprise to anyone who has ever been to a teacher professional development training. Speakers are brought in to sell some new educational gimmick. They present it in the most *rah-rah*, superficial manner possible and then the teachers return to business as usual. The school claims a new cutting-edge pedagogical approach and throws up signs in the hall, but nothing actually changes.

It doesn't matter what values we post on the wall. It is not enough to profess the virtues of a growth-mindset and to occasionally praise effort. These measures won't make a dent in a culture of grade inflation, where students are constantly shown that manipulating perception is what really matters. What makes an impact is the real operating system that drives our culture. Do we celebrate failure and risk-taking? Are students empowered to engage in an honest, high-quality dialectic or do we maintain the illusion that all opinions are equally valid? Praising effort requires a clear standard of excellence. There has to be a sense of the way you *should* conduct your business. Do you play the game the right way?

Most importantly, to appreciate the benefits of a growth-minded culture, teachers must be learners, themselves. Teachers who love learning are always sparking debates and connecting class topics to new ideas that they are learning about. This is the difference between the outcome-oriented developmental strategy that dominates youth development today and one that understands that lifelong learning is essential in order for our children to create fulfilling lives. Learning has merit in and of itself. It is the very essence of a life well-lived.

CHAPTER 16

A NEW VISION
FOR SCHOOLS

"There is fire in the flint and steel, but it is friction that causes it to flash, flame and burn, and give light where all else may be darkness. There is music in the violin, but the touch of the master is needed to fill the air and the soul with the concord of sweet sounds. There is power in the human mind, but education is needed for its development." —*Frederick Douglass*

The core of today's high school curriculum is the same core that you remember:

- Math = Algebra, Geometry, Algebra II, Trigonometry or Calculus
- Science = Biology, Chemistry, Physics, Environmental Science or Astronomy
- Social Studies = World Geography, World History, U.S. History, U.S. Government
- English = Composition, Expository Writing, and themed literature classes

Each of these subjects are valuable and quite beautiful to those who wish to deeply explore them. Yet, in our current public-school model the average student graduates retaining only the most basic algebraic skills, a few meaningless scientific terms like "chlorophyll," a few random historic names, a superficial grasp of the dominant political parties, and depressingly poor writing skills. We silo off subjects from one another, rush through them, and dress them in their most boring, unthreatening, and irrelevant clothes. With nothing to tie them to, each fragment falls away.

As Dorothy Sayers suggested, during the elementary school learning phase all students need a baseline level of math, science, social studies, and English skills. While not alone sufficient, these create a foundation to build upon. I also agree with Sayers's overarching vision of middle school education where formal logic is at the center of most subjects.

Having mastered logic, high school should offer students considerable flexibility. Those more advanced, focused progressions that make up the current high school "core" *should be electives*. Some students will need and love higher level physics and calculus, but a majority will never retain, nor use those skills. They are only necessary for a small segment of the population who has the inclination to learn them. Still, every high school class is not an elective. There are essential lessons and life skills that are truly core to success in the 21st century.

The standard approach to education focuses on checking off boxes that are supposed to guarantee some obscure idea of success. School is an extension of consumerism. We learn to earn. In the process, we miss the point. Even if this model was the best path to bring students financial success (which it isn't), students rarely graduate equipped to create a fulfilling life.

A future engineer will need to understand calculus just as a future doctor will need a firm grasp of biology. But what does that matter if he is depressed, in and out of toxic relationships, and lacks the emotional intelligence to work on his anger and compulsive eating? What will a degree in statistics offer a high school graduate who lacks any interest other than status and immediate gratification? How much more would she be capable of with a strong body, a resilient mind, and clear values? And what will any of this matter if she and her peers don't understand the context in which they live or feel a sense of civic duty?

The true educational core is the foundation that is common to all humans and upon which we are made most capable. These are the lessons that are most timeless and timely for the human experience. The New Core should include:

- The Foundations of a Healthy Lifestyle
- Humanity, Self-Discovery, and Self-Mastery
- Rhetoric and Human Relationships
- Cognitive Bias and the Skill of Learning
- Political Theory, Citizenship, and 20th Century World History
- Essential Financial Strategies

REDUCTIONIST VS. INTEGRATED LEARNING MODEL

Before we examine each of these New Core subjects, let's clarify the overarching educational philosophy. We are teaching the whole person in an effort to create applicable, useful understandings that are stepping stones to future learning and adaptation. Secondary education must transcend subject categories to promote depth and transfer.

Core subjects are not intended to be isolated classes offering narrowly defined skillsets. While each would be designated at least one yearlong course, the skills and ideas must be used across classes. For this core to work best, it must become the language that schools speak in.

For example, high school students should write and read more than they do now, but by high school, English should be part of every subject, not its own. With few obvious exceptions, every course would require writing and every teacher would be well practiced in the writing process. By making writing an integral component of all learning, the overall level of written communication would far surpass what we see today.

Likewise, each core subject would not only permeate all others, but also the way we approach human development. Since each core subject is inherent to the human experience, they will each be an adaptable vehicle to explore every other subject.

To best facilitate integration, each teacher would need to demonstrate mastery across all core concepts. Unlike today when social-studies teachers are baffled by freshman algebra and chemistry teachers have forgotten the causes of Rome's fall, the universal nature of my core creates limitless possibilities for cross-curricular connections that promote real-world application. Learning may be organized by subjects but it knows no bounds.

We need teachers who learn, question, and strive for truth as a way of being—teachers who read every day and are excited to make connections from what they teach to the ideas they are learning about. Such teachers will naturally spark good-natured debates with other teachers and model for students how learning enhances the quality of relationships and life.

Lifelong learning is more than an empty platitude for teachers in high-performing cultures like Finland and Japan. Teaching is a competitive, challenging field that requires rigorous training, but in turn offers tremendous autonomy and respect throughout society. These countries don't have exhaustive curriculums, yearly standardized tests, or bureaucratized evaluation systems that encourage superficial oversimplifications. Rather, teachers are empowered to be developmental experts. Higher standards create a culture where teachers exhibit the values and skills necessary to optimize learning without micromanagement.

The quality of the teachers determines the quality of the school. Not a top-heavy bureaucracy with endless numbers of assistant superintendents, curriculum specialists, human resource czars, and equity officers. These inhibit the learning that would naturally spring from great teachers in a good campus culture. Let's cut all the excess and, instead, funnel our resources to bring in the best people possible. We need talented, empowered teachers to make a more inspired educational experience possible.

The final imperative for schools is to begin treating students like burgeoning adults. Students need to talk about the topics that adults handle because adulthood is the desirable fate they all share. Traditional education sanitizes each topic and puts it in its most unthreatening clothes. We run from fully exploring important, interesting issues such as: death, religion, a life-well-lived, automation, the future of human societies, animal extinctions, the ethical implications of upcoming scientific breakthroughs, mass data collection, how to balance security and liberty, the state of public mental and physical health, race relations, gender relations, romantic relationships, parenting strategies, and corruption, *to name a few.*

These topics bring learning to life and make students more likely to seek greater understanding. But they have the potential to elicit strong emotions and make some parents angry so we shy away from giving them an honest, thorough examination.

How are students to navigate the world if they can't discuss important topics in a contained environment where the rules are set ahead of time? Schools must have the courage to support students' growth regardless of the uncomfortable moments that it might bring. We need to confront all the hard, taboo topics, but in a progressive manner where students have the logical background and the communication skills to navigate these tricky engagements. Our kids are not inheriting a stable, static world. They'll prefer that we made them capable, not comfortable.

And now, a brief overview of each domain within the New Core:

THE FOUNDATIONS OF A HEALTHY LIFESTYLE

> *"Intelligence and skill can only function at the peak of their capacity when the body is healthy and strong. In this sense physical activity is the basis for all the activities of our society."*
> —*John F. Kennedy*

As currently taught, health and P.E. are a joke—relegated to the corners of the building—unseen, unheard, and rarely thought of. And yet, health is our most fundamental need. Every experience and every effort is magnified by greater health and muddied by its absence. We cannot optimize the mind without taking care of the body. Our attitudes and understandings about health directly add or take away years of life and shape the quality of the years we have.

We spend billions each year on diet plans, trainers, and unnecessary prescriptions. Billions more on the preventable consequences of poor health which drive millions into limited, dependent lives. This reactive approach isn't slowing down the epidemic of poor health. Students need to experience an environment that promotes health and human flourishing and they need to be taught the principles of how to take care of their own health.

Perhaps nothing would make a greater impact on students' lives than for each school to develop an inspired P.E. program like Stan LeProtti created at La Sierra High in the late 1950's. LeProtti's program, which was featured in the film, *The Motivation Factor*, developed a high level of physical fitness throughout La Sierra High School. He created a rigorous, individually motivating, yet team-oriented system that promoted strong values, perseverance, and student-coaching. Teachers and former La Sierra students rave about how this program instilled an excellence-driven culture that transferred to the classroom and beyond.

Physical Education has the power to be a unifying educational experience that endears all of society with a respect for health and a basic physical mastery—what many fitness experts call physical literacy. This baseline fitness competency gives people the tools to improve their own health and opens doors to future activities that can be a portal to deep relationships, passions, life lessons, and lifelong health.

Respect for the body can't just be quarantined to P.E., however. Healthy movement habits should infuse every day and every class. Rather than having students sit for six or more hours a day, schools should encourage teachers to include walking lectures and outdoor lessons, and classrooms should feature standing desks. These would have easy up and down adjustment and a high-stool for sitting, but would promote more engaged posture and movement.

In addition to physical literacy, schools should strive to create nu-tritional literacy in the Betty Dickson mold. Students must grasp basic principles so they can practice sustainable, healthy eating hab-its. Even more, schools should be selective about what foods and bev-erages they make available. Halls shouldn't be lined with vending machines. The costs of providing nutritious meals are a far better investment than fancy atriums, showy technology, or other luxuries. There are obvious constraints to cooking for large numbers. Every school won't have a farm full of happy dancing chickens, frolicking streams of wild fish, and rows of fresh-grown produce. Still, the foods available in a school day should be reserved for whole foods, which existed prior to the industrial revolution. Schools should convey the belief that taking care of your health is the beginning of becoming an autonomous adult.

Finally, students must learn more about the mind and the con-ditions that optimize mental health. As the markers of poor mental health proliferate, many states have begun Band-Aid initiatives. In 2019, Texas Governor, Greg Abbot, signed a bill requiring mental health curriculums. This is a step, but I'm afraid it won't be any more effective than modern health classes have been against the growing tide of obesity. One token course means little when saturated in an environment diametrically opposed to it. Students spend their days seated, surrounded by junk food, toggling from app to app, while often lacking sunlight and sleep. To make matters worse, schools have become fragility factories—sheltering students, over-providing excuses, and indoctrinating self-defeating mental distortions.

In addition to fixing these environmental problems, schools should teach students mindfulness practices so they have a basic mental literacy. This is also known as meditation, which apart from the stigmas associated, is among the best tools at our disposal for helping people become happier. As Jonathan Haidt explains in *The Happiness Hypothesis*:

> Suppose you read about a pill that you could take once a day
> to reduce anxiety and increase your contentment. Would

you take it? Suppose further that the pill has a great variety of side effects, all of them good: increased self-esteem, empathy, and trust; it even improves memory. Suppose, finally, that the pill is all natural and costs nothing. Now would you take it? The pill exists. It is meditation.

Meditation also helps you become aware of thoughts and emotions so you can notice unhealthy patterns and take more control of your responses. It helps people drop past assumptions so they can experience a more accurate, unbiased interpretation of the world—pretty advantageous for a learning environment.

Required Reading:
- RAMA: Paradigm 21, by Ed Thomas Ed.D.

HUMANITY, SELF-DISCOVERY, AND SELF-MASTERY

Schools must promote investigation into how humans thrive and explore what it means to be a human. The modern environment could not be further from the conditions expected by our biology. Manipulative entities, heavily incentivized to create addiction and mindless consumption, prey on our every impulse. To ignore this reality virtually ensures dependency and limited living. As we rush into the age of automation this will only increase.

We must study what it means to be human and mine for the universal essentials across the human experience. What environments were we evolved to thrive within? What are the human needs and how do we best operate in this world? From this foundation we can design exercises that promote self-discovery and investigation into creating a meaningful existence in the modern context. This is an ever-evolving process that should be revisited often across many subjects.

In order for our students to create their own future, they must begin to cultivate a more sophisticated sense of who they are and where they derive purpose. From this foundation, they can develop the skills and structure to intentionally identify desirable actions and then follow through.

Early on, this subject is also where students can practice meditation and deep dive into willpower training, habit creation, and and designing their environment, which will facilitate all learning. In particular, there should be a freshman semester course based primarily on James Clear's *Atomic Habits* followed by a semester that specifically addresses the challenges of 21st century time management.

Time is our most valuable resource. Most people feel as if their days are a never-ending game of Whack-a-Mole. They are constantly reacting and being yanked from task to task. Email, texts, tweets, and all the demands of our hectic world pull and prod them in a hundred different directions. We feel busy, but not productive.

Students must learn how to create mental space and focus by creating structures that allow them to manage their time effectively. They should learn the value of deep work, how to create boundaries, batch work, prioritize, and systematize in a fast-paced world. These skills amplify each student's capacity to digest content and direct their own learning. While specific time management courses should probably conclude after freshman year, every teacher and course should expect and reinforce these structures throughout the rest of the student's high school career.

As schooling progresses this subject will delve deeper into the human condition, values, and the pursuit of human excellence. It should communicate the values and expectations of the school culture uniting all behind the ideal of arête. Imagine a student culture that was well-versed in the human needs and trained in the ability to interrupt negative mental patterns, rewire habits, and influence their psychological states by changing their physiology.

The culmination of this field will come at the end of high school when students outline and conquer a rite of passage into adulthood. This will be a rallying point to the entire educational process that requires planning, intellectual competency, physical capacity, and mental will. Think of it as part senior thesis, part Eagle Scout project, and part uniform battery of challenges that all seniors must complete. The goal is to communicate a sense that adulthood is desirable, but it must be earned and it comes with responsibilities of competency, maturity, and capability.

Typical of the integrated model, Humanity, Self-Discovery, and Self-Mastery would feature a heavy emphasis on debate, writing, history, psychology, relationships, philosophy, anthropology, interpreting research, literature, and physical experience.

Required Reading:
- Tribe: On Homecoming and Belonging, by Sebastian Junger
- Natural Born Heroes, by Christopher McDougall
- Man's Search for Meaning, by Victor Frankl
- Zen and the Art of Motorcycle Maintenance, by Robert M. Pirsig
- The Obstacle is the Way, by Ryan Holiday
- Atomic Habits, by James Clear
- Switch, by Chip and Dan Heath
- Getting Things Done, by David Allen

RHETORIC AND RELATIONSHIPS

"When dealing with people remember that you are not dealing with creatures of logic, but with creatures bristling with prejudice and motivated by pride and vanity."   —*Dale Carnegie*

The success of our species is built upon our amazing capacity for communication and coordination. It does not matter how brilliant our ideas are if we cannot communicate them in a way that makes them palatable for others. Furthermore, the quality of our life depends on the quality of our relationships.

In the age of the smartphone, it is more necessary than ever to teach communication skills. Our kids lack social practice and often have a staggering inability to understand body language. We must explicitly teach and facilitate these skills within the school structure. Students need frequent practice speaking publicly and presenting their arguments, findings, or original creations. They would also benefit from the "Yes-and" drills common to improvisational comedians where they learn to be in-tune with partners and find creative transitions.

Additionally, we should reinforce ground rules for honest, good-faith debates that call on students to apply emotional intelligence. Rather than succumbing to common tactics like the straw man, students should practice steel-manning another person's argument by clearly repeating it back to ensure they have characterized it well before building their own case.

We have to teach our students to understand that differences of opinion are essential to our growth and to a healthy society, but, also, that opinions are not all equally valid. These ends are facilitated by a culture where students practice meditation and have been trained in logic.

To dig even deeper, students should begin to study the lost art of rhetoric. To the ancient Greeks, Romans, and Dorothy Sayers, rhetorical training was the culmination of a person's education. As author Jay Heinrichs explains, "Rhetoric gives a real purpose to a liberal education, pulling together all of a student's knowledge while giving her the tools to inspire others. It inoculates her against the kind of manipulation and tribalism that poison our politics. It creates a good citizen. A truly educated one."

Finally, this subject must discuss relationships, even romantic ones, and the differences between male and female experiences and expectations. This is rich, potentially scary territory, but it must be addressed so students have an environment where they can talk and begin to craft more mature understandings about the relationships that will fill their lives.

Rhetoric and Relationships is a large subject that digs into:

- How to package messages so they are better received
- How to create clarity in dialogue

- Reinforcing rules of honest debating
- Writing and speaking better
- How to create healthy boundaries in relationships
- How to better understand different personalities
- Looking at variations of the big five personality traits

Infuse this subject with literature, history, logic, and especially psychology. It is territory ripe for conversation and ever-continuing education.

Required Reading:
- How to Win Friends and Influence People, by Dale Carnegie
- Thank You for Arguing, by Jay Heinrichs
- The Righteous Mind, by Jonathan Haidt
- The Culture Code, by Daniel Coyle
- Talking with Strangers, by Malcolm Gladwell
- On Writing Well, by William Zinsser

COGNITIVE BIAS AND THE SKILL OF LEARNING

"When you know how to think it empowers you far beyond those who know only what to think."   —Neil DeGrasse Tyson

This is an extension of the logic-centric "scholastic discipline" Dorothy Sayers called for in *The Lost Tools of Learning*. This course focuses on cultivating a greater capacity for academic inquiry, more accurate perception, and better judgment. The age of mass media has been built to a consumer base that lacks the basic ability to assess validity. How can we make good decisions if we aren't equipped with a basic capacity for detecting contradictions and biases?

Our world is ever-changing. Those who know how to learn will adapt and thrive. Those who perceive nuance and understand the limitations and patterns of the mind will be invaluable decision makers. Those who know how to deconstruct parts to synthesize new ideas will innovate and create value. Those who understand how the human mind operates and learns best are equipped with the tools to be successful regardless of what life throws at them.

This course would dive deep into meta-cognition (thinking about our thinking), logic, and cognitive biases. Exercises would include recreating psychological experiments, working through trolley problems and other difficult moral questions, dissecting misleading studies, debating, and solving riddles. Einstein's riddle, for example, should become a staple of each person's educational experience. Albert Einstein claimed that 98% of the world could not solve it, but the reality is most people can. It just requires a strategy to organize thinking and a willingness to persist.

Required Reading:

- Bad Science, by Ben Goldacre
- Stumbling Upon Happiness, by Daniel Gilbert
- The Art of Learning, by Josh Waitzkin
- An Illustrated Book of Bad Arguments, Ali Almossawi

POLITICAL THEORY, CITIZENSHIP, AND 20TH CENTURY WORLD HISTORY

"A primary object should be the education of our youth in the science of government. In a republic, what species of knowledge can be equally important? And what duty more pressing than communicating it to those who are to be the future guardians of the liberties of the country." —George Washington

This is really a sub-category under Humanity, Self-Discovery, and Self-Mastery, but it is large enough to warrant its own domain.

Most of the problems society faces today stem from glaring misunderstandings about how human civilization works. Few know how unique representative democracy is within the scope of human history, or what other systems look like in practice. Political theory gives students a foundational exploration of why governments exist, how the various governing philosophies differ, and how they have worked throughout time. From there, students will be able to understand the foundations of representative democracy as well as the tensions across the political spectrum.

This will require a thorough grasp of history since the Enlightenment, with a particular emphasis on the 20th century, where modern technology facilitated multiple world wars, a nuclear cold war, and more deaths from genocide than ever before. To be blunt, it is unlikely that human civilization will last if we don't begin to teach this better. This would be deeply informed by many books from the study of Humanity and Self-Discovery as well as:

- The Lessons of History, by Will and Ariel Durant
- 1984, by George Orwell
- Why We Drive, by Matthew Crawford
- Sapiens, by Yuval Noah Harari
- First Principles, by Thomas E. Ricks

ESSENTIAL FINANCIAL STRATEGIES

"If you understand compound interest you basically understand the universe."   —*Robert Breault*

It may seem odd to include finance after waxing on about the ills of consumerism, but money is a tool to create freedom. Once we understand what is most important, proper money management will contribute to every other area of life.

This does not have to be conceived as an advanced finance course. There are some simple, obvious financial pearls that everyone needs to know. Compound interest can change your life, particularly if you begin investing early enough. Conversely, credit cards and debt can quickly eliminate options and indenture you to a job you dislike.

According to Bankrate's Financial Security Index, only 39% of American households could handle a $1,000 emergency with savings. Money doesn't buy happiness, but intelligent management will bring the opportunity to prioritize rewarding experiences and live with more flow.

These lessons can easily cross-over to other fields, as well. Investing money serves as an appropriate analogy for investing time in order to highlight the difference between skill acquisition and passive entertainment. Budgeting is analogous to balanced eating habits. Individual financial lessons are a doorway to exploring more complex economic systems and the effects that collective spending habits have on the entire country.

As with the freshman level habit and time management courses, this subject could probably be covered thoroughly in a semester or two.

Required Reading:
- The Simple Path to Wealth, by J.L. Collins
- I Will Teach You to Be Rich, by Ramit Sethi

THE WHOLE

The most important element of the integrated approach is crafting the culture and institutional habits of the school itself. People largely act in accordance with group norms. Every time we practice an action, that behavior pattern is hardwired deeper into our personal operating system. Thus, strong institutional habits program students with strong individual habits. By giving students anchor experiences, like daily exercise, meditation, and a gratitude practice, schools could cultivate emotional control and common experiences for students and teachers to refer back to.

Likewise, the entire institutional structure should be built to optimize human flourishing. Schools should factor in research about teenage sleep patterns to determine start times. School schedules should honor the needs of both students and teachers for movement and time outside. Lunches wouldn't be full of students scanning social media as they eat. Schools would implement no-technology policies at lunch, like many districts have already done, in order to promote social skills, connection, and healthy boundaries.

Students attend school for eight hours a day. We know that institutional habits will become their habits. How thoughtless is it to keep them seated, surrounded by sugar and processed food, and exposed to the constant disturbance of their smartphone? How insane is it to distort grades and repeatedly reinforce the expectation that adults will solve their problems? How destructive is it to constantly maneuver standards around the demands of shortsighted parents?

As we examine the pulls on our culture, seemingly forcing us down a path we'd never objectively choose, let's keep in mind the power of culture to do good as well. Imagine if we were pulled towards nutritious foods, activity, competition of ideas, and expectations of personal responsibility.

How much easier and more likely would it be to practice healthy habits if you had exercised and meditated every day at school and been immersed in an environment where only healthy foods were available? Even if you fell away from these habits, you'd have the experience to confidently wade back in and you would live among a population who shared a similar experience. Likewise, how much easier would it be for kids to set technology limits and boundaries if they practiced these as part of their daily school work and lived in a population of people who had done the same?

THE DEEPEST INEQUALITY

"Our awareness seems to shrink in direct ratio as communications expand; the world is open to us as never before, and we walk about as prisoners, each in his private portable cage."
—*Arthur Koestler, The Nightmare that is a Reality*

There is a strong, but relatively small portion of the population, probably 15% or less, who are adapting. They have habits like meditation, gratitude, exercise, journaling, the Wim Hof Method, or charging their phone outside of their bedroom. They read books that change the way they perceive and operate in the world. They learn about concepts such as *first principles thinking, the paradox of choice,* and *growth mindset* and apply their implications to their life. They eat well without dieting, work effectively without overwhelm, and parent well without sacrificing their lives at the altar of youth sports specialization. These people seek wisdom, try to understand their environment better, adapt to offset the pull of market manipulation, and work to create a more fulfilling life.

Then, there are most people. They, like the schools that they attended, are led astray by herd norms. Smartphones, sweets, and sales tactics pull and prod them. They kill time. Their lives are driven by the next dopamine hit. Work and education are a means to material ends. These people may be vaguely aware of the issues their phones present, but social proof tells them it's not that big of a problem. They may occasionally read or try a new hobby, but more often they are resigned to mindless patterns—unsatisfied, yet unable to deviate from their normal way of doing things. They're starving for meaning.

There is a lot of talk about inequality in our world, but this is the greatest and most controllable inequality. Normal people—the "have-nots"—will continue to face disproportionately high rates of obesity, heart disease, suicide, depression, anxiety, drug overdoses, and general despair. By contrast, the "haves" will live higher quality lives. They will overcome obstacles and feel the sense of fulfillment that only comes from pursuing worthy goals. As parents, they will be more likely to insist on intelligent boundaries that optimize the benefit of technology while limiting its destructive capacity. Their children will be more likely to internalize the belief that they can act to influence their future for the better. These kids will play outside, scrape their knees, complete chores, learn to save, read books, and live a healthy lifestyle. They'll grow up with nourishing dinner conversations that stoke their natural curiosities. They'll develop a balanced skill set that opens opportunities and brings a sense of confidence that they can weather whatever life brings.

The gap between the haves and have-nots is growing fast and it is not best-viewed as an economic gap. Sure, a lot of these "haves" are well-educated and well-off. Economics certainly matter, but culture is more important. After all, Ethan Couch and millions of other rich, spoiled youngsters are among the "have-nots" who have been programmed for hedonism, narcissism, and the constant disappointment that tends to accompany entitlement. Conversely, many of the "haves" are living simple lives and even intentionally taking less money for more freedom and authenticity. The real inequality we see in the world today is between the wisdom-seeking adapters and everyone else.

Education is the only solution to this inequality that honors people's freedom and empowers them to take control of their lives. Many of the changes I advocate would be a bitter pill at first. Students who are not used to standards or who have become addicted to smartphones and junk food will not immediately appreciate the benefits of discipline. But the New Core school environment I've proposed would unlock a world of possibility and personal empowerment. Many parents and students would be very upset if schools became what they need to. But we cannot continue to build our systems around shortsighted desires. Schools must lead the fight for human flourishing. They must strive to be the authority in human development, unflinchingly drawing the line against a world that breeds "have-nots."

CHAPTER 17

IS COLLEGE STILL WORTH IT?

"I've never let my schooling interfere with my education."
—*Mark Twain*

In the standard youth development model, college is seen as the culmination of the educational journey. It is the point of all prior academic experiences—the cultural measuring stick of whether parents and schools did their job. As early as elementary school, students are sold the belief that success means getting into a good university. College, they are told, gets you access to all the best jobs and offers the "best four years of your life!" For high school graduates, the decision to go to college is obvious, exciting, and an empowering landmark. But, for most, it is an ill-timed waste of money.

Before 1960, Harvard cost less than $1000 per year. By 1990 it cost $13,085. By 2010, $33,696. And as of the beginning of 2020, a year at Harvard undergrad costs a staggering $51,925 (still thousands less than many other prestigious schools like Stanford, Yale, and Columbia). Most won't go to Harvard, Stanford, or Columbia, but these price changes are emblematic of the entire industry. According to Business Insider, annual college tuition from 1980 to 2014 grew 260% compared with a 120% increase in all other consumer items.

Consequently, U.S. student loan debt has exploded to $1.6 trillion, dwarfing even our notoriously high collective credit card debt.

Rising costs come in spite of the growing number of cheap, accessible education options made possible by the internet and other technologies. We pay staggering fees to sit in lecture halls listening to lessons that are cheaply available in audio lecture series like The Great Courses or through Khan Academy, podcasts, books, apprenticeships, alternate skill certifications, online education memberships like Skill Share, or real work experience. But as the number of opportunities for learning proliferate and the costs grow more absurd, the universities' stranglehold on post-secondary education has only strengthened. U.S. college enrollment has risen to 20.4 million students—up 5.1 million since just 2000. The majority of these students are 18-23-year-olds who lack the life experience and maturity to know how to best allocate such an immense investment.

We're governed by beliefs instilled in a bygone era. The undergraduate degree was once affordable, uncommon and a virtual guarantee that you would have great employment opportunities in an economy that offered stable, long-term careers. The cost-benefit ratio was very high. By contrast, the modern job market is and will continue to be far more dynamic with jobs that tend to have shorter lifespans and lesser benefits. Work will become increasingly performance-based with fewer salary and hourly payment jobs and more independent contractors earning freelance projects.

How impractical to start off your independent life by accruing unreasonable debt, which will require you to immediately earn enough to make large loan payments—often at the expense of other opportunities that could be more educational than college. No wonder 85% of college grads now move home after graduation. Life, exploration, and maturation are further delayed for the comfort and certainty of mom and dad's safety net.

Today, colleges operate more like businesses, governed by the same dollars-over-value mentality as Big Pharma or Coca-Cola. In his book, *The Fall of the Faculty: The Rise of the All-Administrative*

University and Why it Matters, Professor Benjamin Ginsburg highlights how, since the mid-1970s, universities have been adding expensive administrative positions at a far higher rate than tenured professors. These new deans, vice-deans, and equity-officers justify their positions by increasing the number of meetings and bureaucratic hurdles that professors must jump through, but they rarely advance the academic mission. In fact, many professors have been outspoken about how their schools only care that the professors chase grants, write books, and speak at prestigious conferences. Educating students, from the perspective of campus leadership, is a necessary annoyance to continue collecting tuition and fees.

In order to keep this tuition stream constant, universities have lowered student standards. According to a 2020 piece in *The Journal of Basic and Applied Social Psychology,* the amount of time college students spent on academic work has declined from 40 hours per week in 1961, to 27 hours a week in 2003, to less than 12 hours in 2008. Yet, somehow, as work time decreased, A's have become far more common, increasing from 15% of all assigned letter grades in 1960 to 43% in 2006. Even at Harvard, the median undergraduate grade is an A-. Rampant grade inflation appears to be most pronounced in the social sciences.

As professor Jordan Peterson, formerly of Harvard and the University of Toronto explains:

> You can go to Universities to not be something. . . . It's Pleasure Island. And the price you pay for it, especially in the U.S., is debt. You're enticed into it because the administrators can pick your pocket. They rob your future self while allowing you to pretend you have an identity . . . . So tuition fees have shot way out of control. And part of the reason universities don't make more demands on their students and let them get away with all the things they let them get away with is because . . . why the hell would you chase them out? They're $100,000 . . . or more.

Colleges are just as keen to take the money of students who lack basic study skills but also believe they must go to college right after high school. Senator Ben Sasse, formerly the president of Midland University, notes in his book, *The Vanishing American Adult*, that "Four-year universities, despite having lowered standards for freshmen-year performance, now place one-third of their incoming students in remedial reading and mathematics courses. About half the students entering two-year colleges require some degree of remediation." According to a 2016 study, college remediation expenses cost families $1.5 billion annually.

As much as colleges would prefer to continue collecting fees from unprepared students, roughly one-third of college freshmen do not return as sophomores. They may be currently working and want to focus on growing in their job, or they realize they are unprepared and want to focus on other employment opportunities, or their parents just get tired of paying for them to play around. Regardless of the acute reason, its source is the same. People are wasting thousands of dollars because society tells them they have to go to college after high school.

Rather than reinforce this dogma, high schools should help parents and students think through this decision. But currently, they are the greatest purveyor of this oversimplified educational attitude. High schools across the country now offer college credit classes. Despite their lofty titles, the standards for these courses have been lowered to the point where most hardly qualify as acceptable high school rigor. Students graduate high school, generally, far less prepared than students of 1970, but with up to two years of college course credit. Through some bizarre magic trick, we have now deemed the same or lesser high school education as worthy of replacing college classes. If this seems contrary to the university business model, it is. College credit courses are run by community colleges who operate on a very different model but are just as thrilled to get in the door and make sales. Universities will happily take their credits, however, because it means getting another lucrative student.

To summarize, students who are less mature than previous generations are paying exponentially more for a lesser product that holds less value in the job market. Today, it is becoming more and more common for restaurant servers, bartenders, and flight attendants to have a bachelor's degree. There are those who will say this just confirms that you have to get a college degree for almost every job now, but that is just more insanity. Every citizen needs a better K-12 education. Not exorbitantly expensive post-secondary schooling that still rarely covers what their compulsory schooling should have. The faulty belief that 18-year-olds must go to college—that it is an experience any qualified high school graduate would be crazy to miss—creates an environment where colleges can lower their quality and raise their prices.

CONSUMING COLLEGE

"A man is worked on by what he works on."
—*Frederick Douglass*

My own experience, as a 2011 graduate of TCU (in Fort Worth, Texas) would seem to contradict much of my argument in this chapter. I had amazing professors and I would have been thrilled to go on taking new classes forever. But I couldn't help noticing that most of my peers approached college very differently. It's even worse with the students that I encounter today.

Whenever a student tells me that they've picked a college, I always ask what they plan to major in. I light up when they mention something interesting like psychology, graphic design, economics, political science, journalism, or engineering. I can't help but go on about interesting topics, potential careers, and books I assure them they would love. Sometimes students say that they don't know what they want to major in, which also leads me to a rant, this time about how they don't have to know yet—that life is not linear, and that doors will open if you just keep learning. But, most often, the student responds that he or she will major in business. *Whomp, whomp, whomp.*

I should make a more charitable assumption, but what I hear when students say they want to study business is, "I'm not really interested in learning. I'm just supposed to go to college." There are obviously brilliant, passionate business majors, but I can't help but feel the majority of these students are choosing business because they don't know what else to study. They need a diploma to be competitive in the workforce. They just want to be hired by some business, so why not study business. I get it.

In his book *Excellent Sheep*, Yale Professor, Dr. William Deresiewicz critiques how college has shifted from an emphasis on a well-rounded liberal arts approach, to a focus on narrow technical skill sets. More and more elite students restrict themselves to practical degree plans which leave them lacking adaptability, purpose, or any experience that would help them cultivate a philosophy of living. Ginsberg notes a similar trend, in *The Fall of Faculty*, claiming campuses no longer push students to be well-rounded. He attributes this to the expansion of non-academic campus administration who do not appreciate the humanizing goals of a liberal arts education.

If all you really want or need is a narrow skill set, then our expensive college model is a pretty ridiculous one. Students would be much better served by on-the-job experience, a niche technical program, or the apprenticeship model. College has always been as much about cultivating an academic mindset and committing to the pursuit of truth, as it has been about preparing for any specific job.

But for many today, college is more about having a good time than becoming anything. Too often, both students and their parents view the college experience without any expectation or consideration for personal development. Rather, college is a playground to delay maturation and postpone the "real world."

For most college students, classes are a necessary evil—an inconvenient justification for the college pleasure cruise. Students then graduate and gain employment, often in an unrelated field that provides the skill-specific training they'll truly need. Certainly, there are exceptions. Many students work very hard, endure challenging courses, and graduate with experiences that change their lives. Furthermore, there is nothing wrong with enjoying the college experience. I had a very active social life in college and even accumulated a little dumb debt in the process. But most people I went to school with (like most students I see entering college today) seemed to consider partying and playing around the main point of college.

Today, the majority of 18-year-olds (particularly boys) are simply not ready for college. They have no idea who they are, what they are interested in doing, and, most importantly, they have no real appreciation for education. It would be far better to expect that most people don't go to college right after high school. It would be more appropriate for our culture to expect 18-year-olds to work, leave home, and get a few years of adult experience. This would lead to much better new hire training programs and other young adult work initiatives. These young adults would then have the experience necessary to determine whether college was worth the cost-benefit. And if they decided to go to college, they would be far better suited to determine what they wanted to study and to appreciate what was taught.

THE BEAUTY OF SERVICE

"It is easier to act yourself into a new way of thinking, than it is to think yourself into a new way of acting."   —*Millard Fuller*

My friend, let's call him Travis, was the prototypical hard-partying high school slacker and had to take summer school classes in order to graduate high school. Still, most people in his life were pushing him to go the college route. Not one to listen to advice, he joined the Marines instead.

In the Marines, Travis learned discipline and how to act on behalf of something bigger than himself. He sailed across the Pacific, worked and lived with people who'd only known extreme poverty, and created bonds with his fellow service members that are rare in the superficial, civilian world. After four years, Travis left the Marines a man, interested in the world and guided by a sense of duty to live with impact. Travis jumped into college with a newfound interest in other cultures and with free tuition. Today, he is a teacher and is pursuing a Master's degree, also free of charge.

Military experience is often a transformative experience for youth because it provides clear expectations, standards, and goals. It pushes people past perceived limitations, offers skills training, and facilitates bonding with other hard workers. Everyone could benefit from such an experience and it wouldn't have to come from the military.

Retired Four-Star General, Stanley McChrystal is committed to creating a program that pushes every 18-year-old citizen to do a year of service. His vision isn't mandatory military service, but to put citizens from many different backgrounds, races, and creeds together in service opportunities like mentoring students in poorly performing schools, fixing decaying infrastructure, re-training workers from dwindling fields like coal-mining, and much more.

McChrystal's plan would help re-instill a sense of civic duty and would create a clearer deadline to childhood. Parents and schools would know that children have to be made ready for something. Perhaps most importantly, this would expose young adults to different cultures while uniting them through shared experiences.

Something magical happens when you put people together and give them a common purpose. By relying on one another, they build respect and see each other as fellow humans. They have new experiences and begin to understand how good people can come to different opinions. Suddenly the world is nuanced—the solutions complex.

Let's explore the service year idea a step further. Like McChrystal, my vision would not require compulsory military service, but it would utilize some elements of the military model and offer the option to opt out in favor of military enlistment.

As I'd envision it, the initial, for lack of a better term, "Boot Camp Phase," would be twelve-weeks at a randomly selected training "base." This would be geared towards instilling resiliency, discipline, mental toughness, teamwork, and a commitment to service. Young adults would be separated by gender, issued uniforms, and given expectations for cleanliness, timeliness, presentation, and all the basic structures of a military boot camp setting. The day would begin with an early wake-up, physical training, breakfast, and then time spent working on base upkeep until lunch. This could include fixing machines, landscaping, loading and unloading shipments, or farming and tending to local food-production needs. These "cadets" would grow, raise, and process most of the food consumed on the premises.

They would spend afternoons in skills training before units were assigned a nightly mission that required mutual cooperation. Each group would receive dinner only after they finished this task. Weekends would be free for reading, games, and other on sight recreation (tennis courts, archery, rock-climbing, etc.), but there would be no smartphones, television, or entertainment media. Each cadet would be allotted no more than three 15-minute phone calls per week, barring emergencies.

Every fourth week cadets would be dropped off as a group into a remote location with nothing more than a riddle-filled map and a thermos of water. They would have to navigate their way back as a unit within 48 hours or be forced to repeat this challenge each weekend until they were successful. These challenges would escalate in difficulty, culminating in a third and final graduation rite of passage. Units would be given food and monitored, but could not return until successful completion, whether within 48 hours or not. If a unit failed to complete their challenge in 72 hours, they return for an additional two-weeks of extended training before their next attempt.

After the 12-week "boot-camp" phase, young adults should be able to select from a large cadre of tracks that provide further training towards an area of global need where they have an interest. They'd still wake to physical training, but after breakfast, they would be immersed in specific skills education, where their competency was assessed and tracked for future assignments. They'd be free to leave and socialize as they pleased during nights and weekends. This phase would be four weeks culminating in a service placement.

Over the course of the next 14-months, cadets would move from assignment to assignment helping lead service projects ranging from environmental restoration, to disaster relief, community education, care for the sick or dying, and building schools and homes.

This 18-month compulsory service would transform young adults, altering their expectations and worldviews and it would radically strengthen the social fabric of our nation.

While my vision is unlikely to come to fruition, it is important that we begin to question the status quo. For most students and future employers alike, the college experience is largely symbolic. Sure, I'd factor college into my consideration of a work applicant, but most businesses will be better off when conditions favor a more nuanced hiring approach and more varied development.

We've convinced everyone they need a college diploma while colleges make themselves more expensive and less valuable. We've emphasized what college can get you while de-emphasizing the importance of learning and the cognitive skills college was supposed to offer. Many college graduates now begin their work life unprepared, undistinguished, and racked with debt. We have all the ingredients for a massive debt bubble and few indications that anything will change. The future may be hazy, but it is clear that we must be able to adapt far better than this.

NEW OPTIONS FOR A NEW WORLD

"In a world of change the learners shall inherit the earth, while the learned shall find themselves perfectly suited for a world that no longer exists."   —*Eric Hoffer*

There is already plenty of precedent for creating education programs outside the college model. Peter Thiel, the billionaire owner of Thiel Capital, has created the Thiel Fellowship where he finds talented college students and funds their start-up in exchange for them dropping out of college. Legendary author, Robert Greene, pushed Ryan Holiday to drop out of college to be his apprentice. Holiday went on to serve as director of marketing for American Apparel, and is now among the best authors of my generation. Tim Ferriss tells the story of his "real-world MBA" where, rather than spending $120,000 over two years at Stanford's Graduate School of Business, he decided to find a mentor, Mike Maples, and instead use that $120,000 towards an experiential education in angel investing. The fact that he did not lose all the money he invested is arbitrary. He learned more in this experience than a business school could ever offer. How many of us would be better off spending a fraction of the cost of college to chase real dreams and get real entrepreneurial experience? Most of us would no doubt fall on our face, but would learn immensely, acquire a broad network of mentors, and accrue less debt.

Of course, colleges can be an amazing place for learning to take place. Most would aimlessly spin their wheels without the clear structure of a degree program. But as more universities lose sight of their real purpose, we will need to create other avenues.

Other entities could provide invaluable education without the loopholes and the fluff characteristic of today's online education and university culture. Say five noteworthy professors get together to create a liberal arts academy with an emphasis on history, political science, philosophy, religion, and evolutionary psychology. The five of them could congregate in any city or town. In this case, let's say they choose San Antonio and decide to open their micro-academy up to 100 students. At $8,000 per student per year (hardly more than what I pay per child for preschool), the school would gross $800,000 per year. They could rent or buy a small studio for classes, but also feel free to host classes in parks, or throughout the community. Each professor would easily make six-figures.

We should be actively trying to create avenues for professors to create these micro-academies. Once the model was established, droves of professors would jump on board, particularly as administrative oversight grows more stifling and professors feel compelled to flee or censor themselves to avoid the anti-rational social justice ideology sweeping through universities. An amazing education doesn't require expensive administration or luxury housing. Just amazing educators.

Particularly as college degrees become more ceremonial and less valuable, businesses should consider creating more relevant and impactful, in house education models. This could take the form of standard apprenticeships or even a homegrown system that promoted career-long education.

For example, imagine if the K-12 education system took on a rank and promotion system for teachers similar to the military. As it now stands, college degrees in Education are among the most pseudoscientific and dogmatic around. Again, I'll note that there are exceptions (to Dr. Amber Esping, your Psychology of Education and Child and Adolescent Development courses were life-changing). But, for the most part, the only chance most teachers have to get a worthy college education is through their non-Education classes. Teachers then graduate and get hired at schools where they are almost immediately placed on equal standing with teachers who have been teaching for 10, 20, 30, or even 40 years. There is very little difference in pay for each year of experience and very little incentive for teachers to continue educating themselves. The only avenues for distinction are to become a department chair (which most teachers actively avoid) or to leave the classroom to go into administration.

Imagine schools where first year teachers entered at the lowest rank. Before hiring, schools would expend considerable energy recruiting potential teachers so that they could bring in talented applicants, at a good base pay, who knew there was potential for rising to much higher ranks and salary. Schools could then facilitate different standards for

different rank promotions. At the entry rank, this might entail weekly meetings with a mentor, a demonstrated mastery of educational psychology, and good ratings in teacher evaluations. Every teacher would conduct these evaluations so that all teachers remained practiced at critiquing the art of teaching. Teachers would be evaluated on their instruction and their students' improvement, as well as their ability to grade essays and other more "subjective" projects. These are skills that must be cultivated.

At a certain rank, much of this oversight would fall away. Later promotions would require specific admirable service to the school as well as a demonstrated commitment to self-development. Ranks would be indicators of hierarchy. Each school would only have, say, one teacher per department at the highest rank, two in the next highest, three in the next and so on. To facilitate the strengthening of school culture, ranks would also come with corresponding roles in campus traditions like pep rallies, talent shows, or faculty debates.

In this system, teachers would have far more incentive to keep growing and, with more opportunities for promotion, the teaching field would be more competitive, lucrative, and attractive to talented young adults. While imperfect, this is a far better option than the typical, laughable online Master's of Education programs that sap teacher's wallets while teaching them nothing. It is common knowledge amongst educators that a Master's degree in Education takes about 3 hours a week of online busy work. While I'm sure there are better programs, these aren't the norm. Similarly, many principals have told me how their doctoral programs didn't require much more—message board posts and a few papers regurgitating educational dogmas.

Even outside education, many online degrees are little more than purchases with a sprinkling of busy-work to make them look like an education program. Everyone knows this but we continue to require people to pay and jump through the same mindless hoops. Employers need to start asking why they require a degree. What is this requirement doing for them? Is there a better way to get good workers? Could they help fund a micro-academy that becomes a pipeline to their specific business? What experiences do their best workers find to be the best preparation for this work? If we can remember the point of education, then many new doors can open.

THE TRANSITION TO ADULTHOOD

Near the end of each school year, my wife teaches a unit with her high school seniors that she calls, "Adulting 101." Adulting is the slang verb now used to describe all those activities that are second-nature to autonomous adults but which often come as a shock to the newly independent. In the age of bulldozer parenting, this unit has grown to include everything from how to write a check, to how to respond to emails professionally and how much it will cost to live their anticipated lifestyle. Students are caught especially off guard by this last one.

For all the time youth spend in schools, they spend very little time discussing the responsibilities of adulthood and the expectations society has for its independent citizens. Perhaps rightly, these have been left under the purview of parents and local culture. However, that educational gap is often left unfilled.

For most youth, the expectations for transitioning from dependency to adulthood are vague or entirely absent. There is no broader cultural conversation of when this should occur and what, other than the passage of time, is required for becoming an adult. In the absence of any standard, more and more old adolescents come of age expecting all the privileges of adulthood with as few responsibilities as possible.

It is time we thought hard about what it means to become an adult and how society can best promote this progression. Without

278 SETTING THE BAR

reflection, it is unlikely we will create admirable adults with the tools to find fulfillment.

LOST IN THE FINITE. LOST IN THE INFINITE.

"To venture causes anxiety; not to venture is to lose oneself."
—*Soren Kierkegaard*

For most of human history children grew up with a clear model of adulthood. They were being groomed for one specific occupation: survivor. All members of the tribe worked hard to make sure each child was capable of succeeding in a rite of passage that clearly defined the transition from childhood to adulthood and proved their ability to meet the demands of the tribe, specifically, self-reliance and reliability.

The agricultural revolution expanded the number of occupations—farmers, scribes, smiths, etc.—but the majority of people still grew up with few options. Most people took on the same occupation as their parents and their parents before them. Models were obvious, expectations were clear, and the transition to adulthood was a natural extension of their upbringing.

This simple progression began to change after the industrial revolution, however. Suddenly, life was marked by constant change. The number of available occupations multiplied by the year as new technologies replaced old jobs and created new ones. People moved away from their birthplace more frequently and traditional expectations gave way to ever-expanding options for how one could live their life. Today, there are more possible paths than ever before.

The upside to all of these options is that we all have the ability to change our position in the world. We can chase dreams, seek new opportunities, and become almost anything—a doctor, lawyer, banker, marketer, engineer, teacher, insurance salesman, radio broadcaster, electrician, or, to give an example of the vague type of job most fall into today, a director of IT procurement for *7-11*. We can decide to follow any religion or ideology, move anywhere, marry anyone, and live in almost any way we want. Hell, some even decide to change their gender.

The downside to all these options is that humans are notoriously bad at dealing with too many choices. As psychologist Barry Schwartz showed in *The Paradox of Choice*, as the number of choices grows, we become far less rational. For example, in one study, 47% of doctors said they would delay an invasive hip surgery if one potentially helpful arthritis medication was available, but when a second option was made available only 28% would try out medication. Doctors who were happy to delay surgery when there was only one medication option, became convinced it was time to start cutting when a second medication option became available.

As has been shown repeatedly, having more options tends to lead us to our default option—a phenomenon often referred to as analysis paralysis. Give people more 401(k) investment options and they become less likely to invest. Promote more options at your grocery store sample table and people are less likely to make a purchase. And when you give people more options for how to live their lives, they become less likely to do any living at all.

The 19th-century Danish philosopher, Soren Kierkegaard believed that the dizzying number of options available to us in modern societies was leading people to become lost in both the finite and the infinite. Those lost in the infinite are paralyzed by the paradox of choice. The endless number of options and micro-options available in modern affluent societies leaves them anxiously toiling over each potential course and its opportunity costs. Absent a clear best path, they spin their wheels in endless contemplation. This is like a chess novice taking hours to move in hopes that she can think through every option. It is the 22-year-old college graduate who moves home waxing prolific about the things he will someday do, all the while spending his days scrolling social media, playing video games, and critiquing every aspect of a world he has never experienced.

But over-analysis is not the only cause for procrastination. We'll put off challenges for as long as we are allowed to. Unfortunately, there are more easy outs than ever—picking a college just because your friends are going there, living in Mom and Dad's basement, taking the safe job option, and staying long after you grow to resent it. Those lost in the infinite are usually also lost in the finite—the herd norms.

Overwhelmed by choice, the masses follow a broken default model that is supposed to make them happy. They deal with the abundance of worldviews by unquestioningly adopting the predominant patterns and beliefs of those around them. They deal with the infinite number of possible lifestyles by living like everyone else. Go to college. Get a job. Seek status through purchases and posts. Get married. Attend 12-thousand gender-reveal parties. Have kids. Take 73,521 pictures per week. Overprovide. Over protect. Subsist on industrial food. Stare at screens. Sit. Scroll. Buy. Die.

To be clear, work, college, marriage, having children, and embracing your local community can be among the most rewarding life choices you could ever make. But without intentionality, these are far less likely to be portals to depth and fulfillment than sources of regret and self-subjugation.

More people than ever are lost in the infinite, perpetually ignoring the actions they know are necessary, while also lost in the finite, doing what everyone else does because it feels comfortable and safe. But what could be more dangerous than wasting our lives?

For our children to transcend these traps, they'll need exposure to transformative experiences and clear deadlines. Without a clear expiration to childhood, youth are unlikely to accumulate the experiences that would be most meaningful and instructive.

A DEADLINE TO DEPENDENCY

"We often avoid taking action because we think "I need to learn more," but the best way to learn is often by taking action."
—*James Clear*

Parkinson's law states that work expands so as to fill the time available for its completion. Tasks tend to take as long as we allow them to take. We waste time, subconsciously rationalizing the need for every moment prior to a deadline and then, when we have to, we find a new level of focus. Likewise, childhood tends to last as long as we allow it to. All the pep-talks and "breakthrough" conversations in the world mean nothing without a real deadline for dependency. Adulthood cannot really begin until we have the ability to stand on our own two feet.

Age eighteen must mark the expectation of at least a semi-adulthood. Young adults need to direct their own life, suffer consequences, and bear the responsibility of adapting to challenges. Parents might still offer financial assistance, but, ideally, they would be phasing that out as well.

For parents who decide to pay for college or any other expenses, I highly recommend giving only a modest monthly or annual lump sum and requiring the young adult to manage all their own finances. For example, they will know that they get $8,000 per year through college for paying tuition, bills, etc. When the money runs out, they'll have to adapt. If a bill isn't paid on time, they'll deal with the consequences. The money is the gift and the rest is up to the burgeoning adult to figure out. They will look back on these short-term pains fondly for the lessons they brought.

Sooner than later, all young adults must be cut off. When, exactly is not for me to say. I know many families who have raised wonderful, successful adults by clearly communicating that each kid had exactly four years to graduate college, plus a six-month grace period. After that, they had to be moved out and financially independent. Many more have allowed four-years of free rent beginning at age 18, but nothing more. I know wonderful young adults who paid their parents rent during a transition period after college. For the more defiant, challenging young adults, it may be prudent to pull out the entire safety net at age 18 or 19. Sometimes sink or swim is the only lesson that gets through.

The specifics will differ, particularly if you heed my advice and question the college model. But while approaches vary, it is important to clearly communicate an expiration date for dependency and to commit to gradually phasing it out well before the end of high school.

Even if your kids float by for a couple years while living with friends and projecting a desire to never grow up, they will grow naturally from experiencing autonomy. They will learn to adapt and that they must bring some utility to their relationships or these quickly strain. Inevitably, they will be exposed to unfulfilling life choices and come to value the wisdom in their upbringing. Sometimes they just need to actually live in the world to finally appreciate what everyone has been trying to teach them their whole lives.

Author Mark Manson spent years living on friends' couches while on his way to becoming one of the best self-help authors of the modern day. Similarly, writer, Cal Fussman, spent 10-years traveling Europe and South America, with little money to his name. Each day he'd board the train knowing that he had to make such a great impression that one of the passengers would invite him over for a meal and lodging. Out of necessity, he developed a peerless skill for conversation and reading people that propelled him into a prolific journalism career.

Fussman and Manson rose to the top of their fields while experiencing life at a depth most never do, because they were allowed to create their own future absent of the parental safety net. Most people would prefer their children not take such vulnerable routes, but the point remains. Our children have to make their own way.

We so often forget that some of the most transformational lessons we can offer as parents come from simply refusing to enable dependency. We've all seen examples of the young adult who sets off to start working and living on his own only to quit and move home months later. The real world hit hard and he decided he'd rather return to the safety net. But removing that option would probably produce far more growth than the college experience that his parents spent $30,000 per year on. If your real desire is to help your children get an education, the best route is often to let them stand on their own two feet.

Many parents will talk themselves out of necessary tough love. With mature young adults, allowing a grace period for your kids to return home could be a wonderful gesture that helps them find their footing, particularly in an increasingly volatile world. But just because you allowed an older sibling to move back for a few months while they got their careers started doesn't mean all your kids need the same offer. It isn't a matter of fairness. It is a matter of optimal long-term development. What is the lesson he needs right now? What is the education that will make him best in the long-run? More dependency is rarely the answer.

And you can't wait too long. As we saw in chapter 3, it is essential to build antifragility in order to help your children build more resiliency and capability so that they are better able to overcome and learn from their inevitable challenges. But, according to Jonathan Haidt's, *The Happiness Hypothesis,* there is a time limit for when you are likely to benefit from your first major adversity. Haidt references the sociologist Glen Elder's analysis of people who lived through the Great Depression and World War II, writing that:

> Even young men who had not been doing well before serving in World War II often turned their lives around afterward, but people who faced their first real life test after the age of thirty (for example, combat in that war, or financial ruin in the Great Depression) were less resilient and less likely to grow from their experiences. So adversity may be most beneficial for people in their late teens and into their twenties.

It's worth noting that Elder also found that people did better in crises when they were connected to a community and were not also struggling with anomie.

It is hard to watch your kids struggle. You'd prefer they were more prepared. They will not have absorbed and applied all the lessons you hoped they would. But the final steps in their maturation require that they learn the hard way. Necessity tends to erode immaturity and evoke heightened levels of understanding.

For young adults to become admirable people, they must first become independent. They must take risks, chase worthy challenges, fail, and repeat. The greatest education is only available when we let youth fall and pick themselves up. Only then will they have the ability to lift others up.

THE HERO'S JOURNEY

"I don't believe people are looking for the meaning of life as much as they are looking for the experience of being alive."
—*Joseph Campbell*

Chris Rock does a great bit on the difference between a job and a career. As he explains:

> When you've got a career, there ain't enough time in the day.... When you got a career, you look at your watch, time just flies and you're like 'God damn! Whoa! It's 5:35. Damn, I gotta come in early tomorrow and work on my project.' Cause their ain't enough time, when you've got a career! But when you've got a job, there's too much time! You look at your watch like 'Ah shit. 9:08.'

Rock recounts working as a dishwasher at Red Lobster and playing the "time game." He'd say to himself, "I'm not going to look at my watch for two hours. I'm going to sit here and scrape these shrimp." He'd scrape shrimp fighting the urge to look at the clock until he was certain two hours had passed. Then he'd look. "Fuck! 15 minutes."

What Rock notes as the difference between a job and career, extends far beyond workplace endeavors. I spent plenty of my life playing the time game. Killing time, living on other people's terms, and seeking something to shake me back to life. Some degree of this is necessary education. Furthermore, even the best lives will require us to make sacrifices and do things we'd prefer to avoid. But it usually isn't the things we have to do that crush us. I think it is not knowing what we really want to do. It is not being curious, engaged, or driven toward any mission.

We've all had times in our life where we woke up and felt a sense of emptiness—a blah. Life lacked color, urgency, or fun. Work was a job. Relationships felt hollow. Discretionary time dull. Most spend the majority of their existence in this state. Their careers are a means to an end. Their free time is spent trying to fill that hole with pleasures that offer only momentary escape. They lack any sense of mission and the connections this would foster. They long to lose themselves in a worthy endeavor.

When you have a purpose, there is not enough time in a day. The number of projects, interests, and dreams surpasses your immediate faculties. This isn't the headlong pursuit to cross off checklists in pursuit of other people's approval. With a purpose, a fire burns. It isn't that you won't still face repetitive tasks and bullshit. But the juice is worth the squeeze. Life has an intensity that changes how you relate to it.

Unfortunately, purpose can't be handed to us. Over and over, I've found that the right path does not automatically present itself. It won't strike you like a lightning bolt and it is never a steady stream of progress. Life is messy and often requires us to undo our past work. We only find the right way by a constant cycle of action, feedback, reflection, and adaptation.

Ludwig Wittgenstein, a 20th century British philosopher, argued that there were objective truths even in regard to abstract concepts like quality, love, or beauty, but that language was entirely insufficient for revealing them. In his mind, asking someone to describe love, flow, purpose or any of life's most important concepts is completely futile. As host of the *Philosophize This* podcast, Stephen West, put it, "To Wittgenstein, asking a question like 'What is the meaning of my life?' is like inquiring: 'How much red paint would it take to be funnier than sound waves?' It just instantly shows the person's hand as someone that is confused about the limitations of language."

Truths often feel paradoxical because they transcend the bounds of language. By acting, you confront what is real. To be lost in the infinite is to be consumed by the maze of linguistic possibility, constantly confronting the dead-end of utopian delusions. Absent of a clear best path, the safest thing is to sit on the sidelines critiquing others. The modern world works hard to remove as much discomfort and unpredictability as possible. This is beautiful and miraculous, but too much comfort and predictability leave us ill-suited to create a meaningful life.

> *"Remembering that you are going to die is the best way I know to avoid the trap of thinking you have something to lose. You are already naked. There is no reason not to follow your heart."*
> —Steve Jobs

At the end of the day, youth development boils down to this question: What kind of people do we want to be?

Every five-year-old can answer this. Every Athenian, Spartan, or Cretan knew what constituted an admirable life. Every 19th century Lakota Sioux knew what they'd like to be capable of and how they'd like to be remembered. They knew who and what they'd die for, what was worth standing for, and what virtues they wanted to embody.

Children want to be the fighter pilot or the fireman rushing in to save people. They want to be a hero. They want to be capable of doing amazing things. Then, at some point along the way, they start wanting to be a YouTuber who gets rich and famous for their innate awesomeness. They want to avoid work and live opulently. Winning the lottery seems like an ideal life. Yet, we know such dreams won't breed fulfillment.

This is your only life. Each day that goes by is gone, leading you closer to the fate that awaits us all. On your deathbed, what pursuits will have mattered? What is worth the cost of your life? We all pay in one way or another.

We tend to shy away from harsh realities like death. But grappling with our impermanence and other universal human experiences gives essential context that should color our worldview. The human experience is hard and beautiful. We must slowly acquaint our kids with this realistic view of reality.

Despite the egocentric notions that naturally drive our early conceptions of the world, none of us are cosmically special. None of us are entitled to anything. In the infinite scope of time and space, we are infinitesimally small. I don't say this as a call to hedonism or nihilism. Nothing has proven to be less gratifying over time. We can choose to see the amazing size and scope of our world as evidence of our insignificance, or as a call to embrace our humanity and stand in awe of the grandeur that we are a part of.

After seeing an image of earth captured by the Voyager space probe, Carl Sagan noted that all the hopes and dreams of every human who has ever lived are contained on a small, "pale blue dot." If anything, this is a rallying cry—a truly unifying notion. We are part of an amazing, rare, and fragile heritage.

There is an immense legacy of human heroism preceding us. That is who we were born to be. We are meant to live engaged, connected, and guided by a purpose larger than us! You may not be special, but the opportunity to live truly is. Your nature demands that you find missions that are worthy of this gift.

YOUR MISSION, IF YOU CHOOSE TO ACCEPT IT

"These (peak experiences) are moments in which you are lifted out of the daily grind and you sense that there is something larger and more sublime in life that you have been missing . . . . These moments can come from exerting yourself past what you thought were your limits. They can come from overcoming great obstacles . . . . You want to deliberately go in search of such moments. Stimulate them if you can. They have the effect . . . of altering your attitude for good. They expand what you think about your possibilities and about life itself, and the memory is something you will always return to for extreme inspiration."

—*Robert Greene*

While not the most talented athlete, Brian Kim was always one of the hardest workers in the Mansfield High School football program. He never skipped a rep in the weight room, never let up early on a sprint, never lost eye contact when a coach spoke, and never pouted about playing time. This same commitment to excellence helped him earn a top ten class rank and admission into the University of Texas where he studied finance and mathematics with a certificate in applied statistical modeling.

After his first year of college, Brian came back to visit and wrapped me in a big hug. At 19, he spoke with more confidence and maturity than most school employees. Still, he kept insisting that the lessons he learned from his high school coaches were most responsible for his impressive college transition. He named coach after coach recounting specific lessons each had conveyed. But even the greatest programs don't pump out Brian-caliber people. Something about Brian made him receptive to every instructive nugget any coach or teacher uttered. If coaches were able to help Brian, it is because seeds were sown well before he got to us. Kudos to you Mr. and Mrs. Kim.

Two years later, Brian was preparing to ride his bike from Austin, Texas to Anchorage, Alaska as part of the Texas 4000 charity to raise money for cancer. On the charity website, he explained his reasons for riding:

> Life is not defined by adversity. It is defined by your response to it. Throughout my four years playing high school football, Coach Daniel Maberry ingrained this adage into our team. However, I would not comprehend the true meaning of those words until the winter of 2018, when Coach Maberry was diagnosed with stage IV lymphoma.
>
> I had the chance to go see him in person last Christmas break and Coach Maberry greeted me with the same warmth and enthusiasm he'd always displayed when I was in high school. If it wasn't for the antiviral face mask he was wearing or the lack of hair from chemotherapy treatments,

no one would have ever known this man had been battling lymphoma for the majority of the last 12 months. When facing his diagnosis, Coach Maberry led by example, practiced what he preached, and redefined his adversity through his actions and his response to cancer. His toughness, resolve, and positivity over the past year has taught me everything I need to know about what it means to be a leader and a mentor . . . .

In a way, I feel that joining Texas 4000 wasn't a personal decision. Rather, it's a fulfillment of an unspoken obligation to give back to Coach Maberry after all he's done for me.

Sadly, Coach Daniel Maberry lost his fight with lymphoma in February of 2020, at the age of 47. He was a great friend and among the most honorable husbands, fathers, and men I've ever known. Thousands came to his funeral to pay tribute to this life well lived. A couple of months later, Brian's ride was cancelled due to the coronavirus lockdown, but it resumed again in the summer of 2021.

Regardless of how much money the Texas 4000 raises each year, those who ride are the primary beneficiaries. Riding through heat, cold, rain, and mountains, they overcome barriers, create lifetime bonds only possible through shared challenge, and see the world in a way most never could. They will live differently because of these experiences. Adversities and unfortunate events will still happen, but they'll respond with more confidence and more ability to find meaning in the trial.

We all need a mission. Not in order to make the world a better place (although that might be a consequence), but because that is where peak existence lies. This is why people love to shop for other people and love group scavenger hunts. For a brief moment, these projects put us back on the Savannah with a mission that is bigger than ourselves. But Christmas lists aren't enough to sustain us. We need pursuits that stretch us past our comfort zone and give us a sense that we are becoming more.

As children, we are constantly put in new environments—new schools, new sports teams, new classes, new teachers, new skills, new chores, new emotions, new relationships. But suddenly, that all stops. By 30, most people are done with new. We aren't learning new sports like tennis or Brazilian Jiu-jitsu or taking on new skills like the piano or a cooking class. We have the ability to cocoon ourselves in our comfort zones. Same boss, same job, same friends, same daily interactions and an endless cycle of wake, work, TV, bed. Life is busy and this is where social momentum tends to carry us.

If we want to create a more impressive generation, we must become more impressive. If we want our children to live with passion and to chase great missions, then we have to go first. Our model is the most powerful gift we can offer the next generation. As parents and leaders, we can't conceive of ourselves as having reached some mythical endpoint where our purpose is now to simply remain accessible—the wise oracle, spouting wisdom.

We are made for missions which must be replenished as frequently as they are exhausted. What was the last scary challenge you took on? What is worth the inconvenience of effort, sacrifice, and all those antecedents of passion? Life is too short to be normal.

Acknowledgments

This book would not be possible without the immense support of many people. I don't know how I lucked into such an amazing cast of supporters, mentors, and friends, but I am forever grateful to all those who have encouraged, listened, advised and cared for me throughout this process. First, I would like to thank everyone who took the time to read this or anything I've written over the years. It means the world.

To Phil White, thank you for going above and beyond to mentor me. There was no good reason to give me as much time and energy as you have. Your support, direction, and genuine care have been invaluable throughout my years writing this book. I could never repay you, but hope to someday have the opportunity to help someone else as much as you've helped me.

I want to thank Omid and Mindith Rahmat. Mindith, your note after my first article on the need for educational reform sparked the belief I needed to commit to this dream. The opportunity to write for Breaking Muscle fueled my love for writing again and connected me with many wonderful people. Omid, I truly don't know what I did to deserve such amazing support and mentorship, but your wisdom has been invaluable to this project and so many other areas of my life. You are both amazing people and I'm grateful for your immense support.

Justin Lind, I cannot imagine a better friend, business partner, or person. Your fingerprints are all over this book. Hundreds of tiny conversations helped cultivate the thoughts that made this possible. Hundreds of edits on this and my past articles helped refine the style, clarity, and vision of this book. More than anyone, you've been a part of the intellectual evolution that made this book possible. I don't think I'll ever be able to repay you for the amount of generosity, sacrifice, and support you've offered. Thank you, brother.

Mom and Dad. It goes without saying, but none of this would exist without you. In fact, I would not exist without you. More to the point, so much of my passion, sense of purpose, and my worldview are a consequence of your wonderful upbringing. Dad, your early feedback was wonderful, but even more important has been the steady stream of feedback over a lifetime. I love you both!

Griffin and Orion Trotter, I can never repay you for your support and loyalty. Having y'all in my corner has been a source of energy, inspiration, and conviction.

Aunt Amy Jarecki. It doesn't hurt to have an author in the family, but your wisdom and care went far beyond anything I could have hoped for. It was a reminder of how lucky I am to have such amazing people in my family.

Brooke Maddaford and Patti Elliot, thank you both for your genuine care and great insights throughout the editing process. You both went above and beyond to help me communicate better.

Timm Bryson, you were so easy to work with and did such a wonderful job with the book design. Thank you for bringing this project home with such professionalism and mastery.

Ben Altman and Zach Pashea, thank you both for your tremendous feedback, but even more for your friendship and the examples you both set of what it means to live well.

To my awesome in-laws, the Cowen and Muse clans, thank you for taking me in with such love, and for your good humor, and steadfast support.

And, of course, Neely, Ace, and Brix. Y'all are my everything. Ace and Brix, the thought of you two has always been my greatest motivation. I love you and hope more than anything that I've done right by you, here. Neely, no one has borne the brunt of this project as much as you. Thank you for keeping our world running, for being the best mother ever for our kids, for thousands of crucial insights, and for loving me so completely. And sorry about not refilling the soap in the dish scrubber. There is no one I'd rather do life with. Love you like a mermaid.

Endnotes

CHAPTER 1

Criticizing the waltz
Swanson, Ana. "7 Totally Normal Things We Used to Say Only Immature Young People Did." The Washington Post. WP Company, April 29, 2019. www.washingtonpost.com

Stumbling on Happiness, by Dan Gilbert
Gilbert, Daniel Todd. *Stumbling on Happiness*. New York, NY: Vintage Books, 2007, 146.

Obesity has tripled in youth since 1970
"Obesity." Centers for Disease Control and Prevention. Centers for Disease Control and Prevention, September 18, 2018. www.cdc.gov.

Harvard - over half of US Children will have obesity if trends continue
"More than Half of U.S. Children Will Have Obesity as Adults If Current Trends Continue." News, June 22, 2018. www.hsph.harvard.edu.

Increase in teen depression
Schrobsdorff, Susanna. "Teen Depression on the Rise Says New Pediatrics Study." *Time*. Time, November 16, 2016. www.time.com.

Increase in youth severe impairment
Merikangas, Kathleen Ries, Jian-Ping He, Marcy Burstein, Sonja A Swanson, Shelli Avenevoli, Lihong Cui, Corina Benjet, Katholiki Georgiades, and Joel Swendsen. "Lifetime Prevalence of Mental Disorders in U.S. Adolescents: Results from the National Comorbidity Survey Replication--Adolescent Supplement (NCS-A)." *Journal of the American Academy of Child and Adolescent Psychiatry. U.S. National Library of Medicine*, October 2010. www.ncbi.nlm.nih.gov.

Increase in youth suicides
Ruch, Donna A, Arielle H Sheftall, Paige Schlagbaum, Joseph Rausch, John V Campo, and Jeffrey A Bridge. "Trends in Suicide Among Youth Aged 10 to 19 Years in the United States, 1975 to 2016." JAMA network open. *American Medical Association*, May 3, 2019. www.ncbi.nlm.nih.gov.

Increase in teen depression
Twenge, Jean. "Teenage Depression and Suicide Are Way up - and so Is Smartphone Use." *The Washington Post*. WP Company, November 19, 2017. www.washingtonpost.com.

Suicide second leading cause of death for ages 15-34
National Vital Statistics System, National Center for Health Statistics, CDC. Produced by: National Center for Injury Prevention and Control, CDC using WISQARS™.

Drug overdose deaths
"Drug Overdose Deaths." Centers for Disease Control and Prevention. Centers for Disease Control and Prevention, March 19, 2020. www.cdc.gov.

School shootings
Riedman, David. "Incidents by Year." K-12 School Shooting Database, June 14, 2019. www.chds.us.

iGen, Jean Twenge
Twenge, Jean M. "Have Smartphones Destroyed a Generation?" *The Atlantic*. March 19, 2018. www.theatlantic.com.

Victoria Prooday on parenting trends
Prooday, Victoria. "Kids Are Bored, Entitled, Have Little Patience & Few Friends." *Deep Roots at Home*. August 13, 2018. deeprootsathome.com.

Wilt Chamberlain's 100-point game and Mark Granovetter's theory of thresholds
"Revisionist History Episode 03." Revisionist History. Accessed January 10, 2020. revisionisthistory.com.

Defaults and blood donor decisions
Johnson, Eric J., and Daniel G. Goldstein. "Defaults and donation decisions." Transplantation 78, no. 12 (2004): 1713-1716.

Mark Manson on compound learning
Manson, Mark. "Mindf*Ck Monday." *Markmanson.net*, December 29, 2019. www.markmanson.net.

CHAPTER 2
Ethan, Fred, and Tonya Couch
Mooney, Michael J. "The Worst Parents Ever." *D Magazine*, May 2015.

Born to Run, Christopher McDougall
McDougall, Christopher. *Born to Run: A Hidden Tribe, Superathletes, and the Greatest Race the World Has Never Seen*. New York: Alfred A. Knopf, 2016, 180.

Best shoes, Kelly Starrett
Starrett, Kelly. "Keep Your Kid's Heels on the Ground | Feat. Kelly Starrett | Mobility-WOD." YouTube. May 28, 2012. www.youtube.com.

Parenting through the ages, Dan Carlin
Carlin, Dan. *The End Is Always near: Apocalyptic Moments, from the Bronze Age Collapse to Nuclear near Misses*. New York, NY: Harper, an imprint of HarperCollins Publishers, 2020.

Parenting for grit, Angela Duckworth
Duckworth, Angela. *Grit*. London: Vermilion, 2019.

Victoria Prooday, The Silent Tragedy Affecting Today's Youth
"The Silent Tragedy Affecting Today's Children." Victoria Prooday. May 24, 1970. Accessed August 18, 2018. www.yourot.com.

Kyle Maynard's father
Maynard, Kyle. "'My Grandma Told Me That Once I Shake Someone's Hand, My Disability Goes Away.'" OptionB.Org. Accessed February 15, 2021. www.optionb.org.

Kyle Maynard's grandmother
Tribe of Mentors: Short Life Advice from the Best in the World. Boston: Houghton Mifflin Harcourt Publishing Company, 2018, 15.

CHAPTER 3
Theodore Roosevelt's upbringing
Brett, and Kate McKay. "Childhood of Theodore Roosevelt." The Art of Manliness. November 16, 2017.

Millionaires with dyslexia
Flanagan, Ben. "Who Wants to Be a Millioniare?" *The Guardian*. Guardian News and Media, October 4, 2003. www.theguardian.com.

Discipline Equals Freedom, Jocko Willink
Willink, Jocko. *Discipline Equals Freedom: Field Manual* . New York: St. Martin's, 2020, 39.

Antifragile, Nassim Taleb
Taleb, Nassim Nicholas. *Antifragile: Things That Gain from Disorder*. New York: Random House, 2016.

The hygiene hypothesis and auto-immune disorders
Okada, H, C Kuhn, H Feillet, and J-F Bach. "The 'Hygiene Hypothesis' for Autoimmune and Allergic Diseases: an Update." *Clinical and experimental immunology*. *Blackwell Science Inc*, April 2010. www.ncbi.nlm.nih.gov.

Stumbling on Happiness, Dan Gilbert
Gilbert, Daniel Todd. *Stumbling on Happiness*. New York, NY: Vintage Books, 2007, 166.

The Three Great Untruths, Jonathan Haidt and Greg Lukianoff
Lukianoff, Greg, and Jonathan Haidt. *The Coddling of the American Mind How Good Intentions and Bad Ideas Are Setting up a Generation for Failure*. New York City: Penguin Books, 2019, 4.

John Roberts commencement speech
Reilly, Katie. "John Roberts Commencement Speech: Read the Transcript." *Time*, July 5, 2017. www.time.com.

Theodore Roosevelt on Roosevelt Sr.
Grondahl, Paul. *I Rose Like a Rocket: The Political Education of Theodore Roosevelt.*
Free Press, 2015, 54.

CHAPTER 4

Utah free range parent law
Coleman, Korva. "Utah's 'Free-Range' Parenting Law Protects Parents So Kids Can
Roam." NPR. NPR, April 1, 2018. www.npr.org.

Crime declining
Skenazy, Lenore, Jonathan Haidt, and Irshad Manji. "Let Grow Takes a Look at the
Truth About Crime Statistics." Let Grow, February 11, 2021. www.letgrow.org.

Is your child ready for first grade checklist
Lukianoff, Greg, and Jonathan Haidt. *The Coddling of the American Mind How Good
Intentions and Bad Ideas Are Setting up a Generation for Failure.* New York City:
Penguin Books, 2019, 187.

By 1990 48% fewer kids die in accidents
Lukianoff, Greg, and Jonathan Haidt. *The Coddling of the American Mind How Good
Intentions and Bad Ideas Are Setting up a Generation for Failure.* New York City:
Penguin Books, 2019.

Mother investigated for letting kids play in backyard
Staff, CTVNews.ca. "Mother Says She Was Investigated Over Children Playing in
Backyard." www.ctvnews.ca, April 22, 2016. www.ctvnews.ca.

Mom arrested for letting 9-year-old play at park
Friedersdorf, Conor. "Working Mom Arrested for Letting Her 9-Year-Old
Play Alone at Park." *The Atlantic.* Atlantic Media Company, July 16, 2014.
www.theatlantic.com.

Mother charged for running into store
Person. "The Day I Left My Son in the Car." Salon. Salon.com, August 5, 2020.
www.salon.com.

Liability and safetyism
Howard, Philip K. *The Lost Art of Drawing the Line: How Fairness Went Too Far.* New
York: Random House, 2001.

The vital role of play in human development, Dr. Peter Gray
Gray, Peter. "The Decline of Play and the Rise of Psychopathology in Children and Adolescents." *American Journal of Play* 3, no. 4 (2011): 443–63.
www.psychologytoday.com..

Attachment theory
Haidt, Jonathan. *The Happiness Hypothesis: Finding Modern Truth in Ancient Wisdom.*
New York City, New York: Basic Book, 2006.

Kids dosing themselves with appropriate degrees of fear, Dr. Peter Gray
Gray, Peter. *Free to Learn: Why Unleashing the Instinct to Play Will Make Our Children Happier, More Self-Reliant, and Better Students for Life.* New York: Basic Books, 2015.

Piaget water glass experiment
Haidt, Jonathan. *The Righteous Mind: Why Good People Are Divided by Politics and Religion.* New York: Pantheon books, 2012.

E.O. Wilson, soccer moms and FAA pilot accidents
Taleb, Nassim Nicholas. *Antifragile: Things That Gain from Disorder.* New York: Random House, 2016.

Naked streets movement
"The Removal of Road Markings Is to Be Celebrated. We Are Safer without Them Simon Jenkins." *The Guardian.* Guardian News and Media, February 4, 2016. www.theguardian.com.

Increase in distal forearm fractures
Jerrhag, Daniel, Martin Englund, Ingmar Petersson, Vasileios Lempesis, Lennart Landin, Magnus K Karlsson, and Bjorn E Rosengren. "Increasing Wrist Fracture Rates in Children May Have Major Implications for Future Adult Fracture Burden." *Acta Orthopaedica* 87, no. 3 (2016): 296–300. doi.org/10.3109/17453674.2016.1152855.

Self-esteem analysis, Baumeister et. all
Baumeister, Roy F., Jennifer D. Campbell, Joachim I. Krueger, and Kathleen D. Vohs. "Does High Self-Esteem Cause Better Performance, Interpersonal Success, Happiness, or Healthier Lifestyles?" *Psychological Science in the Public Interest* 4, no. 1 (2003): 1–44. doi.org/10.1111/1529-1006.01431.

Good vs. bad self-esteem
"A Framework for Balancing in Article 81 EC." *Article 81 EC and Public Policy*, 2011, 560–68. doi.org/10.4992/jjpsy.81.560.

CHAPTER 5
Best interview question, Peter Thiel
Thiel, Peter, and Blake Masters. *Zero to One Notes on Startups, or How to Build the Future.* London: Virgin Books, 2015.

Docile humans, Yuval Noah Harari
Harari, Yuval Noah. *21 Lessons for the 21st Century.* Melbourne, Victoria: CAE Book Groups, 2019.

Self-actualization, Maslow
"Abraham Maslow and the Psychology of Self-Actualization." *Academy of Ideas | Free Minds for a Free Society*, April 22, 2020. academyofideas.com

Eudaimonia
Gilbert, Daniel Todd. *Stumbling on Happiness.* New York, NY: Vintage Books, 2007.

Rat park, Bruce Alexander
Alexander, Bruce. "Rat Park." Addiction: The View from Rat Park (2010). Accessed February 17, 2021. www.brucekalexander.com

Mental health improves in crisis, Sebastian Junger
Junger, Sebastian. *Tribe: On Homecoming and Belonging.* S.l.: Grand Central Pub, 2018.

Values as preference hierarchies and Edward Bernays, Mark Manson
Manson, Mark. *Everything Is f*Cked: a Book about Hope.* New York City, New York: Harper, 2019.

Television consumption after World War II
Putnam, Robert. "The Strange Disappearance of Civic America." *The American Prospect,* December 19, 2001. prospect.org.

4 to 10,000 advertisements seen per day
Simpson, Jon. "Council Post: Finding Brand Success In The Digital World." *Forbes.* Forbes Magazine, August 25, 2017. www.forbes.com.

1955 Journal of Retailing, Victor Lebow
Lebow, Victor. "Price Competition in 1955." *http://www.gcafh.org/edlab/Lebow.pdf.* Accessed December 30, 2018. http://www.gcafh.org.

"Good" and "bad" values, Mark Manson
Manson, Mark. *The Subtle Art of Not Giving a Fu*k: a Counterintuitive Approach to Living a Good Life.* New York, NY: HarperCollins Publishers, 2016.

Education to counter mass marketing, Dorothy Sayers
Sayers, Dorothy Leigh. *The Lost Tools of Learning. Paper Read at a Vacation Course in Education, Oxford, 1947.* London, 1948.

CHAPTER 6

2015-2020 Dietary Guidelines for Americans Report
"Executive Summary." Chapter 6 Fats. Accessed September 21, 2018. health.gov.

38% of Americans obese
"Obesity." *Centers for Disease Control and Prevention. Centers for Disease Control and Prevention,* September 18, 2018. https://www.cdc.gov/healthyschools/obesity/index.htm.

Harvard, over half of US children will have obesity if trends continue
"More than Half of U.S. Children Will Have Obesity as Adults If Current Trends Continue." *Harvard News,* June 22, 2018. www.hsph.harvard.edu.

Rats and sugar studies
Lenoir, Magalie, Fuschia Serre, Lauriane Cantin, and Serge H. Ahmed. "Intense Sweet-ness Surpasses Cocaine Reward." *Current Neurology and Neuroscience Reports.* 2007. Accessed September 21, 2018. www.ncbi.nlm.nih.gov

Food giants, battle of the Bettys - Salt, Sugar, Fat, Michael Moss
Moss, Michael. *Salt, Sugar, Fat: How the Food Giants Hooked Us.* New York: Random House Trade Paperbacks, 2014.

College costs 1957, 1958
"When Congress Went to College." Demos, February 15, 2018. www.demos.org.

Internet ad revenue 2019
"Internet Advertising Revenue Report: Full Year 2019 Results & Q1 2020 Revenues." *Interactive Advertising Bureau,* May 2020. www.iab.com.

Tristan Harris tricks of the trade
Harris, Tristan. "How Technology Is Hijacking Your Mind-from a Former Insider." Medium. Thrive Global, October 16, 2019. medium.com/thriveglobal.

Media and children
"Media and Children." services.aap.org. Accessed March 22, 2021. services.aap.org

Teen screen time common sense media report
"Landmark Report: U.S. Teens Use an Average of Nine Hours of Media Per Day, Tweens Use Six Hours: Common Sense Media." Common Sense Media: Ratings, reviews, and advice, November 3, 2015. www.commonsensemedia.org

Victoria Prooday, costs of screen time
Jacqueline. "Reasons Today's Kids Are Bored, Entitled, Impatient with Few Real Friends." Deep Roots at Home, February 5, 2021. deeprootsathome.com.

Smartphone and poor mental health correlation
Twenge, Jean. "With Teen Mental Health Deteriorating over Five Years, There's a Likely Culprit." *The Conversation,* The Conversation, 23 Aug. 2018, theconversation.com

An open source literature review posted by Jean Twenge and Jonathan Haidt
Haidt, J., & Twenge, J. (2021). *Is there an increase in adolescent mood disorders, self-harm, and suicide since 2010 in the USA and UK? A review.* Unpublished manuscript, New York University.

Study suggesting increased time on social media does not cause depression
Coyne, Sarah M., Adam A. Rogers, Jessica D. Zurcher, Laura Stockdale, and McCall Booth. "Does Time Spent Using Social Media Impact Mental Health?: An Eight Year Longitudinal Study." Pergamon, October 10, 2019. www.sciencedirect.com.

U.S. 45% of global pharmaceutical sales
Finn, Michael. Issue brief. *Legacy.trade.gov.* International Trade Administration, May 2016. legacy.trade.gov.

Bad Pharma, Ben Goldacre
Goldacre, Ben. *Bad Pharma: How Drug Companies Mislead Doctors and Harm Patients*. New York: Faber and Faber, 2014.

Adderall broadcasting the desire for ADD for all
Schwarz, Alan. "The Selling of Attention Deficit Disorder." *The New York Times*. The New York Times, December 14, 2013. www.nytimes.com.

ADHD Nation, Alan Schwarz
Schwarz, Alan. *ADHD Nation: Children, Doctors, Big Pharma, and the Making of an American Epidemic*. New York: Scribner, an imprint of Simon & Schuster, Inc., 2017.

Dog-shit alley, Lost Connections, Johann Hari
Hari, Johann. *Lost Connections: Why You're Depressed and How to Find Hope*. London: Bloomsbury, 2018.

CHAPTER 7

The Circle
Eggers, Dave. *The Circle: a Novel*. New York: Vintage Books, Random House LLC, 2014.

Cobra effects
Greene, Robert. *The Laws of Human Nature*. New York: Penguin Books, 2019.

The riddle of history solved
Marx, Karl. Private Property and Communism, Marx, 1844. www.marxists.org.

Classical worldview vs. Descartes
Howland, Jacob and Brett McKay. "Podcast #628: The Rise of Secular Religion and the New Puritanism." The Art of Manliness. Brett McKay, June 20, 2020. www.artofmanliness.com.

The Lessons of History
Durant, Will, and Ariel Durant. *The Lessons of History by Will and Ariel Durant*. New York: Simon and Schuster, 1968.

Antibullyism
Kalman, Izzy. "Teaching in the Age of Antibullyism." *Psychology Today*. Sussex Publishers, March 23, 2020. www.psychologytoday.com.
Kalman, Izzy. "Does Informing Schools on Bullying Make It Better or Worse?" *Psychology Today*. Sussex Publishers, October 9, 2019. www.psychologytoday.com.
Kalman, Izzy. "Why Is the Anti-Bully Movement Failing? MercatorNet, May 13, 2020. mercatornet.com.

Blue dot study
Specktor, Brandon. "Are These Dots Purple, Blue or Proof That Humans Will Never Be Happy?" LiveScience. Purch, July 2, 2018. www.livescience.com.
Levari, David E., Daniel T. Gilbert, Timothy D. Wilson, Beau Sievers, David M. Amodio, and Thalia Wheatley. "Prevalence-Induced Concept Change in Human Judgment." American Association for the Advancement of Science, June 29, 2018. science.sciencemag.org.

Bill Maher
Maher, Bill. "Real Time with Bill Maher." Episode. 16, no. 12. Los Angeles, California: HBO, April 20, 2018.

Programming mental distortions of CBT
Lukianoff, Greg, and Jonathan Haidt. *The Coddling of the American Mind How Good Intentions and Bad Ideas Are Setting up a Generation for Failure.* New York City: Penguin Books, 2019.

We all live on campus now
Sullivan, Andrew. "We All Live on Campus Now." *Intelligencer.* Intelligencer, February 9, 2018. nymag.com.

Theodore Dalrymple on historiography
Dalrymple, Theodore. "Against History-as-Nightmare." *Law & Liberty*, August 11, 2020. lawliberty.org.

The Lost Art of Drawing the Line, Philip K. Howard on law
Howard, Philip K. *The Lost Art of Drawing the Line: How Fairness Went Too Far.* New York: Random House, 2001.

Over 80% of Americans think political correctness is a problem
Mounk, Yascha. "Americans Strongly Dislike PC Culture." *The Atlantic.* Atlantic Media Company, October 30, 2018. www.theatlantic.com.

Philip K. Howard TED talk
Howard, Philip K. "Four Ways to Fix a Broken Legal System." TED. Accessed February 24, 2021. www.ted.com.

Righteous Mind Quotes
Haidt, Jonathan. *The Righteous Mind: Why Good People Are Divided by Politics and Religion.* New York: Pantheon books, 2012.

CHAPTER 8

Anders Tegnell Quote
Anderson, Christina, and Henrik Pryser Libell. "In the Coronavirus Fight in Scandinavia, Sweden Stands Apart." *The New York Times.* March 28, 2020. www.nytimes.com.

Sweden COVID response
Sayers, Freddie. "What We Can Learn from the Swedish Paradox." UnHerd, September 8, 2020. unherd.com.

Sweden health
Arnold, Katie. "What Sweden Teaches Us About Parenting and the Outdoors." Outside Online, December 12, 2017. www.outsideonline.com.

Alexis de Tocqueville
Crawford, Matthew B. *Why We Drive: Toward a Philosophy of the Open Road.* New York, NY: Harper Large Print, an imprint of HarperCollins Publishers, 2020.

Bowling Alone - community deterioration
Putnam, Robert. Bowling Alone. Simon & Schuster, 2000.

Increased television consumption
Putnam, Robert. "The Strange Disappearance of Civic America." *The American Prospect*, December 19, 2001. prospect.org.

Social capital
Haidt, Jonathan. *The Righteous Mind: Why Good People Are Divided by Politics and Religion*. New York: Pantheon books, 2012.

Dunbar's number
"Dunbar's Number: Why We Can Only Maintain 150 Relationships." BBC Future. BBC. Accessed July 15, 2021. www.bbc.com.

Why We Drive, Matthew Crawford
Crawford, Matthew B. *Why We Drive: Toward a Philosophy of the Open Road*. New York, NY: Harper Large Print, an imprint of HarperCollins Publishers, 2020.

Idiocracy
Judge, Mike, Mike Judge, Elysa Koplovitz, and Etan Cohen. *Idiocracy*, n.d.

Wall-E
Stanton, Andrew, Jim Morris, Jim Reardon, Ben Burtt, Elissa Knight, and Jeff Garlin. *WALL-E*, n.d.

CHAPTER 9
Loss of shared moral sense increases anomie
Haidt, Jonathan. *The Happiness Hypothesis: Finding Modern Truth in Ancient Wisdom*. New York City, New York: Basic Book, 2006.

Why Honor Matters, honor vs. dignity culture
Sommers, Tamler. *Why Honor Matters*. New York: Basic Books, 2018.

Matthew Crawford, Why We Drive
Crawford, Matthew B. *Why We Drive: Toward a Philosophy of the Open Road*. New York, NY: Harper Large Print, an imprint of HarperCollins Publishers, 2020.

Standards for blue collar work crews, Jordan Peterson
Peterson, Jordan B., Van Ethan Sciver, and Norman Doidge. *12 Rules for Life: An Antidote to Chaos*. Toronto: Vintage Canada, 2020.

Frederick Douglass speech
Blessings of Liberty and Education, Frederick Douglass, September 3, 1894. Public domain, from The Art Institute of Chicago.

Westboro Baptist Church
Phelps-Roper, Megan. *Unfollow: a Journey from Hatred to Hope, Leaving the Westboro Baptist Church*. London: Riverun, 2020.

Zen and the Art of Motorcycle Maintenance
Pirsig, R. *Zen and the Art of Motorcycle Maintenance: an Inquiry into Values*. Bt Bound, 2005.

Public-mindedness, First Principles
Ricks, Thomas E. *First Principles: What America's Founders Learned from the Greeks and Romans and How That Shaped Our Country*. New York, NY: Harper, an imprint of HarperCollins Publishers, 2020.

CHAPTER 9B
Pre-schoolers in Sweden outside six hours per day
Arnold, Katie. "What Sweden Teaches Us About Parenting and the Outdoors." Outside Online, December 12, 2017. www.outsideonline.com.

Victoria Prooday on educational screen-time
Victoria Prooday, Occupational Therapist. "10 Most Common Parental Misconceptions." Victoria Prooday. Victoria Prooday, January 30, 2018. yourot.com

AAP family media plan
"Media-and-Children." healthychildren.org, www.aap.org.

Center for Humane Technology
"Take Control." Center for Humane Technology. Accessed March 23, 2021. www.humanetech.com.

Wait Until 8th
Wait Until 8th. Accessed March 23, 2021. www.waituntil8th.org.

CHAPTER 10
Bret Weinstein on Rubin Report
Life After Evergreen, Evolutionary Biology, and Gender, Bret Weinstein, ACADEMIA, Rubin Report, 2018. youtu.be.

Dan Carlin on History on Fire
Bolelli, Daniele, and Dan Carlin. BONUS EPISODE Dan Carlin's "The End is Always Near". Other, December 18, 2019. http://historyonfirepodcast.com.

Stanley Milgram experiments
Mcleod, Saul. "The Milgram Shock Experiments." *Simply Psychology*. February 05, 2017. www.simplypsychology.org.

John McCain
Relman, Eliza. "As a POW in Vietnam, John McCain Refused Release until His Fellow Prisoners Were Freed, Making Him a Hero in the Eyes of Many." *Business Insider*. August 26, 2018. www.businessinsider.com.

Kidnapping of Nicholas Markowitz
Fox, Sue. "Kidnap Victim Could Have Fled, Witnesses Testify." *Los Angeles Times*. November 01, 2001. articles.latimes.com.

Alpha Dog
Cassavetes, Nick, Sidney Kimmel, and Chuck Pacheco. *Alpha Dog*. United States: Universal Pictures, 2007

Alpha Dog characters based on
Lang, Kevin. "Alpha Dog Movie vs True Story of Real Johnny Truelove, Frankie Ballenbacher." HistoryvsHollywood.com. May 14, 2018. Accessed December 13, 2018. http://www.historyvshollywood.com.

Genome editing
Cribbs, Adam P, and Sumeth M W Perera. "Science and Bioethics of CRISPR-Cas9 Gene Editing: An Analysis Towards Separating Facts and Fiction." *The Yale journal of biology and medicine*. YJBM, December 19, 2017. www.ncbi.nlm.nih.gov.

3D bio-printers
Dvorsky, George. "Scientists Just 3D Printed a Transplantable Human Ear." *Gizmodo*. February 15, 2016. gizmodo.com.

Dr. Nick Bostrum, black ball technologies
Bostrum, Nick. "The Vulnerable World Hypothesis." *Global Policy* 10, no. 4 (November 2019): 455–76. nickbostrom.com.

Daniel Schmachtenberger, 1st, 2nd, 3rd person epistemics
"DarkHorse Podcast with Daniel Schmachtenberger & Bret Weinstein." YouTube, February 10, 2021. youtu.be/YPJug0s2u4w.

CHAPTER 11

Marva Collins Way
Collins, Marva, and Civia Tamarkin. *Marva Collins' Way: Returning to Excellence in Education*. Jeremy P. Tarcher, 1990.

Easy teachers hurt future student performance
Insler, Michael and McQuoid, Alexander F. and Rahman, Ahmed and Smith, Katherine A., Fear and Loathing in the Classroom: Why Does Teacher Quality Matter?. IZA Discussion Paper No. 14036, Available at SSRN: ssrn.com.

U.S. Department of Education's 2001 Baccalaureate and Beyond Longitudinal Survey
Cloud, John. "What Makes a School Great." Time. September 23, 2010. content.time.com.

Finland, South Korea, Singapore attract top teachers
Auguste, Byron, Matt Miller, and Paul Kihn. *Closing The Talent Gap: Attracting and Retaining Top-Third Graduates to Careers in Teaching*. McKinsey and Company, 2010.

Sir Ken Robinson quote
Robinson, Sir Ken. "How to Escape Education's Death Valley." TED. Accessed March 3, 2021. www.ted.com.

Absent Teacher Reserve, back to classroom
Taylor, Kate. "Caught Sleeping or Worse, Troubled Teachers Will Return to New York Classrooms." *The New York Times*. The New York Times, October 13, 2017. www.nytimes.com.

Firing a New York City teacher costs
"Cuomo's Stand and Deliver." The Wall Street Journal. Dow Jones & Company, January 24, 2015. www.wsj.com.

Charter Schools and their Enemies
Sowell, Thomas. *Charter Schools and Their Enemies*. New York, NY: Basic Books, Hachette Book Group, 2020.

CHAPTER 12
Silicon Valley restricts devices in own homes
Weller, Chris. "Silicon Valley Parents Are Raising Their Kids Tech-free - and It Should Be a Red Flag." *Business Insider*. February 18, 2018. www.businessinsider.com.

Deep Work, Cal Newport
Newport, Cal. *Deep Work: Rules for Focused Success in a Distracted World*. Grand Central Pub, 2018.

STAAR Test scoring
Texas Education Agency. "2018–2019 STAAR Raw Score Conversion Tables." Texas Education Agency. Accessed March 3, 2021. tea.texas.gov.

Escaping Education's Death Valley, TED
Robinson, Sir Ken. "How to Escape Education's Death Valley." TED. Accessed March 3, 2021.

CHAPTER 13
First principles thinking
Oshin, Mayo. "Elon Musks' "3-Step" First Principles Thinking: How to Think and Solve Difficult Problems Like A . . ." Medium.com. August 30, 2017. medium.com.

The Psychology of Human Misjudgment
"Charlie Munger: The Psychology of Human Misjudgment (Transcript and Audio)." Farnam Street, September 16, 2018. fs.blog.

Mary's room
Nida-Rümelin, Martine, and Donnchadh O Conaill. "Qualia: The Knowledge Argument." Stanford Encyclopedia of Philosophy. Stanford University, September 23, 2019. plato.stanford.edu.

The Power of Explicit Teaching and Direct Instruction, Greg Ashman
Ashman, Greg. "The Power of Explicit Teaching and Direct Instruction." Thousand Oaks, CA: Corwin, 2021.

Daniel Schmachtenberger 1st, 2nd, 3rd person epistemics
"DarkHorse Podcast with Daniel Schmachtenberger & Bret Weinstein." YouTube, February 10, 2021. youtu.be/YPJug0s2u4w.

CHAPTER 14

The Lost Tools of Learning
Sayers, Dorothy Leigh. *The Lost Tools of Learning. Paper Read at a Vacation Course in Education, Oxford, 1947.* London, 1948.

Matthew Crawford
Brett. "Podcast #619: What Driving Tells Us About Agency, Skill, and Freedom." The Art of Manliness, January 5, 2021. www.artofmanliness.com.

Future authoring program, Jordan Peterson
Morisano, Dominique, Jacob B. Hirsh, Jordan B. Peterson, Robert O. Pihl, and Bruce M. Shore. "Setting, Elaborating, and Reflecting on Personal Goals Improves Academic Performance." *Journal of Applied Psychology* 95, no. 2 (2010): 255-64. doi:10.1037/a0018478.

Dr. Peter Gray, Unschooling
"How Our Schools Thwart Passions: Peter Gray: TEDxAsburyPark." YouTube, July 16, 2018. youtu.be.

KIPP and SUCCESS
Sowell, Thomas. *Charter Schools and Their Enemies.* New York, NY: Basic Books, Hachette Book Group, 2020.

CHAPTER 15

Marshmallow test
Navidad, Angel E. "Marshmallow Test Experiment and Delayed Gratification." Marshmallow Test Experiment | *Simply Psychology*, November 27, 2020. www.simplypsychology.org.

Harvard Treadmill test
"Developing Your Passion and Practicing Perseverance: Is Grit the New It?" Positive Psychology Program - Your One-Stop PP Resource! July 03, 2018. positivepsychologyprogram.com.

Baumeister radish study
Heath, Chip, and Dan Heath. *Switch: How to Change Things When Change Is Hard.* London: Random House Business, 2011.

The Happiness Hypothesis, Jonathan Haidt
Haidt, Jonathan. *The Happiness Hypothesis: Finding Modern Truth in Ancient Wisdom.* New York City, New York: Basic Book, 2006.

Switch, Chip and Dan Heath
Heath, Chip, and Dan Heath. *Switch: How to Change Things When Change Is Hard.* London: Random House Business, 2011.

Carol Dweck, Caution Praise Can be Dangerous
Dweck, Carol. "Caution-Praise Can Be Dangerous." *American Educator,* Spring 1999.

The Art of Learning, Josh Waitzkin
Waitzkin, Josh. *The Art of Learning: a Journey in the Pursuit of Excellence.* New York, NY: Free Spirit, 2008.

Study Finds growth mindset interventions fail
"Study Finds Popular 'Growth Mindset' Educational Interventions Aren't Very Effective." *ScienceDaily.* May 22, 2018. www.sciencedaily.com.

CHAPTER 16

The Happiness Hypothesis, Jonathan Haidt
Haidt, Jonathan. *The Happiness Hypothesis: Finding Modern Truth in Ancient Wisdom.* New York City, New York: Basic Book, 2006.

The Lost Art of Rhetoric, Jay Heinrichs
"Author Jay Heinrichs on Rhetoric and the 'Why' of Words." Penguin Random House Higher Education, May 8, 2018. penguinrandomhousehighereducation.com.

Most Americans can't handle $1000 emergency
Tepper, Taylor. "Most Americans Don't Have Enough Savings To Cover A $1K Emergency." Bankrate. August 02, 2018. www.bankrate.com.

CHAPTER 17

Harvard costs
Olito, Frank. "Here's How the Cost of Harvard Has Changed throughout the Years." *Business Insider.* June 10, 2019. www.businessinsider.com.

College tuition price increases, Business Insider
Jackson, Abby. "This Chart Shows How Quickly College Tuition Has Skyrocketed since 1980." *Business Insider.* July 20, 2015. http://www.businessinsider.com.

Student loan debt 1.6 trillion in 2020
Kurt, Daniel. "Student Loan Debt: 2020 Statistics and Outlook." *Investopedia.* March 16, 2021. www.investopedia.com.

US College enrollment up to 20.4 Million
"Digest of Education Statistics, 2013." National Center for Education Statistics (NCES) Home Page, a Part of the U.S. Department of Education. Accessed September 21, 2018. nces.ed.gov.

85% of college grads move home
@ericamho, Erica Ho. "Survey: 85% of New College Grads Move Back in with Mom and Dad." *Time.* May 10, 2011. newsfeed.time.com.

The Fall of the Faculty: The Rise of the All-Administrative University and Why it Matters, Benjamin Ginsburg
Ginsberg, Benjamin. *The Fall of the Faculty The Rise of the All-Administrative University and Why It Matters.* Cary: Oxford University Press, 2014.

Decline in time college students spent studying per week
Babcock, Philip, and Mindy Marks. "The Falling Time Cost of College: Evidence from Half a Century of Time Use Data," 2010. doi.org/10.3386/w15954.

Made in the USA
Las Vegas, NV
19 October 2021

32646246R00184